NAIS

Journal of the NATIVE AMERICAN *and* INDIGENOUS STUDIES ASSOCIATION

VOLUME 12.2

Fall 2025

NAIS (ISSN 2332-1261) is published two times a year in spring and fall (Northern Hemisphere) by the University of Minnesota Press, 111 Third Avenue South, Suite 290, Minneapolis, MN 55401-2520. https://www.upress.umn.edu

Postmaster: Send address changes to *NAIS,* University of Minnesota Press, 111 Third Avenue South, Suite 290, Minneapolis, MN 55401-2520.

Information about manuscript submissions can be found at naisa.org, or inquiries can be sent to journal@naisa.org.

Books for review should be addressed to *NAIS* Journal, Centre for Indigenous Research and Community-Led Engagement, The University of Victoria, 3800 Finnerty Road, Saunders Annex 130C, Victoria, BC, V8P 5C2, Canada.

Address subscription orders, changes of address, and business correspondence (including requests for permission and advertising orders) to *NAIS,* University of Minnesota Press, 111 Third Avenue South, Suite 290, Minneapolis, MN 55401-2520.

SUBSCRIPTIONS
- **Individual subscriptions to *NAIS*** are a benefit of membership in the Native American and Indigenous Studies Association. NAISA's tiered membership ranges from $25 to $150 annually. To become a member, visit https://naisa.org/.
- For current **institutional subscriptions** and **back issue** prices, please visit: https://www.upress.umn.edu.
- **Digital subscriptions to *NAIS* for institutions** are now available online through Project MUSE at https://muse.jhu.edu.

NAIS

Journal of the NATIVE AMERICAN *and* INDIGENOUS STUDIES ASSOCIATION

CONTENTS

VOLUME 12 ● ISSUE 2

Fall 2025

Articles

Notes from the Field

Critical Review Essays

Reviews

MEREDITH ALBERTA PALMER *and* THERESA ROCHA BEARDALL

Indigenous Data Inclusion and the Colonial Politics of Recognition

Abstract

The COVID-19 pandemic in the U.S. disproportionately harmed Indigenous peoples and brought long-standing calls for increased data collection and data accuracy about systemic issues in Indian Country to national attention. Advocates believe data can help support Indigenous people and address past harms. However, we explore two consequences that arise from data inclusion within the context of Indigenous peoples' relationship with the U.S. colonial state. First, we assert that data demands often lack direct collaboration with Indigenous nations and agencies, resulting in data inclusion that reifies and legitimates exploitative U.S. colonial structures of power and domination. Second, the articulation of Indigenous life using statistical data analyses risks solidifying the racialization and categorization of Indigenous people in ways that obviate their political authority and self-determination by rendering them as populations rather than polities. We conclude by offering two Indigenous-led examples of data collection and data communication that refuse Indigenous erasure and advance Indigenous futures. These represent an invitation for future scholarship to actively consider the multiple ways data can be used and refused in efforts to end U.S. colonial domination, especially given that data has long been used to pathologize and criminalize Indigenous peoples.

Introduction

IN APRIL 2020, one month into the nationwide spread of COVID-19, the Seattle Indian Health Board (SIHB) received an alarming shipment. In response to their urgent request for viral testing materials and personal protective equipment (PPE) from the U.S. federal government, the SIHB received boxes of individually wrapped, zippered, white body bags. Accompanying each bag was a small, beige tag that read "Attach to toe." Health professionals were expected to fill out the tags with identifying information about the deceased, including their name, doctor, and time of death. County health officials later clarified that the delivery of body bags was an error. Nonetheless, the racialized significance of the package served as a chilling reminder to the agency's majority Native staff: the loss of Native life has been so normalized across public agencies that their response to standard requests for lifesaving medical supplies appears to anticipate Native death rather than treatment and recovery.[1]

In response to growing health, resource, and social precarities related to the COVID-19 pandemic (Pirtle 2020), many rights advocates demanded a multidimensional national response, including the collection of publicly accessible disaggregated data to understand who, where, when, and how communities were impacted by the virus. In Indian Country, for example, tribal agencies and advocates such as the SIHB asserted that more and better data could help Native tribes and organizations communicate with various bureaucratic offices and advance their collective needs on their own terms.

Simultaneously in mid-2020, many Native people mobilized their shared affinities with Black Lives Matter movements as communities rose up in the U.S. and around the world to fight anti-Blackness and police brutality. There were renewed calls for reliable data on police violence against Native people, such as those expressed in a report released by the Urban Institute that noted how undercounts prohibit informed efforts to amend this violence (Olugbenga 2017). These calls amplified prior advocacy for more accurate data on Native people, such as arguments for the proper allocation of the $1.5 trillion in funds the U.S. Federal Government owes each year to tribal governments that go to fulfilling basic needs such as water infrastructure, education, and housing.

Considering this context, we examine how data was collected and deployed in two key sites of governance that dominated the U.S. political landscape in 2020: (a) the response to COVID-19 and (b) national organizing and protest against police violence. In these two areas of health and institutional violence, data has been used to pathologize and criminalize Native people historically and today. Contemporaneously in 2020, many tribes and Native data studies scholars argued for more self-determined data to better assess, understand, and advocate around their needs. This conjunctural moment reveals the political and material stakes of Native *legibility* through data inclusion by showing how settler data-making practices attempt to render Native people and their political self-determination[2] into populations rather than polities.

We begin by illustrating the historical relationship between data collection, analysis, U.S. settler state-making, and colonial governmentality. Specifically, we emphasize the historic role that data collection practices have played in efforts to "include" or assimilate Native Peoples into a multicultural U.S. public. Second, we revisit the SIHB during the initial spread of COVID-19 and trace out the connections between data and the unequal allocation of financial resources, essential healthcare equipment, and access to data about Native health. Third, we relate the devaluation of Indigenous life during the pandemic with the genocidal murder of Native people at the hands of police and its sociohistorical parallels to the dehumanization of Black life and the murder of George Floyd in 2020. We conclude by foregrounding two examples that underscore the limitations of quantitative data as a singular mode of communication and futurity: (1) the Akwesasne Mohawks' fight to protect its members from waterway contamination, and (2) the repurposing of the SIHB body bags into a ribbon dress by SIHB Chief Research Officer Abigail Echo-Hawk. Throughout, we train our analysis on the continued implications of ongoing settler domination through data inclusion as a tool of U.S. statecraft, without foreclosing how Indigenous knowledge practices present alternative ways of both using and resisting these techniques.[3]

What does Indigenous data inclusion mean for Indigenous Peoples in the context of 2020 and its aftermaths? To answer this question, we examine how data inclusion is intertwined with the project of U.S. colonial statemaking and the politics of Indigenous recognition (Coulthard 2014, Simpson 2014, Million 2021, Fanon 1952). Glen Coulthard (Yellowknives Dene) names the politics of recognition as a strategy of settler colonial states to include a truncated and depoliticized representation of Indigenous people to maintain colonial domination. This politics of recognition accompanies a structure of human rights in which appeals for justice are reconfigured as appeals for the right to be intervened upon through humanitarian governance. Dian Million (Tanana Athabascan) further links this colonial governance to the creation of "biopolitical misinformation that presents Indigenous worlds" (2021, 395). These politics of recognition and rights are consequential for a critical Indigenous analysis of data inclusion.

The politics of data collection and data accuracy have important implications in Native American and Indigenous studies. First, we connect contemporary Indigenous calls for social justice grounded in the "data inclusion movement" (Hoffmann 2020) with U.S. colonial investments in Native death and elimination. We urge readers to consider the possibility for Indigenous self-determination to be compromised using settler processes of enumeration, data-making, and data relations. Drawing on analyses of colonial politics of recognition (Coulthard 2014) and rights (Million 2013), we hold that the advancement of Indigenous self-determinations and sovereignties requires active refusal of data that function to enable U.S. statecraft. In this way, we seek to bring into generative conversation those scholars who analyze how data-making techniques and practices are *employed* to constitute figures of "the Indian" with other scholars who analyze how data about Native people is *deployed* and operationalized in the world. The intent is to enable an understanding of the history, use, and limits of data in envisioning Indigenous futures that do not reproduce the colonial present. Within this visioning, we highlight how multiple forms of relationality cannot be fully communicated or exhaustively captured through empirical methods (Rocha Beardall 2023). We delineate several reasons and pathways to decouple lived experiences from colonial configurations of legibility through data.[4]

Data Histories of U.S. Colonialism

The political and material stakes of contemporary calls for data inclusion remain rooted in a long-standing U.S. colonial state practice of collecting and analyzing data to transform Native Peoples into subjects of colonial rule. This transformation of people into data is a key tool of colonial governmentality, which, in addition to extraction and exploitation, further maintains colonial relations. Critical Indigenous scholarship has drawn on and critiqued Michel Foucault's frameworks of governmentality and biopolitics to analyze the role of calculation and the construction of "rationality." Foucault (1982) named biopower as the technology by which modern liberal states form and mediate the relationship between individual subjects and larger populations. He focuses on the life of the body politic rather than the individual. His related term "governmentality" refers to the state and extrastate strategies for population management and surveillance through various calculative and regulatory controls and modes of subject formation, such as welfare systems, public health, healthcare policies, environmental law, and psychosocial controls. In the field of geography, Stuart Elden (2007) reintegrates the centrality of *territory* to biopolitics, stating that "territorial strategies themselves should be read as calculative" (562). Both Foucault and Elden, however, do not directly attend to colonialism. By delineating *colonial* governmentality, several critical Indigenous studies scholars have made evident the colonial—and thus territorializing—thrust of calculative strategies whose politics of norming vis-à-vis inclusion impinge upon Indigenous people as place-based, self-governing collectives (Coulthard 2014; Million 2013; Morgensen 2011; Nichols 2017). We join these scholars' insistence that the alternative polities that Indigenous Peoples comprise are not foreclosed within liberal biopolitics and cannot be analyzed as such.

The remainder of this section reviews how data and enumeration emerged as central modes of colonial governmentality in the 1800s amid the bureaucratization of U.S. federal relationships with sovereign tribal nations. We examine a set of connections in the law, the academy, and the U.S. Census in which data collection, data histories, and the bureaucratization of U.S. colonial data sediments colonial violence against Native people. We conclude by examining the SIHB as one contemporary provider of health services that works to ensure the safety and wellness of Native people within these sedimented data histories. In doing so, we reveal the colonial implications of questions such as who was given access to data about Native health, what was done with that data, and how these decisions informed the federal government's COVID-19 response to Native Peoples.

Defining Data and Historical Data Practices in U.S. Colonialism

Human-centered data is commonly understood as information and descriptions about the world gathered through surveys, questionnaires, observations, and informed participation (Lovett et al. 2019). Data is diverse and can include health records, employment history, socioeconomic measures, and demographic and location-based data such as zip codes. In biomedical settings, data includes blood, tissue, or other bodily fluids, including human genes. Data is often subdivided along a quantitative and qualitative binary, separating data that is expressed numerically from data that is expressed descriptively.

These definitions, however, do not reveal the full implication of data—its production, circulation, and mode of communicating—in the lives of Indigenous Peoples. For this, one must understand that the term data comes from the Latin *datum,* meaning "something given"; however, as Johanna Drucker asserts, the reality is that the *data* of Indigenous lives and bodies are more akin to the Latin *capta,* or something taken, captured, or extracted (Drucker 2011). A key difference between data and capta is that the former is supposedly found or collected without searching for it while the latter is actively sought and thus collected into a set of assumptions structuring its object, practice, and analysis. The relationality of these data—whether they were gifted, extracted or obtained to lay claim to a person or place—are particularly salient in Indigenous life in the U.S., especially the capture of information by scholarly and institutional research.

The capture, use, and distribution of data as a state-making tool to surveil and manage Native Peoples emerged in the mid- to late 1800s. During this time, U.S. federal and state agencies sought to assimilate Native Peoples into settler society. This was a project of adverse inclusion that was administered through an increasingly bureaucratic U.S. state with severe social, economic, and political outcomes for Native nations. Importantly, the rise of the bureaucratization of Indigenous relations to lands, waters, and kin was made possible by the "domestic dependent" settler-legal framework found in *Cherokee Nation v. Georgia* (1831), one of three cases collectively known as the Marshall Trilogy. This U.S. Supreme Court decision found that Native nations were "domestic-dependent nations" because they remained in a state of pupilage and in need of federal authority (Duthu 2013). For example, in 1900, U.S. census takers were instructed to note the percent of so-called white ancestry of American Indians for the first time, setting the bureaucratic stage for establishing a baseline of American Indian ancestry below which one could not receive federal services (Snipp 2003). Around the same time, the U.S. Competency Commission was established to determine if so-called Indians were "competent" to control land allotted to them in the 1887 Dawes Allotment Act and be conferred citizenship. Data for this commission included the size of their homes, amount of livestock and farm equipment, and notes on home furnishings (Piatote 2013). These efforts reflected radically shifting political sentiments from earlier overtly violent land annexations and forced removals that had characterized U.S. colonial practice throughout the 1800s. New techniques of bureaucratization emerged that imbued Indigenous-colonial state relationships with procedural uniformity and hierarchical control vis-à-vis a slower violence.

At times, these bureaucracies curbed massacres and forced removal. Simultaneously, they entrenched fundamentally anti-Indigenous administrative concepts and practices within Native communities. For instance, the "post"-Indian War project of Indian assimilation that was driven by a three-pronged approach of education (boarding schools), land allotment (the General Allotment Act of 1887), and citizenship (Indian Citizenship Act of 1924) aimed to manage and limit the political, cultural, and social mobility of Native people, while ushering in capitalist extraction and privatization (Justice and O'Brien 2022). Both the spectacular violence associated with group removal and the slow violence of the assimilation era facilitated the seizure of Native lands, the extraction of rich natural resources, and the removal of Native children from their homes steeped in intergenerational cultural knowledge (Rocha Beardall and Edwards 2021). Both projects also emerged through a growing bureaucratic framework that enumerated and pathologized Native children and their families' health and behavior and that surveyed and recorded land for seizure (Piatote 2013; Palmer 2024).

While these large administrative projects affected Native Peoples in a variety of ways, all had to contend with the consequential dynamics of erasure via "inclusion," namely through efforts to "count" Native people. For example, only those "American Indians" considered "assimilated" were officially counted in U.S. Census documents as Indians, whereas Native people of "mixed blood" heritage living away from tribal lands in white communities were counted as white (Lujan 1990). As Piatote (Nez Perce) notes, this increased bureaucratization appeared as a progressive alternative, and certainly a cheaper alternative, than the costly military strategies of whole group removal and extermination (2013). These enumerations of Native land, families, and health were both the justification *and* the means for continued colonial dispossession.

The bureaucratization of U.S. colonial practices, such as national record-keeping for the distribution of goods and resources, continues today in settler-Native relations and for many people makes the ongoing violence of everyday colonial statecraft appear both banal and innocent. This tightly bound connection between the violence of U.S. colonialism, bureaucracy, and inclusion-by-erasure manifested in other social institutions as well. For example, "the Indian" is a ubiquitous figure in academic production and was central to the formation of distinct academic disciplines (Byrd 2011; Trouillot 2003). In the field of anthropology, for example, Lewis Henry Morgan, Henry Rowe Schoolcraft, Alfred Kroeber, Franz Boas, and Leo Simmons, among others, all established their career trajectories on the extensive and intrusive study of Native Peoples. In fact, Simmons' study of Don Talayesva made this Hopi man the single most documented individual in the world. Simmons collected over 400 formal interviews, 8,000 diary pages, 341 recorded dreams, and multiple psychological tests, all while the Hopi were dealing with multiple colonial incursions, including land appropriation and Indian boarding schools.

Unfortunately, researchers continue to treat Native Peoples as sites of data extraction for career and state building, seemingly undisturbed by the rising ethical concerns surrounding this practice. For example, the biomedical datasets of the Akimel O'odham collected in the mid-1900s have been used for everything from public health and genomic research on diabetes and race, to optimizing predictive algorithms (Radin 2017). Diverse scholars working at the intersection of race, data, and inequality have shown that the ways in which these data are used, circulated, and animated have served to reproduce U.S. colonialism. Other linkages between contemporary Native data inclusion efforts, assimilation-era policies, and bureaucratization can be found in the colonial documents that attempted to control and define Native life and death. Examples include toe tags, census records, biostatistical markers including single nucleotide polymorphisms that make up DNA ancestry markers, surnames, and the standardization of Indigenous place into settler property via land surveys (Arvin 2019; Benjamin 2016; Reardon and TallBear 2012; Snipp 2003; TallBear 2013; Walter and Andersen 2013; Palmer 2020).

These examples illustrate how data-making has been central in academic attempts to render Indigenous life *knowable* and thus manageable. From this perspective, data is produced within distinctly colonial modes of seeing and engaging with the social world and, as such, runs the risk of rein-forcing white possession (Moreton-Robinson 2015). Colonial data-making can take many forms. First, a colonial approach often derives informa-tion *from* Indigenous lives and bodies rather than from Indigenous ways of knowing, analyzing, and determining value for what constitutes Indigenous flourishing. By reproducing the colonial present, this approach recuper-ates Euro-American colonial whiteness through the extraction, collection, amalgamation, analysis, and presentation of Native life and death as fixed, generalizable quantifications of an often racialized reality. Second, catego-ries and numbers impose a universalizing and disciplining norm, allowing users to claim an authority based on the appearance of impersonal distance (Porter 1996). As Theodore Porter writes, "Quantification is a way of mak-ing decisions without seeming to decide" (8). The ruse is that this distance ostensibly eliminates bias and the need or desire for grounded and intimate knowledge of what such data are meant to describe.

In the context of U.S. colonial governmentality, this presumption of objec-tivity and thus empirical authority is wielded by the U.S. colonial state in an attempt to name and manage a singular "population" of disparate Native Peoples who are then defined as a racial subset of the broader U.S. popula-tion. Merging surveillance with governmentality, these data are deployed in a colonial project of truthmaking, in which scientific "facts" and white gen-dered subjectivities are co-constituted over and against Indigenous ways of knowing and being (Arvin 2019; Haraway 1989; Pratt 1992; TallBear 2013).[5] As Coulthard suggests, the paradigm of *recognition* is a "field of power through which colonial relations are produced and maintained" (2014, 17) by "recognizing" and including Indigenous Peoples within the governance of colonial state formation. Inclusion can lead to a host of *mis*recognitions that render Indigenous polities unrecognizable and subordinate in a variety of scientific, medical, and governmental realms. While creating visibility and legibility through data inclusion may appear to be a logical countermeasure to the colonial project of Indigenous erasure, below we continue to show how practices of data-making and data circulation can advance colonial and racial state-making efforts to control Native people.

Indian Health Services Contend with the Data Present
Building from the idea that data is a historical technique of U.S. colonial power, we explore the work of the SIHB, the agency that received body bags in 2020 in lieu of PPE. Created in 1970, this nonprofit 501(c)3 organization was born out of 1960–1970s urban Indian activism and is one of forty-one clinics in the U.S. that provides health services to American Indian and Alaska Native (AI/AN) people in urban areas. The SIHB is funded through

grants from the federally funded Indian Health Services (IHS)[6] and donations from the community and their partners. Though 7 of every 10 Native people in the U.S. live in urban areas, Urban Indian Health Programs receive less than 1 percent of the IHS budget (SIHB 2025). In Seattle, the SIHB today sees about six thousand patients a year, two-thirds of whom are Native American and/or Indigenous. In addition, the SIHB is also the site of one of twelve Tribal Epidemiology Centers (TECs) in the U.S. that serve IHS regions across the nation.

The Urban Indian Health Institute (UIHI), the research division of the SIHB, works on the collection, analysis, and dissemination of public health data. Their stated mission is "to decolonize data, for Indigenous people, by Indigenous people" (UIHI 2020). The organization fulfills this mission by engaging with data-driven initiatives to improve the well-being of Native and Indigenous community members. In 2020, for example, the SIHB published a series of reports on sexual violence against urban women and the missing and murdered Indigenous women and girls (MMIWG) crises in urban and state settings (UIHI 2020). Their goal is to decolonize data to "ensure that it is more accurate and accessible for partners, providers, policy makers, and health advocates and is informed by the people who know the health needs best—Native people" (UIHI 2020). The UIHI are critical of conventional data practices. The conventional use of data within the U.S. excludes Indigenous voices and traditional practices, according to their website, yet it still drives policies, practices, and funding that impact Indigenous Peoples, thus functioning as a tool of colonization. Extensive data are collected about Indigenous Peoples by non-Natives, for example, and these data are often irrelevant to the needs of Indigenous Peoples (Carroll et al. 2019).

Using an "integrated data framework," the SIHB attempts to solve persistent social problems for Indigenous Peoples. By using data that is both legible to the U.S. colonial state *and* reflects Indigenous voices and traditional practices, they work to provide accurate information in order to design and direct services, programs, and policies. The SIHB and its important advocacy work are situated within a field of scholars and policymakers who are invested in collecting data that privileges Indigenous worldviews. Taken together, these advocates are also redirecting the state's trajectory of violence against Native Peoples in ways that promote accountability and transparency and that reimagine Indigenous futures. This work is a form of *counterdata,* which is "collected in contestation of a dominant institution or ideology" (Olojo, in Burrell, Singh, and Davison 2024, 171).

Some practitioners of Native data inclusion maintain that a failure to increase data collection on key issues such as health and mortality runs the risk of Native people being underserviced or, worse, erased in the healthcare system and beyond (Nagle 2020). These health-related concerns combine with the reality that tribal governments are, by design, enmeshed in bureaucratic governance systems that require tribally-specific data to govern their citizens and to make their needs known to other governing bodies, including applications for grant funding. Put simply, tribal governments are expected to perform according to neoliberal forms of colonial governance and calculation to receive their guaranteed resources. For instance, data allows federally recognized tribes to receive funding from the U.S. government, which they can use "for unemployment relief, food programs, and infrastructure projects" (O'Neill 2021). Similarly, in the context of COVID-19, tribal nations and tribal agencies needed access to multiple forms of data to govern the devastating impact of a global pandemic. A lack of such data jeopardized their ability to access resources to care for their citizens. Contextualized within the analyses of Indigenous data studies scholars, these data are made of *relations* that come with multiple obligations: both to the Native nation or community and to the settler colonial state. What, then, are the effects of these dual obligations?

The remainder of this article aims to unsettle two assumptions that have been reiterated within many Indigenous data inclusion efforts: (1) that the lives and value systems of Indigenous Peoples can be accurately or exhaustively communicated through data points and (2) that measuring and demonstrating inequalities will result in the acknowledgment and appropriate resource allocation needed to address ongoing social problems in Indian Country. We explore these implications for tribal nations and Native entities who produce data or request to be included in externally produced data. Further, we give attention to the enmeshment of quantitative techniques with the colonial violence of surveillance and discipline, showing how this affects the endeavors of tribal nations and Native entities to create data that communicate injustice and inequalities experienced by Native people to a non-Indigenous audience.[7]

COVID-19 and the Multivalence of Legibility Through Data

How can calls for data inclusion refashion U.S. colonial structures of power and domination when those structures themselves remain intact? By fall 2024, there had been nearly 1.2 million deaths from COVID-19 in the U.S. alone. These deaths—and the immeasurable grief of this loss—are spread unevenly across geographies and communities, affecting Indian Country with tremendous force (Denetdale, *in press*). To convey the reality of this violence, Native entities are often required by state agencies to communicate using data within the parameters and parlance of the U.S. colonial state, especially when petitioning for and receiving various "benefits" of the nation-to-nation trust relationship. The federal government's response to the spread of COVID-19, specifically its unequal allocation of essential goods, including COVID-19 tests, PPE, and financial resources from the Coronavirus Aid, Relief, and Economic Security (CARES) Act of 2020, illustrates this point.

By May 2020, U.S. Secretary of the Treasury Steven Mnuchin announced that $4.8 billion of the $2 trillion dollars allotted in the CARES Act would be dispersed to tribal governments—60 percent distributed based on population data and the remaining 40 percent based on employment data to cover expenses related to those employed by Indian tribes (Akee et al. 2020). Disputes immediately arose over *how* these funds would be allocated, given that the formula used to determine tribal population was not reflective of tribal citizenship or tribal need (Akee et al. 2020). Allocations were further delayed due to legal disagreements about whether Alaska Native Corporations constituted a tribal government under the CARES Act.

In addition to these procedural and infrastructure inequalities, the very circulation of the virus was overdetermined by the multiple ways U.S. colonialism oppressed Indigenous people: higher rates of comorbidities such as diabetes, higher rates of indispensable frontline yet low-wage jobs, lower rates of insurance, less access to quality health care, and discrimination in health-care settings (Pirtle 2020). These inequalities created the conditions under which marginalized people were also the most vulnerable to the virus's spread. For Indigenous people, these structural inequalities were compounded by the minacious workings of colonial bureaucracies.

Next, amid early reports that Native people were experiencing higher rates of COVID-19 disease and death, federal agency responses—shaped by a U.S. colonial drive toward Indigenous elimination—were entirely inadequate. While the U.S. Center for Disease Control (CDC) website had a special section on COVID-19 for tribal communities, for example, the only Native-specific guidance the CDC provided for the first one and a half years of the pandemic concerned how to bury a large number of deceased people as a result of the virus and how to alter one's behavior to deal with isolation and reduce infection while living in multigenerational homes. Such behavior-based recommendations served to pathologize Indigenous lifeways and, in the process, sidelined understandings of historical colonial structures that perpetuate the lack of housing, health care, and transportation infrastructure in Indian Country (Rocha Beardall 2020).

A third key issue compounded during the COVID-19 pandemic concerned the decades-long phenomenon of sparse and disordered data on Native American health. For instance, the CDC gave individual U.S. states open access to raw COVID-19 data, but it refused multiple requests for this same data from the top twelve tribal epidemiology centers in the U.S. (Government Accountability Office 2022; Tahir and Cancryn 2020). Although the National Indian Health Board and the Urban Indian Health Institute were given the title of "public health authorities" under the 2010 Affordable Care Act, CDC officials refused to cooperate (Wade 2020). Tribal governments were thus excluded or prevented from receiving the resources and disaggregated data that they needed to protect Native citizens using data-informed policies on how to care for their people. In other words, they were not even able to perform as proper neoliberal entities. Specifically, Native people were left out of important health programs, including antibody testing (Goodluck 2020). Native organizations also had no ability to track the spread of COVID-19 across their urban, rural, and reservation populations nor could they determine precisely why Native people were dying at higher rates than other populations. This refusal to share data about Native people *with* Native communities typifies the paternalistic "wardship" approach to nation-to-nation governance that has been central to colonial desires to manage and control both Native life and death.

In response, tribes rethought how they collected data. The Hopi Tribe began separating data by zip codes instead of villages (Curtis 2020), and others such as the Pueblo of Zia, who demanded control over data dissemination, stated that data sovereignty means Indigenous data should only be shared "under our terms" (Bichell 2020). A tribal administrator from Pueblo of Zia noted to reporters that the tribe had been sharing COVID numbers on the Pueblo's Facebook to keep their community and their people safe; however, the administrator and others noticed that statewide press releases and local news outlets were sharing the COVID numbers from the Pueblo's Facebook page, which felt to them like someone was "just coming in and invading our privacy at a very private moment" (Bichell 2020). This enumeration of lost or ill community members was initially shared as a way to gauge the need for caution and keep the public of the Pueblo of Zia informed, but it became open to new interpretations and meanings once it was shared with a broader New Mexican public.

In addition to these examples of withheld data and misdirected policy, data about Indigenous Peoples was, in some instances, turned against Indigenous well-being. This is particularly true in communities that reported higher rates of COVID-19; the rates in the Four Corners region of the Navajo, Hopi, Ute, and Zuni Peoples were some of the highest in the country. One hospital in Albuquerque, New Mexico, profiled pregnant women who arrived in labor: if they looked Native and resided in zip codes located on a nearby reservation, they were singled out as a health threat. These racially and spatially profiled women were first given a COVID-19 test upon arrival and then, after delivery, were quarantined from their newborns until the results came in. Since the hospital used a COVID-19 test that took three days to process, some mothers waited up to three days to hold and bond with their newborns. While health equity epidemiologists rely on zip codes as the best predictor of an individual's health to target interventions in hospitals, emergency rooms, and public health programs (see Krieger 2009), the target in this instance became Native women themselves, and their data was turned against them.

Notably, calls for data inclusion typically imply trust in the count or, at the very least, an obligated recourse to it. As analyzed above, however, modern colonial governance and power are maintained through the racist implications of the making and management of so-called minoritized populations under U.S. colonialism (Small-Rodriguez and Rocha Beardall 2023). Consider the ever-changing enumeration of how to "count" who is and is not Native according to the shifting strategies of the U.S. Census, which itself is a multifaceted biopolitical project charged with creating "populations." The U.S. Census merges hundreds of different Indigenous people-hoods[8] and their members into one broad racial category that is distinctly different from blood quantum and tribally-specific enrollment processes. In public health and policy arenas, this notion of *the count* is complicated further since Native Peoples, if they are included at all, are often placed in an "other" or "something else" category in data analyses that differentiate between racial groups (Nagle 2020). As the SIHB director and chief research officer explained, "By including us in the other category it effectively eliminates us in the data" (Nagle 2020). The small numbers of Native people in a given area, the lack of expertise in counting Indigenous people properly, and the ongoing friction regarding who should be, or wants to be, included in the racial category of "American Indian/Alaska Native," all confound these datasets that still may try to make claims about a "Native American public" or population. As mentioned above, these kinds of omissions and miscounts have material effects; they complicate and shape the allocation of funds and resources.

Together, these examples highlight the stakes of the debate over data inclusion and data exclusion, including whether and under what conditions *inclusion* can be more colonial than data exclusion. This is exemplified in the instance described above when the CDC refused to provide the twelve Tribal Epidemiology Centers with the public health data they needed to care for Native people. Additionally, these examples illustrate that some tribal nations *do* want more data collection about their lives because they understand the consequences of not collecting data at all. Perhaps indirectly, these broader calls for Indigenous data inclusion, which swelled in this moment, point the U.S. toward Indigenous self-determination. They make clearer the colonial implications of the making and management of "Native Americans" as a racialized population, to which we turn in the following section.

Counting Death: Native People and Police Killings

In addition to the rapid, unequal spread of COVID-19 across Native and minoritized communities in 2020, widespread uprisings in the U.S. and around the globe fought back against the ongoing murder of unarmed Black people by police. These organized protests called for municipal action, legal redress, and immediate changes to police policy. Many Native people identified with the Movement for Black Lives and joined this momentum with on-the-ground solidarity during summer protests and by highlighting significant sociohistorical parallels such as the alarming rates of police violence against and incarceration of Native people.

This critical alignment between differently racialized yet intertwined communities raises important questions about the law as much as it does about how one "counts" and is made *legible* within the context of social movement demands. We take up this point by contextualizing how that count shapes what is made legible about Indigenous individuals or collectives to understand what kind of data relations are entered into when the count is used as a claim for redress. We join Kwakwaka'wakw scholar Sarah Hunt (in Holmes et al. 2015, 543), who asks, "Despite this legal recognition and public dialogue, the violence continues. So what is being achieved by this increased visibility?" To attend to this question, we build on our analysis of how data inclusion and exclusion facilitate colonialism by first recognizing the life of John T. Williams, who was taken from his relations in 2010 by Seattle police. In this way, we put aside for a moment the statistics describing the over-policing of Native people and focus instead on *how* these experiences travel through Native communities (Rocha Beardall and Edwards 2021). Next, we explore the making of racialized subjects for enumeration purposes by framing police brutality statistics as a hierarchical unit of being that can be weaponized as a mode of subordination and domination.[9] Finally, we underscore how the "logics of overrepresentation" (Nichols 2017) as a measure of social inequality misframes and dehistoricizes the collective loss caused by settler colonialism and its continuity to the present. Such logics also disadvantage possibilities for coalitional politics with racialized others, particularly our Black relatives. Thus, our analysis illuminates both the colonial technique of forming a depoliticized population using racializing categories and the way that quantifying relations and communicating through *rates* refashions a colonial mode of relationality.

John T. Williams and Accounting for Indigenous Death

John T. Williams, seventh in a long line of Nuu-cha-nulth woodcarvers, began carving wood when he was four. Williams was recognized as a talented artist and would walk throughout his Seattle neighborhood with small carving tools and a piece of wood, making art as he moved through the city. In late August 2010, just after four o'clock on a sunny summer afternoon, Williams used the crosswalk to make his way through a busy downtown intersection. Williams was fifty years of age and hard of hearing. Out on patrol, Officer Ian Birk watched Williams enter the crosswalk and immediately left his vehicle with his firearm drawn. Surveillance footage later revealed Officer Birk motioning for Williams to approach him while yelling, "Put the knife down!" three times in quick succession. Within 4.7 seconds of arriving on the scene, Birk fired five shots, hitting Williams and ending his life. Birk claimed he felt threatened when Williams turned to look at him. Williams's murderer was never convicted, sparking outrage as news traveled widely throughout Indian Country.

A decade later, Williams's memory lives on through his carving community, his Seattle family, and the same city crosswalk, which is adorned with three white deer to honor his life. Williams's memory, and an awareness of the larger problem of police violence, circulates through additional creative works, including the Tribe Called Red song named "Woodcarver" ("The Halluci Nation" 2011). The murder of Williams is not an outlier. Many more Native people have lost their lives to police violence, and yet little has been done to reverse this trend. Similar to Native experiences under COVID-19, a now common response to this violence and the media silence that surrounds it is the demand for more and better data about Native experiences at the hands of the police.

Importantly, these data—and the lack thereof—have long been a point of contention among activists and scholars. The U.S. federal government has yet to fully develop a systematic, mandatory, and publicly accessible database of police violence (Rocha Beardall 2019). As with the COVID-19 pandemic, recent calls for data accountability on police violence rely heavily on arguments originating from public health that this information is critical to community well-being and the prevention of premature death and other health effects of systemic racism (Krieger et al. 2015). Currently, many researchers and advocacy organizations use a combination of public and privately sourced data, including CDC data received from hospitals, to try to assess the magnitude of police violence. This effort is necessary, in part, because police departments often improperly file or fail to file homicide reports, and they fail to reliably list police involvement on death certificates.

Particular to Native experiences with police violence and a lack of police response when they are called, however, is the *jurisdictional maze* (Goldberg-Ambrose 1996) that governs criminal issues in Indian Country. With some combination of local, tribal, county, state, and federal law enforcement officials, this maze leaves Native people living on and around tribal reservations subject to temporally and spatially complex law enforcement agencies that dictate how, when, and by whom criminality (including police violence) in Indian Country can be named, addressed, and punished (Rocha Beardall 2024). This maze also creates new and complex obstacles to accessing specific information when Native people are harmed, killed, or have gone missing. In the urban context, this information is often missing altogether simply because law enforcement officials are not interested and/or not required to capture fine-grained data on Native experiences with violence. This absence of information is compounded by the role of attorneys and judges who oversee such cases and refuse to take action to prosecute violent crimes against Native people generally (U.S. Department of Justice 2016), and on Native women and two-spirit people specifically. When the state fails to prosecute, it compounds the violence Native people experience by refusing to protect them even after they have been victimized.

Amidst calls for better data on police violence, it remains important to note racializing assumptions produced through such data. The enumeration of Indigenous death counts and the insistence on comparing two or more populations for statistical significance are primary modes of this racialization. First, in producing data about racialized people, aspects of individual bodies, lives, and deaths are made to yield measures that produce "facts" that are supposedly representative of an entire racialized population (Fullwiley 2008). Thus, to calculate a rate of a given phenomenon about Native Peoples, one inevitably takes an iteration of a historical understanding of Native Americans as a singular *race* of people: previously called savages, barbarians, Indians, and "American Indian/Alaska Natives" or AI/AN today in U.S. Census and health data. Second, those "facts" about one racialized population are then compared against corresponding "facts" about another racialized population, often in bar graphs that compare different racial groups' rates of death by police. This move to compare populations suggests a mutuality of meaning by the collectors of these data and the communities they purport to count.

In counting Native death by police, as with rates of death from COVID-19 or other phenomena associated with health and social inequalities in the U.S., these rates are constructed by and racially defined within the hierarchies that inform U.S. social relations. These comparative rates are commonplace: white people experience death by police at X%, while Black people experience death at Y%, and on down, sometimes not including Native American people in this schema. In the contexts in which Native people are included in a comparative rate, one (1) Native person is compared against and equal to one (1) white person in a system that locates white people as the statistical baseline. In the U.S. imperial state, which is founded and maintained through the elimination of Indigenous lands, life, and subject positions, this claim that 1 = 1 may appear to be a potent call for equality, a claim that there is (or *should be)* an equal social value between the life of one Native person and one Euro-American settler. Further, this claim indicates that it is an injustice for one racialized population to experience higher rates of death than another.[10]

Valuating Native life in comparative death or disease rates has become common to the point that the implications underlying this quantitative call for equality may be lost. The rest of this section, therefore, considers how statistical techniques that appear neutral in their numerical presentation or even supposedly focus on justice, instead comprise colonial relations and inaugurate colonial approaches toward redress. We first consider the use of statistical techniques in deployments of data that aim to account for Indigenous life and death. Public messaging that compares the rates of different racialized groups' death by police implies that modes of *racial* redress as a categorical identification is appropriate. In other words, in the presentation of "Native American" as a racializing category, it is assumed that redress should be aimed at the level of the racialized population rather than at the level of the Indigenous Nation, or of a particularly situated urban Native community.

Given the prevalent framing of data as an equity tool, this wholesale mode of narrating Indigenous life has understandably shaped how Native Peoples are reckoning with the reality of police violence. It is important, however, to not mistake the messaging and adoption of these racializing counts with a more critical politic of grounded and place-based Indigenous solidarity. A comparative statistical configuration, for example, is itself a recursive "norming" in two senses: (1) whiteness is reproduced as an ideal, and (2) Indigenous Peoples are folded into its own totality without making space for sovereignty and self-determination and difference between peoples. As Peguis Cree scholar Jessica Kolopenuk (2020, 4) writes regarding Native inclusion in biomedical research, "Proportionate distribution of health and disease (within the regime of biopolitics) is believed to contribute to generating equality among biocitizens in a way that makes up for the historical conditions that have caused initial disparities." Importantly, the thrust of Indigenous struggles and demands are not levied toward equal justice as a "race" in the U.S. American project, but rather as a struggle against loss of authority and sovereignty and a refusal to be banished from one's own homelands. Kahnawakero:non scholar Audra Simpson writes, "Race and racialization, some may contend, are symptoms of the problem, not the problem itself" (Simpson 2007, 480). In other words, the problem is ongoing colonial occupation and misrecognition of Indigenous peoplehoods; racialization itself and racism in its structural and interpersonal forms are several symptoms among other and multiple effects of colonial power.

A second set of assumptions ushered in through the deployment of comparative race-based statistics concerns the real and affective relations that are vanished through quantification. Specifically, when these data are made acceptable proxies and approximations of Indigenous life, then the relations of and between Native Peoples become abstracted or disappear through enumerations that are detached from Indigenous life. These fractured misrepresentations of Indigenous life and death are then circulated to bring public recognition and legibility regarding the ongoing violence waged against Native Peoples as a singular population, in this case by U.S. law enforcement. It is understandable that there is a demand for this kind of information within struggles of colonial reckoning. In many cases, it is wielded by Indigenous people as claims upon rights-granting bodies, which may or may not answer to a given demand. Yet, as Frantz Fanon (2008) first asserted, and Coulthard (2014) and Million (2013) situate in terms of *settler* colonialism, seeking recognition or rights via means of colonial governance often reinforces that colonial regime rather than challenging it.

To justify the removal and killing of Native people and the theft and commodification of our lands and resources, the U.S. nation-state has labeled Natives as deviant, savage, or in racial decline (Williams 2012) in ways that render so-called *Indianness* formative to the country's legal and representational presumptions of civility, illegality, and criminality (Byrd 2011). Without this context, the state and other research entities require that Indigenous people or allies produce data to substantiate this harm, to make the "death counts" matter. In other words, those experiencing the injustice of U.S. state violence are the ones who are burdened by the demand to make that violence and death both visible *and* problematic. This demand and trajectory, when the goal is "simply" to create and collate the data alone, leaves critiques of police violence framed in a measurement of overrepresentation in rates of death of racialized people. This line of argument displaces a broader analysis and redress aimed at the ongoing violence of the U.S. colonial state.

Many contemporary demands for producing *more and better data,* open-source data, or the inclusion of Indigenous people in comparative data, fail to center specific Indigenous governance practices and Indigenous responsibilities to and valuations of peoples, places, and nonhuman kin. Instead, these demands rely on the logics of overrepresentation as a standard measure of social inequality (Nichols 2017). A reliance on these data presumes alarm or injustice has only been found when an "overrepresentation" of our relations is killed at the hands of the state. This conclusion indirectly posits the existence of an "appropriate" rate, proportion, or number of Native deaths or assumption of social risks that is above zero.

In contrast, we suggest that *any* prevalence of Native people killed by settler state police is unacceptable, even if it were the same or less than the prevalence among white people. Seeking to render Native peoples' murder by police statistically significant suggests either that there are an acceptable number of murders or that there is some quantum of murders that is insignificant, statistically speaking. If Native deaths by police were accurately counted, the argument goes, it is assumed that the loss of a family or community member would be rendered more legible, or as evidence for a broader claim of systemic injustice. Where funding and research is increasingly focused on Indigenous data initiatives, a focus on addressing both the grief of loss and the necessary structural changes to police/state violence is deferred by a focus on data precision and messaging to quickly circulate shocking facts. An increased visibility of Native death and loss is neither equivalent to nor eventuates its condolence or redress.

Additionally, equating a shared rate of death with authentic coalitional politics on the ground is misleading. This comparison oversimplifies the complexities of political alliances and can, in some cases, reinforce anti-Blackness when Native organizations co-opt the symbolism of abolitionist movements led by Black people. Liu and Shange (2018, p. 190) call this *thin solidarity* or "solidarity based on notions of shared suffering [that] often creates false equivalence between different experiences of racialized violence." Thin solidarity can also manifest in the circulation of data about Native death for a wider audience, which itself cannot replace the localized, relationship-building collective practices of condolence that are necessary for addressing real experiences of grief and loss.

Alternatively, Indigenous people in their communities have a long history of *beginning* demands for safety, justice, and redress within a language of relationality and responsibility, grounded and originating in specific Indigenous governance structures and practices. The following and last section of this article presents two such examples of addressing the settler state's drive toward Native death through Indigenous ethics of care and relational practices.

Reorienting Toward Indigenous Relationality

The material and epistemic subordination of Native life, inclusive of state violence against Native Peoples, is reproduced through the units, measures, and circulation of data. In contrast to data that measures comparative inequalities, Indigenous ethics of care and relational practices confront the social and political limitations of counts and measures (Holmes et al. 2015; Kolopenuk 2020; Liboiron 2021). Such framing interrupts and rejects the standard scholarly measurement of overrepresentation in rates of death in favor of analyses that undermine the U.S. colonial state's claims to corresponding territorial and juridical dominance (Goldstein 2008) by engaging place- and peoples-based analytics, protocols, and critique.

In closing, we bring attention to two examples in which Indigenous people have worked to confront and refuse the colonial power of data: the Akwesasne Mohawk's fight to protect its members from waterway contamination, and the embodied repurposing of the body bags received by the Seattle Indian Health Board into a ribbon dress by their Chief Research Officer, Abigail Echo-Hawk. We visit these examples to think alongside recent efforts of Indigenous scholars who have maintained that we may define historical modes of Indigenous knowledge production, dissemination, and sharing as Indigenous "data."

In the world of colonial data-making, Indigenous researchers and Indigenous nations' employees are confronted with a dual bind: First, Native peoplehoods are coerced and conscripted to engage in practices of data-making that are co-constituted with U.S. state governance (Simpson 2016; Benjamin 2016). Second, colonial structures of recognition require that Native Peoples make themselves legible to colonial governments and agents (Coulthard 2014). Efforts toward Indigenous data inclusion and sovereignty are confronting real issues faced by tribes and Indigenous Nations occupied by the U.S. and Canada, among others; specifically, they are struggling to bring the collection and use of health and genomic data under the purview of tribal governments or Indigenous governance (Hudson et al. 2020).

A feature of this bind is that colonial relations of (mis)recognition shape the context, conditions, and possibilities in which Indigenous Peoples and organizations can and must respond to threats against their health, well-being, and rights as peoplehoods. Their work and ethics of care continuously risk conscription into the discursive and material practices of U.S. colonialism that, as Million (2013) shows, has allowed Indigenous struggles for rights and recognition to be medicalized, pathologized, and co-opted by various institutions in settler colonial states. These structures, however, cannot and do not foreclose possibilities for re-imagining and continuing to create vibrant Indigenous flourishing, acts of care for the people, and data refusal.

Within Indigenous communities and Nations and in urban settings there are many examples of ways that Indigenous-led movements and practices have engaged data as a tool of redress in ways that emerge from emplaced practices of care, consent, and governance. One key example is the work of Katsi Cook of the Akwesasne Mohawk Nation to take control of a research process on environmental toxins on Nation lands (Cook 2003). While previous studies done by Mount Sinai School of Medicine researchers in New York City has resulted in a successful string of publications and funding for distant researchers, the only outcome for the people of Akwesasne was a suggestion that Akwesasro:non discontinue the consumption of local fish: a central aspect of their lifeways and foodways as a people. In response, Cook and others in the Nation enrolled breastfeeding mothers into studies that would aid Akwesasro:non in obtaining data that would argue for a stringent cleanup, and they worked to teach SUNY Albany researchers how to build relationships of integrity with the community. This influenced how data was collected, how it was translated and communicated, and precisely what toxins were measured across the bodies and beings of the multispecies collectivity of people and other beings living at Akwesasne. For Akwesasro:non, this grounded research method was distilled through the development of the Good Mind Research Protocol, that is still in use today and governs what and how research is done and how data is disseminated and stored; it also outlines proper compensation methods. The work of Cook and other Akwesasro:non demonstrates not only how the colonial present requires occupied peoples to become fluent in processes of data-making and of rendering aspects of their lives "legible," but how Indigenous people may still do so on their own terms.

Another way in which colonial drives of data-making are refused is in Indigenous material culture, which challenges the bounded solutions that emerge through data-centric modes of approaching problems and community crises. The body bags received by the SIHB, for example, became the material with which SIHB Chief Research Officer Abigail Echo-Hawk (Pawnee) created the ribbon dress pictured below (figure 1). This dress circulated widely on various social media platforms and was featured in *Vogue* magazine in February of 2021. As a means of processing the horror of the body bag shipment, Echo-Hawk refashioned the material of the body bag into a dress. Along the inner line of the full-length zipper, Echo-Hawk repeated the words in felt pen: "I am a manifestation of my ancestors resiliency I am a manifestation of my ancestors resiliency." The zipper is opened and folded to the side, revealing a bright yellow floral Indigenous print material. This written affirmation and the woodlands-patterned fabric fill the inside of the repurposed body bag with assertions of Indigenous life. Toe

FIGURE 1. Echo-Hawk, Abigail. Ribbon Dress. Facebook, February 9, 2021. Photo by Abigail Echo-Hawk.

tags for the dead were instead sewn into the cuffs of the sleeves and woven like basketwork into silk ribbon. Three layers of ribbon also line the bottom of the dress. By placing three red handprints in a column down the right side of the dress, Echo-Hawk connects the death and stifled voices that the red handprint symbolizes in the Missing and Murdered Indigenous Women and Girls (MMIWG) movement with the death and stifled voices of Native people within a global pandemic. The small, circular mirrors that dot the chest of the dress, Echo-Hawk notes in a public social media post, "deflect and reflect back to those who dare try to cause us harm" (Echo-Hawk 2020).

These two examples—of engaging community concerns about environmental contamination and health from a Kanien'kéha:ka perspective and protocol and of repurposing the body bags sent to an urban Indian health clinic during the COVID-19 pandemic—upend the assumption that more data alone can resolve community crises. Both efforts confront the limitations of data by engaging in practices that affirm and build Indigenous life and futures. In doing so, they oppose the drive toward Indigenous death and settler colonial status quo that is often reinforced by research practices.

Conclusion: Governance of Data, or Data as Colonial Governance?

We have shown in this article how data histories and settler colonialism are co-produced and continue to inform the contemporary call for Indigenous data inclusion. Thus, data and colonial power are always entangled. We have traced these entanglements to urge careful attention to how colonial power shapes data relations. With a focus on the aftermaths of the COVID-19 pandemic and 2020 uprisings against racist police violence, we analyzed how particular ways of being in good relation are foreclosed, how data produces the double binds of legibility, and how the re-racialization of Indigenous Peoples brackets out matters of Indigenous sovereignty and land-based self-determination. In response, we reject a Manichean binary that claims that calculative data is *always* bad and *only* colonial, and that Indigenous Peoples cannot find data-making practices necessary or even beneficial. We therefore close with two questions: Given the historic and ongoing coloniality of data, can data *cum* data be decolonial in the material sense that Tuck and Yang (2012) describe—that is, as a mode of land return and Indigenous resurgence? Additionally, *must* data be part of a decolonizing project if there seem to be no better options for Indigenous Peoples to sustain themselves?

We do not claim to hold answers to these questions. By turning away from logics of Indigenous erasure and the politically evacuated promises of inclusion and recognition that undergird normative practices of data-making, Indigenous relations and resurgence can, in fact, be centered in knowledge production. Indigenous Peoples have found ways to refuse our subjectification as Indians in need of care by the U.S. government or as a group who require legibility to colonial actors. Indigenous Peoples have also shown that we need not prove that our practices and modes of accounting, responsibility, and valuation are "data" in order to be valid and useful (Carroll et al. 2019; Liboiron 2021; Walter and Andersen 2013). Stuart Hall (1997) aptly demonstrated that historical identity, here Indigeneity, has no foundational political guarantee, and so even Indigenous people and tribal governments themselves can engage in and produce colonial relations of data. Despite this, as we have shown above, there are times when urgently needed data have been *withheld* from tribal nations, excluding Native Peoples from engaging in necessary, life-saving, data-making practices. Future research may consider under which conditions data inclusion is the best possibility for the immediate care of Native people. Critiques and frameworks must be built that take these prospects seriously.

Indigenous people are constantly ensuring the flourishing of their peoplehoods and broadening the conversation we engage here by sharing and learning from and across community-driven engagement with data and legibility. Each Indigenous peoplehood, urban Native community, and organization will continually work out their relationships to these data and the relationships made through investments in the power of this data. Rather than standing behind a specific way forward, our sentiments in this paper echo the current Indigenous data sovereignty movement: Indigenous Peoples must ultimately be in charge of decisions about their own data. As we have shown in this article, a data point is not an end in itself; instead, as a means toward other ends, data must be negotiated carefully. By considering both the colonial stakes and the valuable potential of data, insights about a group's collective relations to and within those data can emerge. In all cases, data will always put Indigenous Peoples, communities, and organizations in relation with others in a historically and geographically specific way that is rooted both in colonial power and in Indigenous, nonextractive relationalities.

MEREDITH ALBERTA PALMER (Tuscarora, Six Nations of the Grand River) is an assistant professor of geography and Indigenous studies at the University at Buffalo. She is a critical Indigenous geographer who researches technologies of colonial dispossession and works to amplify and build ways in which they are refused.

THERESA ROCHA BEARDALL (Oneida/Sault Ste. Marie/Mexican) is an associate professor of sociology at the University of Washington. Her research critically examines how U.S. legal systems and state agents engage in structural violence against marginalized communities, specializing in issues of race, law, family, policing, dispossession, and tribal sovereignty.

References

Akee, Randall KQ, Eric Henson, Miriam Jorgensen, and Joseph Kalt. "Policy Brief #2: Dissecting the U.S. Treasury Department's Round 1 Allocations of CARES Act COVID-19 Relief Funding for Tribal Governments." Harvard University, Cambridge, MA, 2020. http://nrs.harvard.edu/urn-3:HUL.Inst Repos:42672265.

Anderson, Kay. *Race and the Crisis of Humanism.* Routledge, 2007.

Arvin, Maile Renee. *Possessing Polynesians: The Science of Settler Colonial Whiteness in Hawaii and Oceania.* Durham: Duke University Press, 2019.

Bichell, Rae Ellen. "Pandemic Complicates Tribes' Quest For Data Sovereignty." *KUNC.* July 13, 2020. https://www.kunc.org/health/2020-07-13/pandemic -complicates-tribes-quest-for-data-sovereignty

Benjamin, Ruha. "Informed refusal: Toward a Justice-Based Bioethics." *Science, Technology, & Human Values* 41, no. 6 (2016): 967–90. https://doi .org/10.1177/016224391665605.

Burrell, Jenna, Ranjit Singh, and Patrick Davison. "Keywords of the Datafied State." *Available at SSRN 4734250* (2024).

Byrd, Jodi A. *The Transit of Empire: Indigenous Critiques of Colonialism.* University of Minnesota Press, 2011.

Carroll, Stephanie Russo, Desi Rodriguez-Lonebear, and Andrew Martinez. 2019. "Indigenous Data Governance: Strategies from United States Native Nations." *Data Science Journal* 18:31, 1—15.

Cook, Katsi. "Cook: Women Are the First Environment." Indian Country Today, December 23, 2003. https://indiancountrytoday.com/archive/cook-women -are-the-first-environment.

Coulthard, Glen Sean. *Red Skin, White Masks: Rejecting the Colonial Politics of Recognition.* U of Minnesota Press, 2014.

Curtis, Chelsea. "Hopi Tribe releases ZIP code data, but COVID-19 data for Arizona's 22 communities is confusing." *AZ Central.* June 4, 2020. https:// www.azcentral.com/story/news/local/arizona-health/2020/06/04/corona virus-arizona-indigenous-communities-cases-covid-19-data-hopi-navajo /3091650001/

Deloria, Philip Joseph. *Indians in Unexpected Places.* University Press of Kansas, 2004.

Deloria, Vine Jr. *Behind the Trail of Broken Treaties: An Indian Declaration of Independence.* University of Texas Press, 2010.

Deloria, Vine Jr. "Intellectual Self-Determination and Sovereignty: Looking at the Windmills in our Minds." *Wicazo Sa Review* 13, no. 1 (1998): 25—31.

Denetdale, Jennifer Nez. "`Building the Perfect Body to Invade': An Analysis of the Dikos Ntsaaígíí (COVID-19)/From Bordertowns to the Navajo Nation," *Indian Cities: Histories of Indigenous Urbanism* (University of Oklahoma Press, in press)

Duthu, Bruce. *Shadow Nations: Tribal Sovereignty and the Limits of Legal Pluralism.* Oxford University Press, 2013.

Drucker, Johanna. "Humanities Approaches to Graphical Display." *Digital Humanities Quarterly* 5, no. 1 (2011): 1–21.

Echo-Hawk, Abigail. "It's done. After six months of starting and stopping . . ." Facebook. (December 14, 2020). https://www.facebook.com/permalink.php ?story_fbid=pfbido2zvhTW1Jj7DzzeyBay1K3RTM26ZEdvQynvns7Meus SUGLjsLKyJS7TLQodTfepjznl&id=1260036730787825

Edwards, Frank, Hedwig Lee, and Michael Esposito. "Risk of Being Killed by Police Use of Force in the United States by Age, Race–Ethnicity, and Sex." *Proceedings of the National Academy of Sciences* 116, no. 34 (2019): 16793–16798.

Elden, Stuart. "Governmentality, Calculation, Territory." *Environment and Planning D: Society and Space* 25, no. 3 (2007): 562–580.

Eze, Emmanuel Chukwudi, ed. *Race and the Enlightenment: A Reader.* Wiley-Blackwell, 1997.

Fanon, Frantz. *Black Skin, White Masks.* Grove press, 2008.

Foucault, Michel. *Security, Territory, Population: Lectures at the Collège de France, 1977–78.* Springer, 2007.

Foucault, Michel. "The Subject and Power." *Critical Inquiry* 8, no. 4 (1982): 777–795.

Fullwiley, Duana. "The Biologistical Construction of Race: 'Admixture' Technology and the New Genetic Medicine." *Social Studies of Science* 38, no. 5 (2008): 695–735.

General Allotment Act of 1887, 25 U.S.C. ch. 9 § 331–337 (1887), (repealed 2000).

Goldberg-Ambrose, C. Public Law 280 and the Problem of Lawlessness in California Indian Country. *UCLA Law Review* 1405, 1996.

Goldstein, Alyosha. "Where the Nation Takes Place: Proprietary Regimes, Antistatism, and U.S. Settler Colonialism." *South Atlantic Quarterly* 107, no. 4 (2008): 833–861.

Goodluck, Kalen. 2020. "Indigenous Data Sovereignty Shakes up Research." *High Country News.* October 8. https://www.hcn.org/issues/52-11/indigenous -affairs-covid19-indigenous-data-sovereignty-shakes-up-research/

Government Accountability Office. "Tribal Epidemiology Centers: HHS Actions Needed to Enhance Data Access," March 4, 2022. https://www.gao.gov /products/gao-22-104698

Hall, Stuart. 2021. "Race, the Floating Signifier: What More Is There to Say about 'Race'?" In *Selected Writings on Race and Difference*, edited by Paul Gilroy and Ruth Wilson Gilmore, 359–73. Duke University Press.

Hansen, Elise. 2017. "A Forgotten Minority in Police Shootings." *CNN.* November 13. https://www.cnn.com/2017/11/10/us/native-lives-matter/index.html.

Haraway, Donna Jeanne. 1989. *Primate visions: Gender, Race, and Nature in the World of Modern Science.* Psychology Press.

Hoffman, Anna Lauren. 2020. "Terms of Inclusion: Data, Discourse, Violence." *New Media and Society:* 1–18.

Holmes, Cindy, Sarah Hunt, and Amy Piedalue. 2015. "Violence, Colonialism and Space: Towards a Decolonizing Dialogue." *ACME: An International Journal for Critical Geographies* 14, no. 2: 539–570.

Hudson, Maui, Garrison Nanibaa'A., Rogena Sterling, Nadine R. Caron, Keolu Fox, Joseph Yracheta, and Jane Anderson et al. 2020. "Rights, Interests and Expectations: Indigenous Perspectives on Unrestricted Access to Genomic Data." *Nature Reviews Genetics* 21, no. 6: 377–384.

John, Maria K. 2020. "The Violence of Abandonment: Urban Indigenous Health and the Settler-Colonial Politics of Nonrecognition in the United States and Australia." *Native American and Indigenous Studies* 7, no. 1: 87–120.

Justice, Daniel Heath, and Jean M. Brien, eds. 2022. *Allotment Stories: Indigenous Land Relations Under Settler Siege.* University of Minnesota Press.

Kolopenuk, Jessica. "Miskâsowin: Indigenous Science, Technology, and Society." *Genealogy* 4, no. 1 (2020): 21.

Kolopenuk, Jessica. "Provoking Bad Biocitizenship." *Hastings Center Report* 50 (2020): S23-S29. https://doi.org/10.1002/hast.1152.

Krieger, Nancy. 2009. "Putting Health Inequities on the Map: Social Epidemiology Meets Medical/Health Geography——An Ecosocial Perspective." *GeoJournal* 74, no. 2: 87–97.

Krieger, Nancy, Jarvis T. Chen, Pamela D. Waterman, Mathew V. Kiang, and Justin Feldman. 2015. "Police Killings and Police Deaths are Public Health Data and Can Be Counted." *PLoS Medicine* 12, no. 12: e1001915.

Liboiron, Max. *Pollution is Colonialism.* Duke University Press, 2021.

Liu, Roseann, and Savannah Shange. "Toward Thick Solidarity: Theorizing Empathy in Social Justice Movements." *Radical History Review* 2018, no. 131 (2018): 189–198.

Lovett, Raymond, Vanessa Lee, Tahu Kukutai, Donna Cormack, Stephanie Carroll Rainie, and Jennifer Walker. 2019. "Good Data Practices for Indigenous Data Sovereignty" in *Good Data,* edited by Angela Daly, S. Kate Devitt, and Monique Mann. Amsterdam: Institute of Network Cultures.

McKittrick, Katherine. 2014. "Mathematics Black Life." *The Black Scholar* 44, no. 2: 16–28.

Million, Dian. 2013. *Therapeutic Nations: Healing in an Age of Indigenous Human Rights.* University of Arizona Press.

Million, D. 2021. "Resurgent Kinships: Indigenous Relations of Well-Being vs. Humanitarian Health Economies." *Routledge Handbook of Critical Indigenous Studies*, 1st ed., 1:392–404. Routledge.

Moreton-Robinson, Aileen. *The White Possessive: Property, Power, and Indigenous Sovereignty.* University of Minnesota Press, 2015.

Morgensen, Scott Lauria. 2011. "The Biopolitics of Settler Colonialism: Right Here, Right Now." *Settler Colonial Studies* 1, no. 1: 52–76.

Nagle, Rebecca. 2020. "Native Americans Being Left Out of US Coronavirus Data and Labelled as 'Other'" *The Guardian.* April 24. https://www.theguardian.com /us-news/2020/apr/24/us-native-americans-left-out-coronavirus-data.

Nichols, Robert. 2017. "The Colonialism of Incarceration." In *Legal Violence and the Limits of the Law,* 49–67. Routledge.

Olugbenga, Ajilore. 2017. "Native Americans Deserve More Attention in the Police Violence Conversation." *Urban Institute,* December 4. https://www.urban.org /urban-wire/native-americans-deserve-more-attention-police-violence -conversation.

O'Neill, Eilis. 2021. "Unrecognized Tribes Struggle Without Federal Aid During Pandemic." NPR. https://www.npr.org/2021/04/17/988123599/unrecognized -tribes-struggle-without-federal-aide-during-pandemic.

Palmer, Meredith Alberta. "Rendering Settler Sovereign Landscapes: Race and Property in the Empire State." *Environment and Planning D: Society and Space* 38, no. 5 (2020): 793–810.

Palmer, Meredith Alberta. 2024. "An Indigenous Geographic Position on Producing Data in Colonial Conditions." *Geography Compass* 18, no. 5: e12746.

Piatote, Beth H. 2013. "The Indian/Agent Aporia." *Studies in American Indian Literatures* 25, no. 2: 45–62.

Pirtle, Whitney N. Laster. 2020. "Racial Capitalism: A Fundamental Cause of Novel Coronavirus (COVID-19) Pandemic Inequities in the United States." *Health Education & Behavior* 47, no. 4: 504–508.

Porter, Theodore M. 1996. *Trust in Numbers.* Princeton University Press

Pratt, Mary Louise. 1992. *Imperial eyes: Travel Writing and Transculturation.* Routledge.

Radin, Joanna. 2017. ""Digital Natives": How Medical and Indigenous Histories Matter for Big Data." *Osiris* 32, no. 1: 43–64.

Ramirez, Renya K. 2007. *Native Hubs: Culture, Community, and Belonging in Silicon Valley and beyond.* Duke University Press.

Reardon, Jenny, and Kim TallBear. 2012. "'Your DNA is Our History' Genomics, Anthropology, and the Construction of Whiteness as Property." *Current Anthropology* 53, no. S5: S233-S245.

Rocha Beardall, Theresa Ysabel. 2019. "Transactional Policing: Reframing Local Police-Community Relations Through the Lens of Police Employment." Ph.D. diss., Cornell University. https://ecommons.cornell.edu/items/4adc96a5 -1433-4bdd-9d37-6bb42501b531.

Rocha Beardall, Theresa. 2020. "Social-Distancing the Settler-State: Indigenous Peoples in the Age of COVID-19." In *Social Problems in the Age of COVID-19,* 39–50. Policy Press.

Rocha Beardall, Theresa, and Frank Edwards. 2021. "Abolition, Settler Colonialism, and the Persistent Threat of Indian Child Welfare." *Colombia Journal of Race and Law* 11, no. 3: 533–574.

Rocha Beardall, Theresa. 2023. "Toward a Sociology of Indigenous Placemaking." In *New Approaches to Inequality Research with Youth,* 13–28. Routledge.

Rocha Beardall, Theresa. 2024. ""Imperialism Without Imperialists" and the Settler-Colonial Logics of Reservation Policing." In *Police and State Crime in the Americas: Southern and Postcolonial Perspectives,* 49–70. Springer International Publishing.

Seattle Indian Health Board. 2025. https://www.sihb.org/about/.

Simpson, Audra. 2007. "On the Logic of Discernment." *American Quarterly* 59, no. 2 (June): 479–491.

Simpson, Audra. 2014. *Mohawk Interruptus: Political Life Across the Borders of Settler States.* Duke University Press.

Small-Rodriguez, Desi, and Theresa Rocha Beardall. 2023. "Tribal Sovereignty and the Limits of Race for American Indians." In *The Oxford Handbook of Indigenous Sociology*, edited by M. Walter, T. Kukutai, A. Gonzales, and R. Henry. Oxford University Press.

Snipp, C. Matthew. 2003. "Racial Measurement in the American Census: Past Practices and Implications for the Future." *Annual Review of Sociology* 29, no. 1: 563–588.

Tahir, Darius, and Cancryn, Adam. 2020. "American Indian Tribes Thwarted in Efforts to Get Coronavirus Data." *Politico.* June 11. https://www.politico.com/news/2020/06/11/native-american-coronavirus-data-314527.

TallBear, Kim. 2013. *Native American DNA: Tribal Belonging and the False Promise of Genetic Science.* University of Minnesota Press.

"The Halluci Nation—Woodcarver (Official Video)." 2011. YouTube video. "The Halluci Nation." March 20, https://www.youtube.com/watch?v=sx4JLPBMUxo.

Trouillot, Michel-Rolph. "Anthropology and the Savage Slot: The Poetics and Politics of Otherness." In *Global Transformations:* 7–28. Palgrave Macmillan, 2003.

Urban Indian Health Institute. 2020. https://www.uihi.org/about/.

Tuck, Eve, and K. Wayne Yang. "Decolonization is Not a Metaphor." *Decolonization: Indigeneity, Education & Society* 1, no. 1 (2012).

U.S. Department of Justice Indian Country Investigations and Prosecution. 2016. https://www.justice.gov/tribal/page/file/1032116/download#page=1.00&gsr=0

Wade, Lizzie. "COVID-19 Data on Native Americans Is "a National Disgrace." This Scientist is Fighting to be Counted." *Science* (2020). https://www.science.org/content/article/covid-19-data-native-americans-national-disgrace-scientist-fighting-be-counted.

Walter, Maggie, and Chris Andersen. 2013. *Indigenous Statistics: A Quantitative Research Methodology.* Left Coast Press.

Williams, Robert A. 2012. *Savage Anxieties: The Invention of Western Civilization.* New York: St. Martin's Press.

Notes

1. Throughout this paper we use four terms to refer to the Indigenous people who are the original habitants of lands now territorialized as the United States: Native, Native American, Indigenous, and American Indian. We use some of these terms interchangeably to be inclusive and respectful of the myriad ways that people identify with their Indigenous status. Additionally, we designate our use of the term American Indian when referring to federal law, policies, and administrative processes associated with healthcare, census designations, and other formally bureaucratic processes.

2. In a 1998 article, Vine Deloria Jr. describes how the term "self-determination" specifically arose in a post–World War I context against Woodrow Wilsonian ideas and policies of assimilation. Deloria writes that the term aimed to open up space between tribal governments and the federal government and was therefore defined by a colonial relationship.

3. We would like to thank reviewer #1 for their insights and succinct clarification of our argument. We have adapted their phrasing here.

4. In this paper we are invested in exploring and understanding Indigenous ways of knowing, being, and relating that cannot be held or communicated with numerical data. We appreciate the often-cited examples of Indigenous modes of counting as validation that Indigenous Peoples have "always done data" or to prove that Indigenous Peoples have used numbers differently, therefore provincializing Western modes of counting. However, we are interested in analyzing how modes of counting are imbued with logics, assumptions, and expectations of the social world that, in their attempt to render and speak experiences as universal, collapse Indigenous life and relations into a set of monolithic assumptions.

5. Pratt (1992) terms the historic universalizing reach of knowledge production *planetary consciousness,* which was figured by early European explorers and travel writers as neutral, ordered, and universal. Haraway describes how "men became man in the practice of modest witnessing" (1997, 92) and analyzes how the transparent modesty of early experimenters produced the illusion that the "nature" they were studying was speaking for itself as "God" intended. Such pronouncements of neutrality and universality embody the "god-trick" of science, in which an all-knowing "conquering gaze from nowhere" was in fact racially and geographically constituted as an Anglo male.

6. The U.S. federal government is required by a trust agreement—rooted in early treaty stipulations that promised medical care to tribes coerced to sign over their lands—to provide medical care to Native people who are enrolled tribal members at no cost. Clinics such as the SIHB are vital spaces of care and connection for Native people who are more often made invisible in cities (Deloria 2004; Ramirez 2007).

7. We differentiate these dynamics and note not all techniques of data-making converge with aspects of the Indigenous Data Sovereignty movement described above. We do not focus explicitly on the broad and emerging field of IDS, nor on the propensity of non-Native entities who create data "about" Native people and histories and traffic in it for their own ends.

8. In this article we use "nationhood" and "peoplehood" somewhat interchangeably. While both are used to distinguish Indigenous collectivities separate from common yet apolitical and culturally based distinctions as "communities," the term *peoplehood* denotes an historic intersociality that is broader than the state-based associations of a Euroamerican sovereignty.

9. Critical Race Theory and, more recently, critical humanist analyses emerging from Black studies have mapped the many ways that differences between "humans" came to be placed on a hierarchy and made material in the world (Anderson 2007; McKittrick 2014). The conjecture that so-called Native American people, encompassing various wholes or parts of the Indigenous Peoples that lived anywhere in the American continents before 1492, are a distinct class, variety, or kind of human is a tenet of early racial theories and philosophies that emerge in European philosophies (see Pratt 1992; Eze 1997; Williams 2012), and proliferated in U.S. institutions of academia, government,

and medicine and health. Thus, we stress the importance of understanding the co-constitution of colonialism and racism. Concepts of race were at work in the world and in U.S. imperialism long before they came to be biologized and made into a science in the late 1800s, and before they became population-based units of the modern nation-state. Nonetheless, racism and colonialism cannot be collapsed.

10. There are data, then, to be found about Native death at the hands of police in the U.S. For example, recent analysis show that Natives are three times more likely to be killed by police than whites (Hansen 2017), and Native women are twice as likely as white women to be killed by police (Edwards, Lee, and Esposito 2019). Recent data also indicate that Native deaths caused by police shootings nearly doubled in recent years, increasing from 5.49 per one million people in 2015 to 10.13 per one million people in 2016. Data also indicate that Natives ages 20–24, 25–34, and 35–44 were three of the five groups most likely to be killed by police among all social groups in the U.S. To read or hear these rates at which police kill Native people is alarming and unsettling, if rarely discussed in policing scholarship and in mass media. We have chosen to place these numbers in an endnote to illustrate that so-called disparities in rates exist, and perhaps most importantly, to allow readers a chance to examine their own reactions to these rates and their attempt to enumerate, value, or represent Native life.

JUSTIN GROSSMAN

Who Saved Edinbur Randall?
The Wampanoag of Gay Head, Race,
and the Telling of a Fugitive Slave Escape

Abstract

In 1854, members of the Wampanoag Tribe of Gay Head on the island of Martha's Vineyard rescued an escaped enslaved person named Edinbur Randall and led him to safety. All traces of an Indigenous presence in the story were erased when local and regional newspapers reported on the escape. Contrastingly, members of the Wampanoag Tribe, which has a long history of incorporating outsiders of different races, told and retold the story of Randall's rescue in ways that highlighted their Native identity, but simultaneously downplayed their African ancestry. During a period when Massachusetts was using strict blood interpretations of race to support policies designed to eliminate Native tribes, the different ways in which the identity of Randall's Wampanoag rescuers were portrayed in these accounts shows how members of the tribe both actively challenged Euro-Americans' conceptions of Native extinction and racialized Indianness even as Wampanoag identity became tied up with notions of racial belonging. Looking at how Native and non-Native authors from different generations characterize race in their telling of the Edinbur Randall story therefore reveals how the Wampanoag negotiated defining their own identity in ways that allowed them to survive eliminationist policies that would later be replicated across North America.

IN 1921, more than sixty years after her grandparents William and Beulah helped the fugitive slave Edinbur Randall escape from Martha's Vineyard, Netta Vanderhoop revisited the affair in an article she wrote for *The Vineyard Gazette*. Titled "The True Story of a Fugitive Slave: Or the Story a Gay Head Grandmother Told," the author highlights the Indigenous identity of her grandparents but says nothing of their African heritage.[1] There are multiple ways to read Netta's account of her grandparents that reflect underlying tensions at the heart of the Tribe's own understanding of racial identity. The first view, expressed by Netta's mother and William and

Beulah's daughter-in-law, Mary A. Cleggett Vanderhoop, is that the inclusivity and openness of Wampanoag society is what made it special and allowed it to survive colonization. In this account, having some non-Native ancestry has no bearing on one's belonging in the Tribe, for Indianness is based on culture, values, and kinship.[2] Alternatively, Netta's omission of her grandparents' African lineage could be seen as a pragmatic response to a settler colonial framework of race that was and continues to be used to categorize and eliminate Native people.[3] Within a context in which race was a tool of discrimination and threat to Tribal sovereignty, it follows that this prejudice was internalized to a certain degree as notions of racial purity seeped into disputes over land, access to Tribal resources, and later federal recognition status.[4] Therefore, Netta's silence can be read as revelatory of the inconsequential nature of skin color to belonging in Wampanoag Gay Head, a purposeful omission carefully navigating how settler colonial authorities and local interests weaponized racialized Indigeneity and anti-Blackness to disregard Tribal sovereignty, or some combination of the two. In this way, the subsequent telling and retelling of Randall's escape offers a way to track how the Wampanoag negotiated the role that race played in their own identity as the Tribe fought to preserve and pass along their heritage for future generations within a colonial "context of coercion."[5]

The Escape

While the accounts of Randall's story are littered with ambiguity with regard to race and identity, his testimony and Netta Vanderhoop's article align on most of the details.[6] Randall hid himself in the cargo hold of a ship leaving Jacksonville, Florida, sometime in 1854. Overheating and in desperate need of water, Randall was forced to reveal himself to the crew after a few days at sea. The captain, whether out of proslavery leanings or frightened by the consequences of subverting the recently imposed Fugitive Slave Act of 1850, threatened to "put [Edinbur] on board the first vessel . . . bound for the South."[7] This was perhaps more charitable than some earlier suggestions to "throw him overboard," although Randall later states this would have been preferable to a return to bondage.[8]

Considering these threats, Randall decided to jump ship when the captain docked at Holmes Hole on the island of Martha's Vineyard off the coast of Massachusetts.[9] The sailors on the ship, who had befriended, fed, and clothed Randall after his discovery, told him that, "if [he] went to the south-westerly part of the Island, [he] should find friends among the Indians."[10] Randall took the sailors' advice and started making his way toward Gay Head.

At this point, William Vanderhoop, Beulah Salsbury, and the other Wampanoags living on the island enter the picture. Although Netta's account and Randall's later testimony differ slightly, the local deputy sheriff offered William Vanderhoop a reward to help find "a man who had run away from a ship," a request that was overheard by Beulah Salsbury, William's wife.[11] On returning to Gay Head, Salsbury got word of a man hiding in a nearby swamp. Figuring that he was probably a fugitive slave, she coaxed Randall out of the swamp, disguised him in women's clothes, and arranged for his escape. The people of Gay Head, "armed with guns, pitchforks, clubs, and almost anything that would do to fight with," stood guard against the pursuing sheriff, while a boat was fashioned by Samuel Peters, also of Gay Head, who proceeded to take Randall to the abolitionist hotbed of New Bedford.[12] After a few weeks in the city, Randall safely sailed to freedom in Nova Scotia, Canada, where he remained until after the Civil War.

While the details surrounding Randall's escape generally line up in these accounts, themes of race and identity vary depending on the author's perspective. Euro-American reporting at the time, by contrast, wrote William Vanderhoop, Beulah Salsbury, and the people of Gay Head out of the story entirely. The various narratives surrounding Randall's escape reveal dynamic and competing views toward race both between Euro-Americans and the Wampanoag Tribe and within the Tribe itself. By analyzing how race is portrayed or hidden in these accounts, their Native and non-Native authors demonstrate its contested role in shaping Wampanoag and New England society.

Race in Native New England

Since the 1990s, after years of silence on the history of Native people in New England after King Phillip's War, scholarship on the continuing presence of these Tribes in the region has flourished. As part of that research, some historians have started to grapple with the issue of defining race in Native New England since the onset of colonization.[13] Nancy Shoemaker, for example, examines how Native whalers' self-fashioned and perceived racial identity changed depending on where in the world they were, who they were in contact with, and the gender dynamics between the (mostly) men operating the ships and women living on.[14] She also highlights how state authorities struggled to fit Native people and their increasingly global communities into the neat Black/white spectrum of racial categorization that became common in the United States in the nineteenth century.[15]

While Shoemaker's focus is on Native people's racial identity, the scope of her work as a story of Atlantic and then global proportions means that views of race within the Tribes receive less attention. Other studies take a more localized approach to studying race within Native New England generally and the Wampanoag Tribe specifically. Much of this research is centered on the Massachusetts Enfranchisement Act of 1869 and the privatization of communal land.[16] Elliotte D. Draeger and David Silverman note how land privatization caused tension between Black, nonproprietor men who had married into the Tribe, and Native, mostly female, proprietors.[17] The state of Massachusetts carried out allotment, which split up Indian "plantations" into individually held lots, using their own gendered assumptions of men as the heads of households and owners of property.[18] This meant that Native women who controlled access to land under Tribal law and were married lost jurisdiction to their spouses even if they were non-Native. The men could then sell the privatized lots to individuals outside of the Tribe, making it difficult to maintain communal land practices and Tribal cohesion. Using town property records, Draeger shows how this contributed to a precipitous drop in Native land holdings at Mashpee in the late nineteenth and early twentieth century.[19] Meanwhile, Silverman asserts that the Wampanoag at Gay Head were able to continue their communal land practices because of their control over the newly created town government but that this did not occur without a newly virulent anti-Blackness among some individuals in the Tribe.[20]

Lastly, Ann Marie Plane and Gregory Button's scholarship ties together local and regional perceptions of race.[21] By using the law as a lens through which to view the state's racialized notions of Massachusetts's Native people and as a catalyst for changing notions of race within the Tribes, they analyze the fluidity of race in the 1860s from multiple perspectives. The Massachusetts Enfranchisement Act of 1869 was a precursor to the nationwide contests over racial belonging within Native Tribes that would later be spurred by the Dawes Act. In both cases, settler colonial authorities, first the Massachusetts State Legislature and later Congress and the Bureau of Indian Affairs (BIA), enacted policies of blood quantum and allotment that threatened to sever Native people from their land and Tribal identity, and Native people, while successfully resisting assimilation and preserving their heritage, were forced to do so within a context in which Indianness as a racial category took on greater legal meaning.[22] However, like most historians to date, Plane and Button take a short-term outlook of racial identity centered on the 1869 Massachusetts Indian Enfranchisement Act. While the law has an important place in the history of race in Native Massachusetts, the scope does not let us see how these ideas persisted and/or changed in subsequent generations. Most notably, as federal Indian policy evolved in the twentieth century, the unrecognized status of most New England Tribes left them without access to many of the protections and BIA resources available to the recognized reservation-based Tribes further west.[23] Eventually, this forced many Eastern groups to subject themselves to the "Faustian bargain" of federal recognition and the federal acknowledgment process (FAP), which demanded that Tribes prove their political, cultural, and community cohesion in a way that fit the BIA's racialized definition of Native nationhood.[24] Within such constraints, the Wampanoag had to continually delineate and negotiate their own identity. Thus, the competing and changing portrayals of the people involved in Randall's escape offers an important throughline as a conduit for the examination of race and racialization in modern Wampanoag history.

Indians on the Underground Railroad

As the nation approached the Civil War, issues of race were on the minds of many New Englanders. Just a few years after the region had freed the last enslaved persons, secret societies, vigilance committees, and newspapers devoted to abolition were springing up in port cities such as New Bedford and Boston. Men such as William Lloyd Garrison, Frederick Douglass, and Henry David Thoreau railed against the evils of slavery.[25] In 1850s New England, a fugitive slave escape like Edinbur Randall's was something to celebrate, and indeed it was. However, it was also a story in which a Wampanoag presence did not line up with non-Native New Englander's views of Native people.

At the time of Randall's escape, coastal New England was home to thousands of Native people and dozens of Tribal communities. Those communities recognized by the state of Massachusetts such as the Wampanoag at Gay Head, Christiantown, Chappaquiddick, and Mashpee were organized into Indian "districts" or "plantations" which were supposed to be governed by a state-appointed "guardian." Massachusetts state authorities created these paternalistic designations, which turned Native people into wards of the state, with the intention to "Christianize" and "civilize" them, and were an offshoot of the earlier "praying towns" set up by missionaries at the beginning of the colonial era.[26] While the corruption of some of these guardians invariably led to further reduction in many of these Tribes' land and resources, at Gay Head the prospect of land privatization and seizure of land as debt collection spurred the Wampanoag to overthrow their guardians in 1811.[27] Therefore, up until the plantation system was abolished in 1869, distinctive Tribal communities were common in the state of Massachusetts and no group enjoyed more autonomy than the self-governing Wampanoag Tribe at Gay Head.

The strong presence of Native communities throughout New England did nothing to dissuade Euro-Americans of the notion that Indigenous people verged on extinction. Jean O'Brien coined the term "lasting" to describe how New England communities actively wrote Native people out of their histories by the nineteenth century, reimagining the region as an Anglicized space by claiming that such-and-such a person was the "last of their race."[28] In the early 1850s, Wampanoag in the neighboring town of Chilmark and the nearby island of Nantucket had already been subject to "lasting," even though their descendants still lived in these communities.[29]

It is no surprise, therefore, that in the contemporary reporting on Randall's escape there is no mention of Gay Head's Indian Plantation status and the Wampanoag identity of William Vanderhoop, Beulah Salsbury, Samuel Peters, and the rest of the community. In 1854, the *Vineyard Gazette* published a story "A Runaway Slave," an account that anglicized Randall's escape.[30] In this reporting, Beulah Salsbury, the Wampanoag woman who coordinated the rescue, is instead replaced by two unnamed women from "the lovely village of Holmes Hole."[31] Samuel Peters, the Wampanoag boatman who transported Randall to New Bedford, is recast as "a good pilot" also from Holmes Hole, an all-white town.[32]

Last in this process of disappearing the Wampanoag presence from the escape is a discrepancy as to the sheriff's whereabouts. In later accounts, upon hearing of the scores of armed men rising up at Gay Head to guard Randall before his rendezvous with Samuel Peters, the sheriff thought it the wiser to not make an appearance.[33] However, the *Vineyard Gazette* article from 1854 reports that the sheriff was approaching Menemsha as Randall was leaving, "but all was still and silent as the grave, save the music of the trickling water-brook, and the clear sharp notes of the feathered warblers, which sang freedom's sweetest, wildest song of jubilee. The sheriff was entranced, he forgot his mission, the reins fell from his hand, and he thought of nothing but nature, and music, and the goodness of God."[34] In this way, a beautiful evening, good conscience, and divine intervention make for a more plausible explanation as to the absence of the sheriff than a Wampanoag community's hand in a fugitive slave's escape and their own display of autonomy against an intrusion of white law enforcement.

The *Vineyard Gazette* reporting from 1854 suggests that for many white New Englanders at the time Indianness and the Underground Railroad were incompatible. The abolition movement was part of that "city upon a hill" mentality, which saw regional pride develop around the extension of citizenship and equality to Black people.[35] As Silverman writes, "The Bay Staters' pontifical air found justification in that the commonwealth had achieved the highest degree of civic equality for blacks of any state in the country."[36] Amidst this zeal of enlightenment with regard to the local Black population, Massachusetts lawmakers and most white voters found the district and guardianship system, which considered Native people wards of the state and incapable of voting, a lamentable divergence.[37] As the state grappled with its undemocratic approach to Native governance, the solution white leaders found was not to incorporate Tribes into government on these Tribes' own terms, but to do as the *Vineyard Gazette* had done and simply make them disappear.

Racial Purity and Indian Enfranchisement

In a speech addressed to the Massachusetts General Court on January 9, 1869, Governor William Claflin made a case for ridding the state of its Indian districts, disregarding any Tribal authority or sovereignty, and privatizing Tribal land for individual allotment. Race was central to his argument. Claflin stated, "These persons are not Indians in any sense of the word. It is doubtful there is a full-blooded Indian in the state."[38] Even before the first English settlement on Martha's Vineyard in 1642, intermarriage and incorporation of outsiders had been a part of Wampanoag life. This became even more prominent in the eighteenth and nineteenth centuries as a search for economic opportunities led to a steady outflow of young men from Gay Head. The importance of the whaling industry in coastal Massachusetts is well documented, and the Wampanoag whose lands make up the region were especially involved in and impacted by the industry's economic impacts and global scale.[39] Estimates indicate that almost 40 percent of whalers were Native during the late eighteenth century, and by 1792 one can already see the demographic results of absent, missing, or killed men in Gay Head as a census taken that year showed fifty-five adult women and only twenty-seven adult males.[40] This gender imbalance and the influx of men engaged in whaling and other seafaring occupations made for a large increase in the number of marriages between Wampanoag women and free men of color. William Vanderhoop was one of these men. Born in Suriname, Vanderhoop had been working on a merchant ship when he met Beulah on the mainland before the two married and moved back to Aquinnah in 1837.[41] John Salsbury, Beulah's father, was a Black nonproprietor born in Hudson, New York, who had fought and been captured by the British during the War of 1812. It was on his way back from imprisonment in Bermuda that Salsbury found his way to Gay Head and married Naomi Occouch, Beulah's mother.[42]

According to white New Englanders at the time, the intermarriage of Wampanoag and other Native groups was further proof of their imminent extinction. Plane and Button have shown how state and local authorities not only amalgamated Native and Black people into the indistinguishable label of "people of color," but also how they used this racial theory to deny the cultural distinctiveness of Indian communities. Plane and Button quote Benjamin Marchant, the town clerk of Edgartown on Martha's Vineyard, who in 1859 blamed all of the problems local Native people faced on "the mixture of blood-that of several races flowing in the same veins."[43] According to the clerk, this took on a gendered dimension in that Native men no longer felt any responsibility toward their people and therefore left at a young age, leaving the Tribes without leadership.[44] The dangers of racial mixing and a loss of Indian characteristics were similarly broadcast by an editorial in the *Boston Daily Advertiser* that said on the topic of young men leaving in search of work, "Their places have been filled by men of other races, till there is left as little of the pure Indian blood as of the traditional characteristics of the race."[45] For Marchant, race and blood were interchangeable and predetermined a culture's characteristics. White New Englanders following similar logics saw Native communities that incorporated outsiders as no longer Indian.[46]

As Plane and Button demonstrate, Native people in New England contested the state's attempt to equate mixed-race heritage with a loss of Indianness. The state used the political sentiments of men like William Claflin and an 1859 report on the racial purity of Native people within the state as rationales to end the recognition of its Tribal communities with the Massachusetts Indian Enfranchisement Act of 1869.[47] This law not only turned the Indian Districts into towns like any other, erasing the state's legal acknowledgment of these Tribes' existence, but also demanded the privatization of the Tribes' communal lands. Native communities such as the Wampanoag at Gay Head used a different definition of Indian identity, which focused on kinship and proprietorship rather than race, to challenge the changes wrought by the Act of 1869. As Plane and Button explain, "For the majority of Indians . . . the Enfranchisement Act attacked some of the most fundamental symbols of Indian ethnic identity. These included the communal holding of land and other resources, and the care of their own sick, elderly, and poor."[48] This was certainly true for the Wampanoag on Martha's Vineyard prior to 1869.[49] Instead of defining belonging in terms of blood purity, the Wampanoag welcomed outsiders who married into the Tribe as nonproprietors of the land, but their children were granted full Tribal status regardless of race. In the case of William Vanderhoop and Beulah Salsbury, this meant that their children were recognized as Wampanoag even though only one of their grandparents was born into the Tribe.[50] However, what Plane and Button do not remark on is how families like the Vanderhoops (though not the Vanderhoops themselves) had their Wampanoag identity and access to land challenged on racial grounds. Even before township became a reality for Gay Head in 1870, friction within the Tribe over who was racially Indian began to rise to the surface. This tension between inclusive incorporation of outsiders and a stricter race-based interpretation of who was Wampanoag would become a divisive issue in Gay Head and impact how the Edinbur Randall story would be told and understood in later years.

A Tribe of Kin

Netta Vanderhoop's 1921 article on her grandparents' heroics, written two generations after Randall's escape and the incorporation of Gay Head as a town into the state of Massachusetts, serves as a reminder that Native people remained on Martha's Vineyard. Unlike the *Vineyard Gazette* reporting from 1854, Netta's article casts William Vanderhoop and Beulah Salsbury as the protagonists of the story and they are understood to be Wampanoag. Gay Head's reputation through the twentieth century as the island's "Indian Town," Netta's inclusion of the phrase "Gay Head Grandmother" in the article's title, and Vanderhoop's family history in the editor's note indigenize the story. This is especially true in the section in which Vanderhoop explains why the sheriff failed to apprehend Randall. She writes:

> By the time the Sheriff returned with his men the whole reservation was aroused by this man-hunt in the North. Ninety-nine per cent of the men were determined that the slave should not be taken . . . On shore there gathered a large number of men, armed with guns, pitchforks, clubs, and almost anything that would do to fight with. In case the sheriff came with armed men and demanded the slave's release these men had made up their minds to resist him to the end, even though they had to kill or be killed. In some way the sheriff got wind of the true state of affairs and failed to put in an appearance.[51]

Here, Vanderhoop not only makes it clear that the "reservation" was Native but also that the men who made up the community were moral, brave, and just. They not only come together to help this stranger but do so out of a commitment to the idea of freedom which is held so strongly that they are willing to sacrifice their personal safety.

This account of the Wampanoag people as a tight-knit group with noble values reflects Vanderhoop's own upbringing and view of her Tribal heritage. Her mother, Mary A. Cleggett Vanderhoop was a white woman from Pennsylvania working in Arkansas when she met and married Edwin Vanderhoop, the son of William and Beulah. The newlyweds moved back to Martha's Vineyard, and Mary A. Cleggett Vanderhoop became a scholar and writer of Wampanoag history, culture, and cosmology.[52] Perhaps due to her own experience marrying into the Tribe, Cleggett Vanderhoop was one of the strongest proponents of the argument that Wampanoag society was uniquely welcoming and deft at incorporating outsiders. In articles on the Tribe that she wrote for the *New Bedford Evening Standard* in 1904 and 1905, she frames racial inclusion as a Wampanoag virtue. In a quote that has often been used by later historians to highlight the Tribe's understanding of Indianness, she wrote, "In the offspring of the intermarriages the strongest blood may show externally and the predominant features are those of either the white or the negro, but the Inner Self, the ego, the soul, the mind, the living principle, is wholly and always and forever-Indian."[53] Cleggett Vanderhoop further praised the Tribe's assistance in slave escapes in a way that would be reflected in Netta's account. In 1904, seventeen years before her daughter's article appeared, Cleggett Vanderhoop wrote of the benefits of interracial cooperation and relationships, stating, "Gay Head's share constitutes merely an atom, but therein analysis reveals today the blood of Indian men who fought in the Revolution mingling with that of the Vineyard's first born Caucasian daughters, who honored themselves by their assistance to Negro fugitive slaves at a time when such a thing required the greatest moral courage and personal bravery."[54] In this way, Cleggett Vanderhoop argues that racial mixing is not only easily compatible with Wampanoag life but is also a reflection of the Tribe's righteous morals. John Winthrop's Boston is replaced by the cliffs of Gay Head as the beacon the rest of the world should look to as a model for justice.

While this emphasis on Wampanoag virtue is reflected in Netta Vanderhoop's later account, she does not take her mother's assertive position on racial mixing. In fact, "The True Story of a Fugitive Slave: Or the Story a Gay Head Grandmother Told" is silent when it comes to there being any Black presence in the story other than Randall's. As mentioned before, William Vanderhoop was from Suriname and was listed as colored on the 1860 census.[55] Beulah Salsbury, who was listed as from Gay Head on the same census because of her proprietor status, also had a Black father. Samuel Peters, the boatman who sailed Randall to New Bedford, was the son of an enslaved man named George Peters who had married Anna Tackanash, a proprietor at Christiantown, another Wampanoag community on the island.[56] Netta makes no mention of the racial dynamic of the Wampanoag Tribe as a possible reason for their community being a known haven for fugitive slaves.[57]

The absence of Blackness in Netta's account stands in stark contrast to her portrayal of Wampanoag identity. However, there are two possible ways to read into her intentions, which reflect the unresolved dispute over the role of race in Wampanoag belonging. One possibility is that Netta's failure to identify the African heritage of the main characters in the story demonstrates that she viewed it as unremarkable. Her mother was white, her dad was three-quarters black, yet she considered herself Wampanoag.

For Netta, as for her mother, race had no bearing on whether someone could belong to the Wampanoag Tribe or identify as Native. This view resisted Massachusetts' claims that it had eliminated Tribes living in the state by refusing to recognize them. Following Netta's lead, Plane and Button, as well as journalist Gerald Kelly in his 1995 retrospective feature on the escape "Vanderhoop and the Runaway," featured the persistence of Gay Headers' Wampanoag identity as proof that they had survived the state's attempt to erase them.[58]

The Island's "Indian Town:" Self-Government, Racial Discrimination, and Anti-Blackness at Gay Head

It is possible that Netta did not want to highlight her own or the Tribe's African ancestry. While the invocation of race in debates over Wampanoag identity preceded the Massachusetts Indian Enfranchisement Act of 1869, as Button and Plane show, the law accelerated its growing importance.[59] The legislation, which extended the state's jurisdiction over Native people by claiming that they were no longer Native, was supposed to eliminate Massachusetts' Tribal communities by stripping these Tribes of their sovereignty over their land.[60] In many cases, the state was successful. As historian Deborah Rosen writes on the law's impacts, "not surprisingly, the outcome of Indian citizenship in later years was further loss of Indian land to Americans, as well as forced assimilation of Natives into the European-American economy."[61] Following these trends on Martha's Vineyard, Christiantown and the Wampanoag Tribe at Chappaquiddick would slowly dissipate, leaving Gay Head Aquinnah as the only remaining Tribe on the island by the 1880s. Notably, the Wampanoag at Gay Head survived because they were able to maintain a separate town government run by Tribal members that upheld communal land rights.[62] However, the matter of racial belonging remained an issue for the Tribe as their fight for autonomy faced new challenges in the township era.

In the years since Randall's escape and the incorporation of Gay Head as a town in 1870, race had often been used as a means of questioning the newly enfranchised Gay Headers' ability to self-govern and partake in island-wide politics. During the election campaign of 1879, the first one in which Gay Head Wampanoag were eligible to vote as citizens, Democratic politicians from Edgartown, the largest, most affluent, and most segregated town on the island, sued to throw out Gay Head's ballots (which had swung the election in the Republican's favor) on the grounds that Gay Head town officials had failed to carry out the proper protocols for notification of the election.[63] Though unsuccessful, this challenge was based in racial prejudice as made obvious by a satire of a popular minstrel show titled "Gay Head Gleanings" which circulated widely through Edgartown after the election. Notably, the poem demeaned the town's voters not as Indians but as "N-words," resurfacing the rhetoric of the governor and other lawmakers that characterized Tribal members with non-Native ancestry as not real Indians.[64] Netta's father, Edwin, was a Gay Head selectman at the time of the first election, and his later campaigns for island-wide office would be characterized by similar, if not quite so overt, racial animus. In the 1881 campaign for representative to the state legislature, fellow Republicans attacked him as being antiprohibitionist, a politically untenable position due to the local Party's strong support for temperance because they did not want a "Gay Header" on the ticket in the upcoming election.[65] Six years later, Edwin would finally be elected to the Massachusetts state legislature, but even this victory was marred by racial prejudice.[66] Thus, while there is nothing explicit in Netta's article itself to suggest that she purposefully omitted William and Beulah's African ancestry, pressures from living within a settler colonial context and state policies that tied Wampanoag sovereignty rights to race provided ample motivation for Tribal members to push aside their Black heritage.

As government policies based on racialized notions of "Indianness" started to have more power over defining Wampanoag identity and Tribal members continued to face anti-Black discrimination at the personal level, some within Gay Head began to use similar rhetoric to delineate who was and was not Indian. Continuing into the twentieth century, Tribal members faced discrimination from non-Natives who could not always distinguish between their Native and African ancestry but nevertheless treated them as inferior.[67] To combat this discrimination, the Wampanoag made a point to highlight their identity as "Indians" and separate themselves from any notion of Blackness. Thus, the combination of prejudiced legislation and the persecution against them as "people of color" shows how settler colonialism and racism intersected and infected the self-perception of what it meant to be a Gay Head Wampanoag.

The racial animus that shaped dynamics into the nineteenth century accelerated in later years, as Tribal members became more exposed to the personal and legal ramifications of appearing phenotypically dark-skinned. Interactions with non-Natives from outside Gay Head or off-island provide ample evidence of the Tribe projecting their Indianness as oppositional to being categorized as Black. For example, during one field trip to Boston led by June Manning, as part of a Wampanoag education program she ran in the early 1970s, she remembered that when the bus stopped to ask for directions, a person stuck their head in and asked what the group was. One of the kids shouted, "What do you mean? This is the Indian bus!" And all of them cheered.[68] Pan-racial pride, though, could quickly drift into anti-Blackness. In a collection of interviews done in collaboration with the Martha's Vineyard Museum in 1999, Tribal member Patsy Malonson remembers facing racism in the 1950s when she left the mostly all Wampanoag Gay Head school, which only ran through the fifth grade. In Vineyard Haven, where she and many Tribal children went for middle and high school with students from all over the island, Malonson recalls being told by the principal that she would not be allowed to attend a field trip to Washington, D.C., because she could not stay in the same hotel as the rest of her classmates. When Malonson asked the principal why this was, he responded, "Well, you know, you are a little darker."[69] It is noteworthy that in retelling this story of discrimination, Malonson makes a point to distinguish herself from Black students. She goes on to say, "Of course, we did see the division among the blacks and us (Wampanoag) once we got there (the Vineyard Haven school)." Therefore, the individual prejudice Tribal members felt outside of Gay Head influenced their need to distinguish between themselves and "blacks."

Internalized discrimination was felt by some within the Wampanoag community as well. In an interview I conducted in the summer of 2022, Grace Reeves (a Tribal member in her eighties who had moved off island in young adulthood before returning in the 1980s) remembers growing up in Gay Head in the 1940s and 1950s. Although the tenor of Reeve's interview was overwhelmingly positive and she felt entirely included in Tribal events such as powwows and church gatherings, she nevertheless recalled being looked down on for having darker skin and her father, who was a non-Native African American, facing prejudice while living in Gay Head.[70] Wampanoag historian Helen Manning spoke to the tension between race and identity within the Tribe in an interview she gave to Linsey Lee as part of the Martha's Vineyard Museum Oral History project. Manning remarked when asked about her Black mother, "I had a rich background in Black history and it is something to be proud of. You know, a lot of times people, especially Wampanoags, feel as though to be Black is just to be like the worst thing in the whole world. And they'd do anything to get away from it. Anything to be less cognizant of who they really are. I think it's this thing of prejudice against one or the other."[71] Here, Manning shows the tension that existed and continues to exist between Wampanoag racial and Tribal identity and how that can sometimes manifest in the form of internalized anti-Black prejudice.[72] In a context in which their authenticity as "Indians" was always under threat and Gay Head's autonomy rested on their distinction as the island's "Indian Town," the Tribe often had little choice but to present their Indigeneity in a way that was legible to non-Natives and therefore opposed to "Blackness."[73]

"Power Over This Unfortunate Race": Federal Recognition and the Use of Race to Challenge Wampanoag Sovereignty[74]

Despite non-Native attempts to dismiss the Wampanoag's ability to self-govern on racial grounds and the discrimination faced by darker-skinned individuals inside and outside the community, by the time Netta's article was published in the 1920s, the Tribe had managed to strengthen the town government and use it to exercise their sovereignty over Gay Head.[75] Over the course of the twentieth century, however, non-Native land ownership and encroachment accelerated to the point that they represented an existential threat to the Wampanoag's ability to survive as a Tribal community in the town by the 1970s.[76] As a last resort, the Wampanoag reincorporated the Tribal Council and sued the town for return of their common lands that had been illicitly taken from the Tribe by the state of Massachusetts in 1870.[77] The case was taken to the Massachusetts State Supreme Court where, due to their unrecognized status, the Wampanoag found themselves in a legal paradox in which the state court dismissed the case because, although the state had illegally seized the land from the Tribe in 1870, the Tribal Council could not be said to represent the Tribe because they were no longer recognized by the state or federal government. This "context of coercion" boxed the Tribe into an imperfect settlement that allowed non-Native interests to leverage the Wampanoag's need for federal recognition into an agreement that strictly limited the extent of the Tribe's ownership and sovereignty over the land of Gay Head.[78]

Even once the agreement was reached, winning federal recognition was far from assured.[79] To seal the settlement, the Wampanoag were forced to submit a petition through the FAP and have their Tribal nationhood judged by parameters determined by the BIA. Like the Massachusetts Indian Enfranchisement Act of 1869, the FAP uses a racialized definition of Indigeneity to diminish Tribal sovereignty.[80] Viewed together, these two policies show how the enduring contest over race's place in Native New England continued to impact the Wampanoag's understanding and presentation of the Edinbur Randall story and their own racial identity in the twentieth and into the twenty-first century.

When the Wampanoag Tribal Council submitted their application in 1986, the BIA initially rejected their petition based in part on the Tribe's failure to provide evidence that they were a community of American Indians "distinct from other populations in the area."[81] Again, this is an example of settler colonial authorities using a Euro-American understanding of Indianness to allow (limited) Native sovereignty only if they remain culturally and, to some degree, racially separate. Therefore, when the Wampanoag

Tribe successfully rebutted these claims one year later, it was with evidence showcasing "Native" practices and connections to ethnic kin off-island that left no room for alternative understandings of Wampanoag identity more closely aligned with Cleggett Vanderhoop's deemphasizing race.

The pressure to fit Wampanoag identity into the racialized stipulations of the FAP can best be viewed through a close examination of how and why the BIA rejected the Tribe's first petition for federal recognition in 1986, the rejoinders the Tribal Council added in order to appeal the decision, and the rationale the BIA used to explain why they changed their ruling when they ultimately granted recognition in 1987. As part of their initial finding against the Tribe, the BIA determined that the Wampanoag had failed to meet two of the seven criteria: "criteria b" (that Gay Head was a historically and continuously distinct Tribal community) and "criteria c" (that the petitioner maintained political influence or authority over its members through to the present day).[82]

In relation to the former, the BIA's "Evidence for Proposed Finding Against Federal Acknowledgement of the Wampanoag Tribal Council, inc." declares that by the 1930s social cohesion within the Tribe had disintegrated and that outmigration and failure to maintain contact with those living off-island meant that most "Gay Head Indians" no longer identified themselves as Tribal members.[83] Rejecting the community ties of the Tribe on these grounds reveals that the BIA was acting under the premise that race and ethnicity were the only determining factors in who was or was not part of the Tribe.[84] Not all Tribal members defined belonging in this racialized manner. Instead, some focused on the local history, culture, and values more akin to what Cleggett Vanderhoop thought made Gay Head special. Rejecting the pan-ethnic term "Wampanoag," they instead self-identified as "Gay Headers," an abbreviation of their longstanding appellation as "Gay Head Indians." Former town selectman during the years of the lawsuit, former Tribal Council member, and current Aquinnah town clerk Jeffrey Madison, explained in an interview that considering oneself a "Gay Header" was a statement proclaiming one's deep connection to the land and community that has lived there since time immemorial. When I asked Madison how being a "Gay Header" was different than being "Wampanoag" he explained that those who lost contact with the community "no longer knew what Gay Head was like."[85] In contrast Madison exclaimed that he was "proud to be a Gay Header" because "my grandparents raised me to be proud," because "I know what it was like to be here in those old days."[86]

Madison wasn't alone in insisting that Tribal cohesion was rooted more in knowledge of Gay Head's land and history than simple ancestry. In interviews that Grabowski conducted with anonymous Tribal members for her dissertation in 1982, she found that most Gay Head Indians identified them-selves as "Gay Headers" and that this meant that they were *both* descen-dants of families that had lived in Gay Head when it was an Indian District *and* that they lived in the town or were raised their as children.[87] Summariz-ing the importance of these dual aspects of being a "Gay Header," Grabowski remarks that many of those she interviewed were irritated by the fact that their identity was being called into question and were angry that they had to prove they were Indian when "Indian people have always been here at Gay Head."[88] Grabowski observes that the use of the word "always" was fun-damental to how Gay Headers saw themselves and was frequently used to place their personal histories within that of the Tribe. The use of the abso-lute "always" "invoked tribal continuity, authoritatively sealing the space between then and now and situating the speaker within that continuum, she explains. Having established their bona fides, Grabowski continues that "what followed could only be understood in the context of 'still'-that is, Gay Head Indians still live here and what I tell you I do as a Gay Head Indian."[89] Notable about this understanding of what makes one a "Gay Header" is that while having ancestry rooted in the Tribe prior to incorporation matters, race does not. Just like Madison, then, those that Grabowski interviewed predicated Tribal belonging on more than mere blood lines but also on being educated and serving witness to the history and active community life of Gay Head. Being Wampanoag did not make one a Gay Header, and it was the latter rather than the former who the Tribal Council claimed to repre-sent. The BIA's judgment, following the view that Tribal membership must be static and racially based, rejected the ideas of locals aligned with Cleggett Vanderhoop who had a more dynamic and fluid understanding of what it meant to be a Gay Head Wampanoag.

The need for federal recognition, though, meant that the Tribal Council had to reshape its petition, and eventual criteria for Tribal membership, to fit the racialized definition of Native nationhood underlying the FAP. To rebut the BIA's assertion that the Tribal council did exert authority and retain connections with Wampanoag off-island, the Tribe presented new evidence of how the town government prioritized the interests of and gave preferential treatment to Wampanoag kin over what was best for the town. They also described how Council leaders such as Harrison Vanderhoop, Napoleon Madison, and Donald Malonson had used their roles to maintain connections and disseminate information to Wampanoag living off-island.[90] In this way, the FAP's criteria forced the Council to shift their definition of Tribal belonging from the local, community orientation of the "Gay Head Indian," to the pan-ethnic, racially defined "Wampanoag."[91] This meant that when the Tribal Council finally received recognition and became a formally acknowledged Tribal nation, their legitimacy at least partially rested on presenting themselves as racially homogenous in a way that left little margin for acknowledging aspects of their history that complicate the meaning of Wampanoag identity.

Despite receiving recognition in 1987, the role of race in determining Native status carried on as a threat to Wampanoag sovereignty.[92] In a context in which settler colonial policies continued to push the Tribe to deemphasize their African heritage, it is not surprising that as the story of Edinbur Randall has been retold, characterizations of the Wampanoag rescuers highlight their distinctiveness as a Native community. Even within these constraints, though, room for ambiguity and alternative definitions of Tribal belonging persist. For example, in Gerald R. Kelly's 1999 *Martha's Vineyard Times* feature that included Mary Cleggett Vanderhoop's quote on the "inner Indianness" of the racially inclusive Wampanoag, Kelly follows Mary's daughter Netta's lead in never mentioning the family or Tribe's African ancestry. That said, Kelly relies largely on Vanderhoop's narrative and the interview with Randall, so it is unclear if this was done purposefully or out of ignorance. Kelly also interviews Ann Allen, a member of one of Chilmark's oldest non-Native families and the founder of CHiP, a community history program on Martha's Vineyard that works with the Tribe and provided the impetus for the article. Allen stated, "The Indians were an armed posse protecting this runaway and you get the feeling that it was not the first time they had done something like this."[93] Just as Cleggett Vanderhoop had done in her *Evening Standard* articles, here Allen extols the virtues of the Tribe only without mentioning the Tribe's African heritage.

In addition to these media accounts, when Tribal members tell of their community's role in Randall's escape entirely in their own words, they focus on celebrating their Indigenous identity while creating narratives that leave open other possibilities. At a 2002 commemoration of two African American Heritage Trail sites recognizing Wampanoag participation on the Underground Railroad, Tribal member Adriana Ignacio spoke to her people's moral courage but not the shared lineage with those they rescued. She remarked, "Our story is one of bravery and compassion of people doing what is right when to do so meant breaking the law."[94] Similarly, when William and Beulah Vanderhoop's great-grandson Charles Vanderhoop recalled his family's heroism in an interview with the MV Museum Oral History Project, he pointed out that aiding a fugitive slave was a regular occurrence in Gay Head.[95] Framing the story as a tale of interracial reciprocity, Vanderhoop focused on how the Tribe's moral clarity created a connection between the Native community of Gay Head and the African slaves that endured even after the Civil War. Recalling how some of them and their families returned to the island for a summer to help Beulah and William when they fell ill, Vanderhoop remarked, "So although (Beulah had) done a great deal for them, they turned around and, (showing) respect, paid her back."[96] Here, space for interpretation is left. While Vanderhoop never explicitly acknowledges Beulah, William, and his own African ancestry, his version of the story concentrates on the lasting bond that could join his Wampanoag great-grandparents and former Black slaves in a relationship of reciprocity closely resembling kinship. As with Netta's *Gazette* account, then, there is ambiguity as to if Charles Vanderhoop and Adriana Ignacio were following Cleggett Vanderhoop's view that race was irrelevant to Wampanoag identity, did not find it politically expedient to discuss Tribal members' African ancestry, or some combination of the two.

So . . . Who Saved Edinbur Randall?

Perhaps this is the wrong question. What concerns us is not who saved Randall but rather who gets to decide how the rescuers' heritage fits into and shapes a contemporary understanding of Wampanoag identity. These enduring tensions continue to hold tangible influence on not just Tribal members' sense of self but also hold huge consequences for the power to recognize or reject Indigenous claims to sovereignty, as dramatically demonstrated in the case of the Mashpee.

At present, the Wampanoag and other Native Tribes are still engaged in these battles over the role of race in determining Native status as part of their fight to survive ongoing efforts of erasure and secure enduring acknowledgment of their political authority. In 2020, the Trump administration revoked the federal recognition of the Mashpee Wampanoag, on the grounds that since they were not considered a Native Tribe when the Indian Reorganization Act was passed in 1934, their land could not be considered reservation land and put into Trust.[97] Such rulings would have the devastating consequences of revoking the Tribe's ability to govern, use, and protect their land, and it was feared that they could be similarly applied to the Wampanoag at Gay Head and other New England Tribes. The decision also ignored the ways that race factored into Massachusetts' and other states' rationale for terminating Native Tribes in the nineteenth century. The Biden administration would reverse the policy in 2021, but it highlighted the vulnerable position even federally recognized Native Tribes find themselves in when their sovereignty can be threatened or upheld based on the political landscape of the day.[98] By showing the contested and contingent views of the place of race in Wampanoag identity, the narrative surrounding Edinbur Randall's escape serves as a reminder of the false premises and ideologies that informed settler colonial Native policies in the past. Challenging the simplified notions of race underlying these earlier decisions enables Tribes and their allies to eradicate these policies' impact on the present so that they can create a future in which Native people once again have the freedom to define belonging entirely for themselves.

JUSTIN GROSSMAN is a University of Rochester Ph.D. candidate in history.

Notes

1. Netta Vanderhoop, "The True Story of a Fugitive Slave: Or the Story a Gay Head Grandmother Told," *The Vineyard Gazette,* February 3, 1921. In different sources Edinbur Randall is also referred to as either Edgar Jones or Randall Burr. Due to his own testimony and the remarkable similarities between the stories, it is safe to assume that these were aliases used by Edinbur. I will use the name Edinbur Randall unless quoting sources directly, as this was the name he gave when later interviewed by the Boston Vigilance Committee after his freedom was assured. John W. Blassingame ed., *Slave Testimony: Two Centuries of Letters, Speeches, Interviews, and Autobiographies* (Baton Rouge: Louisiana State University Press, 1977), 320.

2. The Wampanoag name for Gay Head is Aquinnah and those that live there are part of the Gay Head/Aquinnah Tribe. However, for the purposes of this paper I will use the term "Gay Head" because that is what it was called at the time and to differentiate between those living in Gay Head with the larger Wampanoag Nation. Many Tribal members, especially elders, continue to distinguish between their identity as "Gay Headers" and the more general term "Wampanoag." Christine Tracey Grabowski, "Coiled Intent: Federal Acknowledgement Policy and the Gay Head Wampanoags" (Ph.D. diss., City University of New York, 1994), 304. The town changed its name back to Aquinnah in 1998 to reflect its Wampanoag heritage, although the terms are still used interchangeably on the island today.

3. Starting in the 1860s, the state of Massachusetts used a racialized definition of Indianness to enact policies that terminated Native Tribes, allotted common lands into private holdings, and led to the political elimination of Native sovereignty and sale of most of the Tribes' previous landholdings into non-Native hands. Ann Marie Plane and Gregory Button, "Massachusetts Indian Enfranchisement Act: Ethnic Contest in Historical Context, 1849–1869," *Ethnohistory* 40, no. 4 (1993): 587–618. In this way, Massachusetts predated more well-researched and larger scale Bureau of Indian Affairs (BIA) policies that also used racial definitions of Indigeneity to reduce the number of people who legally qualified as "Indian." Katherine Ellinghaus, *Blood Will Tell: Native Americans and Assimilation Policy* (Lincoln: University of Nebraska Press and the American Philosophical Society, 2017).

4. Federal recognition became essential to the Tribe's survival in the 1970s and 1980s. As an unrecognized Tribe, the Wampanoag had to petition the BIA

through the Federal Acknowledgement Process (FAP), which has seven criteria that determine whether a Tribe qualifies for recognized status. Bureau of Indian Affairs, "Evidence for Proposed Finding against Federal Acknowledgment of the Wampanoag Tribal Council of Gay Head, Inc," *The Federal Register* 51, no. 125 (June 30, 1986). For more on the historical context and political considerations informing the creation of FAP and asserting the BIA's hegemony over determining federal recognition status for unrecognized Tribes, see Mark Edwin Miller, *Forgotten Tribes: Unrecognized Indians and the Federal Acknowledgment Process* (Lincoln and London: University of Nebraska Press, 2004).

5. "Context of coercion" is a term coined by anthropologist Gloria Levitas to describe how the U.S. government and state of Massachusetts ignores their historical disregard for Tribal self-government to justify their ongoing circumscription of the autonomy of Native Nations. Gloria Levitas, "The Burden of Proof: Coercion, Autonomy and Justice in Gay Head," *Dukes County Intelligencer* 19, no. 4 (May 1978), 126.

6. Several of these details are contradicted by reporting done by *The Vineyard Gazette,* the paper of record on Martha's Vineyard at the time of the escape. However, there are reasons to believe that Randall's testimony and Vanderhoop's writing, which line up in their accounts, are a more accurate representation of the story. This will be explained in full in subsequent pages.

7. John W. Blassingame, *Slave Testimonies,* 322.

8. Ibid.

9. Holmes Hole is known as Vineyard Haven today.

10. John W. Blassingame, *Slave Testimonies,* 322. The race of the sailors is also not mentioned, although, based on the demographics of Atlantic maritime crews in the mid-nineteenth century, it would be surprising if at least some of them did not have Native or African ancestry or some combination of the two. For more on the connection between sailors and Black abolitionism see Matthew D. Brown, "OLAUDAH EQUIANO AND THE SAILOR'S TELEGRAPH: 'The Interesting Narrative' and the Source of Black Abolitionism," *Callaloo* 36, no. 1 (2013): 191–201.

11. Netta Vanderhoop, "The True Story of a Fugitive Slave."

12. Ibid.

13. Significant contributions include Lisa Brooks, *Our Beloved Kin: A New History of King Philip's War* (New Haven: Yale University Press, 2018); Christine DeLucia, *Memory Lands: King Philip's War and the Place of Violence in the Northeast* (New Haven: Yale University Press, 2018); Ruth Wallis Herndon and Ella Sekatau, "The Right to a Name: The Narragansett People and Rhode Island Officials in the Revolutionary Era," *Ethnohistory* 44, no.3 (Summer 1997). These works highlight the erasure of Indigenous' histories and identities by ways of violence both physical and textual, and the weaponization of race towards those ends. Herndon and Sekatau, for example, use the term "documentary genocide" to highlight how the legal classification systems severed the Narragansett people from their collective governments and identities. Jean O'Brien also notes how the census and other methods of racial categorization bureaucratically erased Native belonging. Jean O'Brien, *Firsting and Lasting: Writing Indians out*

of Existence in New England (Minneapolis: University of Minnesota Press, 2010). However, most of the historical scholarship on the intersection of race and settler colonialism in New England is focused on the period before, or ends with, the mid-nineteenth century when many states in the region terminated their recognition of Tribal governments. While anthropologists and legal scholars have done exceptional work on how the framework of race has continued to threaten and constrain Tribal sovereignty in the twentieth century, historians have been slow to examine its ongoing implications.

14. Nancy Shoemaker, *Native American Whalemen and the World: Indigenous Encounters and the Contingency of Race* (Chapel Hill: University of North Carolina Press, 2015).

15. The unrecognized status of the Wampanoag Tribe of Gay Head puts them in line with other Native groups living in the uncertain legal context that defined race as either Black or white. Malinda Maynor Lowery, for example, explores how the Lumbee strategically negotiated this uncertainty in the American South. Just like the Wampanoag, the Lumbee maintained their identity as "Indian" even though non-Natives and settler colonial authorities ignored their existence or assumed that Native people had disappeared. The case of the Wampanoag shows that this black/white thinking extended well into New England and shaped policies toward Native people there as well. Malinda Maynor Lowery, *The Lumbee Indians: An American Struggle* (Chapel Hll: University of North Carolina Press, 2018).

16. The Massachusetts Indian Enfranchisement Act of 1869 was a complete overhaul of the state's relationship to Native people. It eliminated the plantation system and any Indian Districts, granted citizenship and voting rights to Native individuals, and incorporated Tribes into preexisting or newly created townships. This served the dual purpose of ridding the state of any financial obligation to these groups while also eliminating corporatist practices such as communal land holding. Generally, these measures were opposed by Native people throughout Massachusetts although nonproprietors living among the Tribes favored these measures, which granted them access to land and citizenship. See Elliotte D. Draegor, "Losing Ground: Land Loss Among the Mashantucket Pequot and the Mashpee Wampanoag Tribes in the Nineteenth Century" (Ph.D. diss., University of Connecticut, 2009) and David Silverman, *Faith and Boundaries: Colonists, Christianity, and Community Among the Wampanoag Indians of Martha's Vineyard 1600–1871* (Cambridge: Cambridge University Press, 2005).

17. Proprietor and nonproprietor refer to a person's status in the Wampanoag Tribe with regard to communal land. Black men who married Native women were considered nonproprietors in that they could only use the land through their wife's access. The children of these marriages would be considered proprietors. The proprietorship system in combination with the Tribe's gender imbalance at the time made women in effect the stewards of Wampanoag communal land during the plantation era. Draegor, "Losing Ground."

18. Before the 1860s Massachusetts' Native Tribes were organized on "plantations" which were effectively reservations for which the state appointed

guardians to oversee Native people who were considered wards of the state. These "plantations" consisted of commonly held land whose access was determined by the Tribes, which in many cases were matrilineal and therefore passed land rights on through the mother.

19. Draegor, "Losing Ground."

20. David Silverman, *Faith and Boundaries.*

21. Plane and Button, "Massachusetts Indian Enfranchisement Act."

22. This continued when the BIA set its parameters for federal recognition in 1978. Grabowski, "Coiled Intent." For more on the Dawes Act of 1887, allotment as an eliminationist policy, and Native resistance to the Act see Patrick Wolfe, "Settler Colonialism and the Elimination of the Native," *Journal of Genocidal Research* 8, no. 4, 387–409; Nicole Tonkovich, *The Allotment Plot: Alice C. Fletcher, E. Jane Gay, and Nex Perce Survivance* (Lincoln: University of Nebraska Press, 2012); Daniel Heath Justice and Jean O'Brien, *Allotment Stories: Indigenous Land Relations Under Settler Siege* (Minneapolis: University of Minnesota Press, 2021). For similar accounts of Native Tribes' increasing the role of race in defining belonging as a result of white imposed allotment see Alaina Roberts, *I've Been Here All the While: Black Freedom on Native Land* (Philadelphia: University of Pennsylvania Press, 2021).

23. These policies ranged from those that promoted Tribal Nationhood such as the 1934 Indian Reorganization Act, which sought to strengthen Tribal self-governance and sovereignty, to the termination and relocation policies of the 1950s and 1960s, which were informed by settler colonial ideologies of assimilation. For a broader overview of these policies generally, and their origins and impacts see Donald L. Fixico, *Bureau of Indian Affairs* (London: Bloomsbury Publishing, 2012). For more on how recognized Native communities navigated the BIA's handling of education, medical care, land and financial transactions in the twentieth century see Brenda J. Child, *Holding Our World Together: Ojibwe Women and the Survival of Community* (New York: Viking Press, 2012); Margaret D. Jacobs, *White Mother to a Dark Race: Settler Colonialism, Maternalism, and the Removal of Indigenous Children in the American West and Australia, 1880–1940* (Lincoln: University of Nebraska Press, 2010); Daniel Heath Justice and Jean O'Brien, *Allotment Stories: Indigenous Land Relations Under Settler Siege* (Minneapolis: University of Minnesota Press, 2021); Brianna Theobald, *Reproduction on the Reservation: Pregnancy, Childbirth, and Colonialism in the Long Twentieth Century* (Chapel Hill: University of North Carolina Press, 2019).

24. Grabowski, "Coiled Intent," 274. Grey uses the term "Faustian Bargain" to describe the trade-off by which "New England tribes derisively subject themselves to federal recognition and its bothersome demands for bureaucratic textual production, (because) federal recognition is prized as a means by which at least some ancestral land can be recovered and as a mechanism by which poor tribes can receive benefits in the form of subsidized tribal housing, health care, and affordable education." Jacquelyn L. Grey, "Beyond Words on the Island of Noepe: Mediating Power, 'Blood,' and the 'Law' in Indigenous New England" (Ph.D. diss., Columbia University, 2008), 8. Part of this subjugation involves conforming to FAP's racialized criteria for approval. As Fletcher describes,

Native nations thus find themselves in a paradox whereby according to federal laws "an American Indian tribal nation is either too 'Indian' to be constitutional in this modern American legal regime, or it is not 'Indian' enough to sustain its status as a separate sovereign." Matthew L. M. Fletcher, "Race and American Indian Tribal Nationhood," *Wyoming Law Review* 11, no. 2 (2011), 317. For the long history of the differentiation and changing understanding of Native political groups as "tribes" or "nations" see Gregory Ablavsky, "'With the Indian Tribes': Race, Citizenship, and Original Constitutional Meanings," *Stanford Law Review* 70 (2018): 1025–1076.

25. Kathryn Grover, *The Fugitive's Gibraltar: Escaping Slaves and Abolitionism in New Bedford Massachusetts* (Boston: University of Massachusetts Press, 2019).

26. The English set up praying towns to attract Native converts in the first decades after they settled at Plymouth. These included Christiantown on the island of Martha's Vineyard, which was set up by Thomas Mayhew in 1659. For a detailed albeit non-Native, account of the lives of the Native people of Christiantown see Experience Mayhew, *Indian Converts or some Account of the Lives and Dying Speeches of a considerable Number of the Christianized Indians of Martha's Vineyard, in New England* (London, 1727).

27. Evidence for Proposed Finding against Federal Acknowledgement of the Wampanoag Tribal Council of Gay Head, Inc., Bureau of Indian Affairs, *The Federal Register* 51 no. 125, (Monday June 30, 1986), 4. On the power and consequences of the guardian system see Elliotte D. Draegor, "Losing Ground."

28. Jean O'Brien, *Firsting and Lasting: Writing Indians out of Existence in New England.*

29. In Chilmark, the last Wampanoag families had sold their land and moved to the Indian District of Gay Head, but the ties between the town and Gay Head remained. For example, they shared a post office until 1873. Meanwhile on Nantucket, after an epidemic of smallpox in the 1790s, many Wampanoag had intermarried with African descendants living in a neighborhood known as "Guinea" on the island. While this space was characterized as "black" by white Nantucketers, it still maintained a strong Indian identity. Essex Boston who was born to African slaves on Nantucket in 1822 later wrote, "We hereby certify that there are among the coloured people of this place remains of the Nantucket Indians, and that nearly every family in our village are partly descended from the original inhabitants of this and neighboring places." Frances Ruley Karttunen, *Other Islanders: People who pulled Nantucket's oars* (Spinner Publications, 2005), 56; Charles Edward Banks, *History of Martha's Vineyard: Volume II* (Dukes County Historical Society, 1966), 31; Frances Karttunen, "The Notion of the 'Last Indians,'" *Historic Nantucket* 69, no. 4 (Fall 2019), 18–27.

30. The paper was only a couple of years old at that point and did not have the resources to do much of its own reporting. Therefore, many early issues of *The Vineyard Gazette* contain stories aggregated from other papers.

31. *The Vineyard Gazette,* "A Runaway Slave," https://vineyardgazette.com/news/1854/09/22/runaway-slave, September 22, 1854.

32. Holmes Hole was all white at the time even though no official segregation existed. See Ibid.

33. Netta Vanderhoop, "The True Story of a Fugitive Slave."

34. *The Vineyard Gazette,* "A Runaway Slave."

35. City upon a hill refers to John Winthrop's characterization of the establishment of Puritan Boston as a model city which could serve as a moral example for the rest of the world. John Winthrop, "A Model of Christian Charity, (Holyrood Church, March 21, 1630).

36. Silverman, *Faith and Boundaries,* 256.

37. Ibid.

38. William Claflin, "Address of the Governor to the General Court. Massachusetts Acts and Resolves, 833—44. (January 9, 1869).

39. For more on whaling's social and cultural impacts see Gioia Dimock, "Images of America: Whaling in Massachusetts" (Mount Pleasant, South Carolina: Arcadia Publishing, 2017), Nathaniel Philbrick, *In the Heart of the Sea: The Tragedy of the Whaleship Essex* (New York: Penguin Books, 2000). Nancy Shoemaker, *Living with Whales: Documents and Oral Histories of Native New England Whaling History* (Amherst: University of Massachusetts Press, 2014).

40. Silverman, *Faith and Boundaries,* 226.

41. Andrew Pierce and Jerome D. Segel, *Wampanoag Families of Martha's Vineyard: The Wampanoag Genealogical History of Martha's Vineyard, Massachusetts Volume II: Part B* (Berwyn Heights, MD: Heritage Books, 2016), 1013.

42. Ibid, 814.

43. Plane and Button, "The Massachusetts Indian Enfranchisement Act," 595.

44. Ibid.

45. Ibid.

46. The characterization of white New Englanders as generally affirming a racialized notion of Indianness is supported by Jean O'Brien's *Firsting and Lasting.* Using local histories and accounts of King Phillip's War written in the nineteenth century, she demonstrates the pervasiveness of these ideas not just in the minds of state authorities such as William Claflin and Milton Earle but also those in the small towns and everyday citizens who used them to privilege their own heritage over recognition of Indigenous identities. This imposition of settler colonial notions of race to erase Native people would later be expanded as part of the federal government's Indian policies following the Dawes Act in 1887. According to Katherine Ellinghaus, BIA officials used eugenics, blood quantum, and other pseudoscientific applications of race as part of this strategy. On the use of blood quantum in Tribal enrollment calculations, she quotes one such official, Francis Leupp (Commissioner of Indian Affairs, 1905—1909), as stating, "If we can thus gradually watch our body of dependent Indians shrink, even by one member at a time, we may congratulate ourselves that the final solution is indeed only a question of a few years." Ellinghaus, *Blood Will Tell*, xxiii.

47. John Milton Earle, the commissioner hired to by the state legislature to carry out the report appeared sympathetic to Tribal self-government, at least in the case of the Gay Head Wampanoag. With regard to Tribal laws of communal land sharing, he stated that "from its apparently favorable working, (it) is probably well adapted to their conditions and circumstances." Yet even though

Earle thought the Tribe was running the district smoothly, he could not help but question the validity of their Wampanoag identity due to the Tribe's history of intermarriage. He wrote that "the Indian names have almost become extinct, and but for two or three families, a list of their names would never suggest an idea of their aboriginal origin. The admixture is much like that of the other plantations, with, perhaps, a less infusion of the African than in some of them." Evidence for Proposed Finding against Federal Acknowledgement of the Wampanoag Tribal Council of Gay Head, Inc., 26.

48. Plane and Button, "Massachusetts Indian Enfranchisement Act," 597.

49. Brooks's reimagination of King Philip's War shows how the bonds of Wampanoag kinship were tied together in a "webbed landscape" that was able to survive colonial violence. Brooks, *Our Beloved Kin,* 255. The Wampanoag of Martha's Vineyard notably avoided outright warfare with Euro-American settlers even during larger region-wide conflicts such as King Philip's War.

50. The family would have nine children and hold considerable status within the Tribe through the present day. Their son Edwin (Mary's husband and Netta's father) became the first Wampanoag to serve in the state legislature when he was elected representative in 1887. To read more about the history of the Vanderhoop family in the twentieth century see: Mary Jane Carpenter, "On the Cliffs in Aquinnah, History is Alive at the Vanderhoop Homestead," *The Vineyard Gazette,* November 23, 2015, https://vineyardgazette.com/news/2015/11/23/cliffs-aquinnah-history-alive-vanderhoop-homestead. The term "by blood" is how race is characterized in the Wampanoag genealogies of record. Andrew Pierce and Jerome D. Segel, *Wampanoag Families of Martha's Vineyard.*

51. Vanderhoop, "The True Story of a Fugitive Slave."

52. Antoinette Powell and Linda Muldoon, "Mary Amelia Cleggett Vanderhoop," *Neighborhood News: The Newsletter of the Old Third Ward Neighborhood Association, Inc.,* Spring 2016, http://www.oldthirdward.org/news letter-2016-spring.pdf

53. Evidence for Proposed Finding against Federal Acknowledgement of the Wampanoag Tribal Council of Gay Head, Inc., 28.

54. Gerald R. Kelley, "Vanderhoop and the Runaway," *Martha's Vineyard Times,* February 16, 1995, 18–19.

55. The 1860 Indian Census of Gay Head (Aquinnah), Mass. *Indians of Massachusetts:* Gay Head Tribe, in Mass. Senate no. 96 publication (March 1861).

56. Ibid, 733.

57. The Tribe had previously rescued several other fugitive slaves and the crew of the ship where Randall was stowed already knew of Gay Head's reputation as a friendly place for runaways. African American Heritage Trail, "Wampanoag Tribe, Aquinnah," June 12, 2023, mvafricanamericantrail.org.

58. Kelley, "Vanderhoop and the Runaway."

59. Plane and Button, "Massachusetts Indian Enfranchisement Act," 589.

60. As Deborah Rosen shows, state governments were often at the forefront of negotiating questions of sovereignty between Native people and the larger community. She finds that states tended to act in any way that justified direct rule over Native people and that for all of Massachusetts' rhetoric

about racial equality this, along with the economic benefit of opening up Tribal lands, was among the primary motivations behind the Massachusetts Indian Enfranchisement Act. Deborah A. Rosen, *American Indians and State Law: Sovereignty, Race, and Citizenship, 1790–1880* (Lincoln: University of Nebraska Press, 2007).

61. Ibid, 178.

62. Ibid, 270.

63. Gay Head was incorporated as a town in 1870 but due to delays in the allotment process and transition to town governance, 1879 was the first election in which the Wampanoag voted as full citizens of the state of Massachusetts.

64. In a particularly vulgar section, the poem claims that Gay Headers unthinkingly voted as a group, ending with the applause of one of the Republicans praising "the little N-words," who helped in the fraud." "Gay Head Gleanings," RU 340 Box 1 Folder 17 MV Museum.

65. Vanderhoop Flyer to Prohibitionists, "To Prohibitionists," MV Museum collections RU 401: Politics, B1, F22.

66. On their way to the polls, supporters reportedly voiced their enthusiasm by shouting "we're going to vote for the coon," ironically misrepresenting the first Native American representative to the state legislature as Black during his historic election. "Election of Edwin Vanderhoop," *Vineyard Gazette,* November 11, 1887.

67. As Gay Head became a tourist destination in the twentieth century, there are numerous articles that reference visitors' disappointment that the locals do not "look Indian." As one 1975 *Boston Globe* article reported on a boy asking his father "Where are the Indians?" when visiting Gay Head. When the father pointed out a girl selling trinkets in a shop by the cliffs, the boy responded "That's an Indian? How can you tell?" Tony Chamberlain, "Vanishing Americans: Indians of Northeast see others making gains while real natives are left in backwater," *Boston Globe,* October 10, 1975. There are far more examples of this type of confusion in *The Vineyard Gazette* than space to include here. For reference and how the Wampanoag "Played Indian" to appeal to early twentieth-century tourists, see "Vineyard Vagabond Finds He Can't Write About Colored Clay When There Are Human Beings Around," *The Vineyard Gazette,* August 1, 1941, Ellen Stokes, "Says Silver Work Would Fit Gay Head," *The Vineyard Gazette,* June 20, 1952, and Philip J. Deloria, *Playing Indian* (New Haven: Yale University Press, 1998).

68. The program was started after the closure of the Gay Head school and was funded by a $45,000 Federal Title IV grant earmarked for Indian cultural education. Chamberlain, "Vanishing Americans."

69. Patsy Malonson, "Helen Manning Oral History Collection," Martha's Vineyard Museum Repository, 1973, 1983–1988.

70. "Grace Reeves Interview," 11:00–12:00, conducted by the author at the Totem Pole Inn, Aquinnah, MA, 6/28/2022. Christine Tracey Grabowski, a consultant hired by the Wampanoag to help them prepare their petition for federal recognition, conducted interviews with Tribal members as part of her research.

She found that within the Gay Head community slurs were frequently used against those with darker skin. Grabowski, "Coiled Intent," 295.

71. Linsey Lee, *Vineyard Voices: Words, Faces and Voices of Island People* (Edgartown, Mass.: Martha's Vineyard Historical Society, 1998), 211.

72. Wampanoag historian Helen Attaquin uses the phrase "learning racism" to highlight how the divisive place race plays in determining "authenticity" in contemporary Native America seeps into Tribal politics. She rhetorically laments, "Why have Indians readily adopted the cruelty of the dominant society to their own ambitious purposes, to the obtaining of authority, power, and personal control." Helen Attaquin, "There Are Differences," in *Dawnland Voices: An Anthropology of Indigenous Writing from New England,* edited by Siobhan Senier, (Lincoln: University of Nebraska Press, 2014), 462.

73. Gay Head was colloquially known and advertised to tourists as "The Indian town" throughout the township era. One 1941 advertisement in the *Vineyard Gazette,* for example, highlights Gay Head as "The Indian town. Owned solely by the descendants of the original Indians, and administered by them." See *The Vineyard Gazette,* April 25, 1941. The *Gazette's* description of their racialized ownership and administration of Gay Head thus shows how the Wampanoag were able to use their "Indian" identity to maintain authority separate from outsiders.

74. Legal scholar Bethany Berger uses the phrase "power over this unfortunate race" as the title for her article on the 1846 *Rogers* Supreme Court case that she argues shifted federal Indian law away from viewing Tribes as sovereign governments. Instead, the Court saw them not as political entities but as collections of individuals tied together by ethnicity that could be subjected to federal authority. Bethany R. Berger, "Power Over This Unfortunate Race: Race Politics and Indian Law in United States v. Rogers," *William and Mary Law Review* 45, no. 5 (April 2004): 1957–2052.

75. Wampanoag historians documented in their petition to the BIA for federal recognition how the town government was administered almost entirely by Tribal members, continued to enforce communal land practices, and extended preferential treatment to individuals and economic projects that would benefit the Tribe. "Gay Head Wampanoag Tribe Recognition Petition," submitted by Wampanoag Tribal Council of Gay Head, Inc., Gay Head, Mass., 1986.

76. Gladys Widdiss, president of the Tribal Council testified before Congress in 1986 that without Wampanoag control over the historically and culturally significant common lands, affordable housing to allow exiled Tribal members to return home, and federal recognition the dramatic increases in land values and underdeveloped year round island economy left the Tribe "in danger of being destroyed by the forces of the marketplace." Public hearing before the Select Committee on Indian Affairs, United States Senate, S. 1452, April 9, 1986, Washington, D.C., 22.

77. The Tribe enlisted the help of Tom Tureen, a lawyer with the Native American Rights Fund (NARF), who had used the same argument in a successful land claims suit that won thousands of acres of land for the Passamaquoddy Tribe of Maine in the early 1970s. Susan Sanders and Debbie Thomas, "Native

American Rights Fund: Our First 20 Years," Clearinghouse Review 26, no.1 (1992): 52.

78. The Settlement agreement of 1983 included provisions that the Wampanoag would give up any land claims outside of the common lands received in the agreement and that this communally held Tribal land would still be subject to state and local zoning laws. Ian Fein, "Town, Wampanoag Tribe of Gay Head Trace Their Disputes Across Decades," *The Vineyard Gazette,* September 2, 2006.

79. In another instance of the circular logic of settler colonial policies and legal frameworks, because the deal could only be enforced and supported if the federal government acknowledged the authority of the Wampanoag Tribal Council to represent the Tribe and therefore receive the promised money for cultural education, economic development, and repurchasing additional land, the Council needed to formally receive federal recognition as a Tribal nation. To do this, the Tribe had two options: convince Congress to pass special legislation granting them recognition, which they had done that year for the Mashantucket Pequot in Connecticut, or petition the BIA through the FAP. The Tribal Council pursued both options, but with strong local opposition from rich and powerful non-Natives and a larger regional backlash against New England Native-American rights claims in the 1980s, partisan politics made the legislative route ineffective, leaving FAP as the Tribe's only option. Christine Tracey Grabowski, "Coiled Intent," 206.

80. Fletcher, "Race and American Indian Tribal Nationhood"

81. Ibid, 2.

82. "Evidence for Proposed Finding against Federal Acknowledgment of the Wampanoag Tribal Council of Gay Head, Inc," 2.

83. Ibid, 3.

84. Ibid.

85. Jeffrey Madison Interview," conducted by the author February 12, 2024.

86. Ibid.

87. Grabovski, "Coiled Intent," 276.

88. Ibid, 275.

89. Ibid, 278–79.

90. This included the town government not collecting arrears from Tribal members, giving them first rights to lease the town's common lands at the cliffs and herring creek, and siding with fellow Native people on political issues within Gay Head regardless of non-Native opposition. Bureau of Indian Affairs, "Recommendation for Final Determination that the Wampanoag Tribal Council of Gay Head, Inc., exists as an Indian tribe pursuant to 25 CFR 83, (Federal Register, Washington D.C., 1987), 1–15.

91. Again, the issue here isn't that those aspects of the Tribe's history didn't occur or were things the Tribal Council didn't want to divulge, but that the BIA became the arbiter of what a Wampanoag nation at Gay Head could look like and used that power to limit the extent of Tribal Sovereignty. More broadly, legal anthropologist Matthew Fletcher writes about how racial definitions of Native nationhood have been used to undermine the legitimacy and political

authority of Tribal governments. According to Fletcher, because Tribal membership is always at least partially based on some racial component, settler-colonial states have claimed that Native nations have an inherent "democracy deficit" and therefore cannot exert jurisdiction over outsiders even if they reside on Tribal land. After the Wampanoag Tribal Council received recognition, local non-Natives would use this logic to justify granting the Tribe full sovereignty over their common lands and economic development projects. Fletcher, "Race and American Tribal Nationhood."

92. In 2001, the Tribe lost a Massachusetts Supreme Court case which reaffirmed the subjugation of Tribal authority to the rules and regulations of the town government. The court's judgement assumed that prior laws and agreements that weaponized race against the Tribe were still legitimate precedents and had to be followed. Grey, "Beyond Words," 97.

93. Gerald R. Kelley, "Vanderhoop and the Runaway," *The Vineyard Gazette,* 18–19.

94. The African-American Heritage Trail of Martha's Vineyard, "Fugitives from Slavery Escape via Menemsha, Aided by the Wampanoags," *Menemsha—MV African-American Heritage Trail,* accessed December 1, 2020.

95. Correcting the record, he stated "the *Vineyard Gazette* wrote her up as freeing one (fugitive slave), she actually freed eight." MV Museum Oral History Channel, "Beulah Vanderhoop and The Gay Head Underground Railroad," told by Charles Vanderhoop, October 13, 2021.

96. Ibid.

97. Phillip Marcelo, "Feds Revoking Reservation Status for Tribe's 300 Acres," *Associated Press,* March 30, 2020.

98. "Feds Drop Legal Battle Over Tribe's Reservation Status," *Associated Press,* February 20, 2021, https://www.wbur.org/news/2021/02/20/mashpee-wampanoag-tribe-legal-victory.

PHIL HENDERSON

With Allies Like These . . . : Promises and Pitfalls in the Anticolonial Theories of "Ally Toolkits"

Abstract

Since the mid-2010s there has been a proliferation of "ally toolkits" that purport to offer guidance or actionable ways for those who view themselves as "allies" or supporters of various movements. The politically resurgent movements of Indigenous Peoples in Canada, for example, have been accompanied by and formed the backdrop of a considerable literature of toolkits produced for would-be settler allies. These toolkits are written for an imagined or desired ally and imagine ends or political horizons toward which allyship is striving. These toolkits can be understood as documents of political theory in order to critically engage the models for political change that are being advanced. Ultimately, allyship and the terms on which it is established within the examined toolkits are situated as an overly thin political theory when confronting social forces of ongoing settler colonialism and racial capitalism.

THE EVERYDAY CRISES of settler imperialism give rise again and again to a question both concise and often explosive in its consequences: What is to be done? The narrower question of what is to be done *by settlers* encapsulates the problematic of how those who are interpellated *within* the social totality of settler imperialism can struggle *against* it. Examination of the political framing of *allyship* and *alliance-building* through critical discourse analysis can reveal important considerations/conditions within the theories of change implied by much of the discourse on settler allyship. While also reviewing relevant scholarly literature, I draw most extensively from an activist archive of ally toolkits written within the Canadian colonial context in order to interpret this discourse as part of a politics rooted in grassroots movement activity. Of particular interest is how the authors of these toolkits frame allyship as an attempt to have settlers divest from their investments in colonial processes.

This article is divided into four sections. Rather than merely presume the importance of critically studying allyship—as well as the terms and theories through which it emerges—I begin by outlining why critical scholars should be interested in these questions. As this section shows, this is a matter of importance for those committed to anticolonial work precisely because the solidarity that Indigenous movements have built with settlers and other non-Indigenous people is clearly viewed as effective, and therefore threatening, by colonial security apparatuses. The second section reviews "alliance-building" literature as a crucial development in the scholarship on colonialism. I suggest that this literature has been particularly innovative for its focus on movements and localized political dynamics (primarily focusing on literature from Canada), even though I note a growing methodological individualism as the concept of the ally comes increasingly to the fore. The third section reviews an activist archive comprised of five ally toolkits, produced by nongovernmental organizations (NGOs), labor unions, and grassroots community organizations. These toolkits are the primary materials I use to study the discourse of allyship as it is mobilized in actionable ways. In the final section, I ask two questions of both the scholarship and the activist archive: How is the ally discursively constructed and imagined as a political subject? Second, what is the political horizon of allyship—what, concretely, does it seek to achieve?

Ultimately, I suggest that the theories of allyship and the figure of the ally that emerge in both scholarship and this activist archive are unhelpfully dyadic—that is, binary. By operating only at the scale of one constitutively antagonistic relationship, the theories of allyship I examine here lack a social theory by which to work through the internal contradictions of a given settler society (much less the imperial world system of which such societies are an integral part) that could be leveraged into anticolonial political commitments and struggles. I suggest that theories of allyship constitute an overly *thin* account of the sorts of political mobilizations that are necessary to struggle in and against Project Canada (Green 2001). Informed by an understanding of Canadian settler imperialism as part of a *world system* of differentiated but interrelated and co-constitutive processes of dispossession, expropriation, extraction, and exploitation, I note that the allyship literatures explored below tend to rely upon and reproduce a domesticating conception of political activity that is particularly dissatisfying. Which is to say, ultimately, I am skeptical that the approaches of this political tendency can match the actual challenges of getting beyond the colonial present and may inadvertently reproduce core elements of the power structures undergirding settler rule.

Why Study Allyship at All?

The colonial dynamics of settler societies are not reducible simply to actions of the state or state officials. Rather, such colonial dynamics function through and depend on the formation of what Stuart Hall (developing an antiracist/

anticolonial reading of Antonio Gramsci) calls a historic bloc. That is, an internally differentiated and complex unity, produced as the relatively stable alignment—or "articulation"—of otherwise disparate social forces (Hall 2019a, 2019b). Rife with internal contradictions, historic blocs are stabilized through collaboration—secured through incentives toward compromise and disincentives against conflict—that attempts to suspend or sufficiently institutionalize competing interests that might otherwise manifest as social struggle (Henderson 2024). As Gerald Horne (2014, 2018, 2020) has memorably shown, settler societies and the imperial orders centered on them ought to be understood as collaborationist projects. Any given historic bloc is helpfully understood as itself an alliance-building process dependent, in the case of settler colonies, upon forms of negative solidarity aiming to advance the interests of some through the dispossession and exploitation of others.

Mediated, always, through shifting regimes of (dis)ability, gender, and racialization, personal property in land—as an active or aspirant possession—is the sine qua non of historic blocs centered on settler rule. Property in land is the social technology that (re)produces settlers as a class, incentivizing their collaboration within the ruling historic bloc (Federici 2014; Harris 1993; Linebaugh 2014; Macpherson 1978; Moreton-Robinson 2015; Taylor 2019). Gina Starblanket and Dallas Hunt (2018) make clear that this collaboration has deadly consequences. They argue that dominant property relations deputize settlers (but especially white, able-bodied men) as colonial functionaries, incentivized to continue the violent project of dispossessing and displacing Indigenous Peoples in order to maintain their own *personal* property by lethal violence if it is deemed necessary. These "ordinary" settlers are, more generally, also deputized to defend *collective* settler possession as regulated through whiteness, masculinity, and production for the purposes of capital accumulation. Settlers, write Starblanket and Hunt, are constantly presented with the possibility of becoming like the imagined "farmer serving as king of this realm—and of his castle—whose responsibility it then becomes to protect against intrusions." While it is always an offer attenuated by proximity to power, settlers are incentivized into reinvesting themselves, personally and collectively, in the ruling historic bloc. Importantly, though, this reinvestment is never guaranteed. The future of Canadian settler imperialism is in constant need of buttressing because of both its own internal contradictions and the external challenges leveled against it. In this way, it is the same as all other ruling historic blocs. And it is because of the challenges that settler societies face in reproducing themselves as complex unities that the question of social movements and grassroots alliance building is fundamental for anticolonial struggles.

While there has not been a *mass* movement of settlers challenging Canadian imperialism, those movements that have occurred and their potential to be followed by still broader/deeper shifts represent a serious concern for the regime's power elite—as they represent fissures in the social basis of the historic bloc. This is perhaps most clearly evinced by the responses of the security apparatus (including the police, intelligence services, and armed forces) to Indigenous-led social movements. It is well documented that in what is presently Canada, a central function of the police has been to regularize the surveillance, dispossession, and displacement of Indigenous Peoples in the service of accumulating land and thereby producing settlers (Monaghan 2013; Stark 2016; Whitaker, Kealey, and Parnaby 2012). Moreover, despite piecemeal reform, the institutional relationship of police to Indigenous Peoples today remains fundamentally violent (Morin 2021). Investigating the Royal Canadian Mounted Police's (RCMP) Project SITKA, a mass surveillance program targeting Indigenous community leaders, Miles Howe and Jeffery Monaghan (2018, 328–29) observe that after several years of pursuing a "negotiated management model [which] allows for a 'right' way and a 'wrong' way to protest," police forces are increasingly reverting to a model of movement policing premised on overt antagonism toward all community mobilization. This "strategic incapacitation" model of policing social movements uses mass data collection to create "risk profiles" both of individual community leaders (who are then often targeted for criminalization) and of whole movements. Through *Access to Information Act* requests, Howe and Monaghan obtained documents used by the RCMP to create a "public order profile scale" that "measures" the "risks" associated with a given movement. The RCMP score movements against a list of twenty different criteria, with a risk factor scaling from one (very low) to five (very high). Howe and Monaghan note that "an option of 0 [or no risk] is not a possibility" within the RCMP's assessments. Here, the overt antagonism of police toward movements is made clear, as *any* community mobilization *must* carry some risk, thus authorizing the security apparatus surveillance and likely intervention.

The precise criteria against which this risk profile is built are particularly striking. These include such descriptions as "the protest group is very well known and credible," "the group is supported by many other groups," "the group has high public support," and "there are linkages from the main issue to others" (Howe and Monaghan 2018, 328–29). Movements are deemed to be *greater* risks the more they are characterized by these features. Despite much rhetoric about fear over extremism, internal police documents acquired by Howe and Monaghan confirm the more pervading concern among the security apparatus is over social movements that are broadly supported, that speak to clear and long-standing grievances, and that are effective at building their struggles in relationships of reciprocal solidarity with the struggles of others. In short, the security apparatus's concern is that Indigenous movements have the capacity to—and indeed are already proving capable of—destabilizing Canada's historic bloc by articulating new solidarities that challenge the colonial status quo. Indigenous social movements are remarkably effective at building solidarity within and across Indigenous communities and nations but also with settlers and other non-Indigenous communities as well. And it is for precisely this reason that the security apparatuses seek to strategically incapacitate these movements. That is, in the words of an internal Canadian Security Intelligence Service document, they aim to disrupt the "connectivity between Aboriginal issues and allied groups" through the targeted surveillance and subsequent criminalization of key community members (quoted in Howe and Monaghan 2018, 338; see also: Rutherford 2020).

The scale of the resources mobilized by Canada's security apparatuses to disrupt social bonds *within* Indigenous movements, and in these movements' linkages with settlers and non-Indigenous groups, indicates that those relationships are taken as very serious threats by the state (Barrera 2021). The "threat," in the eyes of the security apparatuses, arises from Indigenous movements continuing to show settlers and other non-Indigenous people that an otherwise to imperial modes of living is both possible and desirable. Given how seriously these matters are taken by colonial security apparatuses, opponents of settler imperialism should also take seriously the work of understanding how to break settlers from their historic and ongoing roles collaborating in global processes of dispossession. *Not* because settlers represent any kind of essential historical subject; we do not. Rather, because at present the ongoing reinvestment of settlers in imperial modes of living represents one of the sturdiest bulwarks against the self-emancipation and self-determination of peoples dispossessed by Canada around the globe (Coulthard 2014, 173; Henderson, forthcoming).

From Alliances to Allies

Kiera Ladner notes (2017, 167) that while there has been a recent proliferation of scholarship on Indigenous politics in Canada within dominant disciplines, it has focused largely on "the interplay between Indigenous people and the settler-state" (see also Mowatt, Wildcat, and Starblanket 2024). This predominating approach is what I describe as the study of *Canadian-Indigenous relations* and is helpfully distinguished from a smaller but growing body of scholarship that I characterize as studying *settler-Indigenous relations* in the Canadian context. This literature is beginning to escape the state-centricity that Ladner identifies as so problematic in the dominant study of Indigenous politics. It shifts attention to grassroots political relations between nonelite settlers—those capable of exercising only relatively marginal institutional, social, and/or political power (Táíwò 2022; Mills 1956)—and a variety of Indigenous actors, with especial emphasis on social movements.

Among the earliest direct efforts at making this shift Davis, O'Donnell, and Shpuniarsky (2007, 96) note that "Aboriginal-settler relationships have been long studied, particularly those with governments and increasingly, with industries." They suggest that there is nevertheless "an area of relations little examined in Canada," that being "the growing partnerships, alliances, and coalitions between Aboriginal peoples and social movements." Their article explores how settler and Indigenous community-organizers led campaigns that successfully called for a public inquiry into the so-called Ipperwash crisis of 1995, during which Dudley George of Stony Point was murdered by the Ontario Provincial Police while reclaiming Aazhoodena (see also Aazhoodenaang Enjibaajig 2022). The study of such grassroots settler-Indigenous relations opens productive analytical space in which the structural logics of settler imperialism contend with the agential possibilities of everyday life—where processes of settler rule are simultaneously reproduced *and* contested.

Crucially, however, this analysis has to be done without romanticizing grassroots actors. Just as much as this shift has made visible the positive solidarity of social movements marked as alliances between settlers and Indigenous Peoples, it has also shown the negative solidarity among settlers (especially white settlers) acting in ways that are *more* assertively colonial than state policy. Studying both Ipperwash and the 2006 land dispute at Six Nations/Caledonia, Michael Morden tracks reactionary grassroots movements of settlers who pushed local and provincial politicians to more aggressively confront Indigenous movements: and where these efforts bore little fruit, these settlers took to the streets themselves in order to provoke direct conflict. In this context of settler-driven backlash against both Indigenous movements *and* the state, Morden (2014, 46) notes that the "level of analysis" in much of the scholarship on Canadian-Indigenous relations is "focused at the level of high politics, and there is a broad conflation of settlers with the institutions and structures" of the state. Against this, approaching solidarity—in both its positive (anticolonial) and negative (colonial) manifestations—as the social basis for political activity, reveals a cacophonous disarray of competing drives and interests, which evince a number of distinct potentialities for shifting alliances and counteralliances. And, as Zoltán Grossman (2017) details, many times the particular alliances can be of a surprising or "unlikely" character if prejudged from the typically urbane remove of academia.

Further, emerging scholarship has been much more attentive to co-constitutive regimes of power and the interrelationships formed in and against those regimes by a variety of grassroots actors. As Amar Bhatia (2013, 41) notes while discussing the place of racialized migrants in treaty discourses, the dominant focus of research on the "relationship between racialized immigrants and Indigenous Peoples is *vertical.*" That is, it studies these communities almost exclusively *through* their "regulation by the British Crown and then the Canadian state," seldom considering their direct interrelations with each other. This verticality also produces an image of both racialized communities and Indigenous Peoples as merely objects of regulation, rather than as communities striving toward self-determination amidst the adverse conditions produced by Canada's co-constitutive regimes of white supremacism and colonial dispossession. New scholarship is increasingly attentive to a distinct form of internationalism long practiced as solidarity in the streets, in the prisons, on the job, or on the land (see Desai 2021; Dhamoon 2021; Dhillon 2019; Lethabo King 2019; Mays 2021; Sullivan-Clarke 2020; Tabar and Desai 2017).

Yet, even while it is displaced from its typical position of centrality, the state is never wholly absent in the study of settler-Indigenous relations. In many cases the shift to studying settler-Indigenous relations better accommodates the ethical and political commitments of both researchers and their interlocutors in their often-fraught relations with the colonial state. Paulette Regan (2010, 4) typifies this sentiment when she writes that "as Canadian citizens, we are ultimately responsible for the past and present actions of our government," and it is this sense of responsibility that animates her commitment towards reconciliatory work as a process of "unsettling" colonial sentiments primarily through education (see also Mackey 2016). In another seminal text on settler-Indigenous relations, Roger Epp (2008, 126) asks the challenging but fundamental question: "Whose work is reconciliation?" As Ladner, Mowatt et al., Regan, and Epp show, state-centric approaches tend to point to courts, government ministries, or modern treaty-negotiators. Epp, by contrast, highlights both the ethical distinction and the political possibilities that the settler-Indigenous relations literature draws attention to. He writes that in the project of reconciliation, "the subject under closest scrutiny becomes 'ourselves,'" because when the institutions of state are no longer assumed to be the *necessary* central mediating force, reconciliation is seen as a response not to "the 'Indian problem' but the 'settler problem.'" The settler-Indigenous relations literature studies reconciliation not in the form of (typically cynical) statecraft, but in processes of grassroots alliance-building. In this way, it bears a resemblance to framings of relationality within critical Indigenous studies (Starblanket and Stark 2018; Simpson 2017; see also Asch 2014).

Lynne Davis's edited volume *Alliances* (2010), remains not only a foundational text but also a methodological weathervane in studying settler-Indigenous relations. While the volume's contributors are all interested in the study of alliances between settlers and Indigenous Peoples, they also take care not to overdetermine this phenomenon. Davis and Shpuniarsky (2010, 346) write that there are "certainly Indigenous leaders for whom alliances and coalitions with non-Indigenous people are peripheral or are to be avoided." The authors note that some leaders demur from such relations for important political reasons, as these may be interpreted as diminishing their "Nation-to-Nation relationships and [such leaders prefer instead to] deal with state actors directly." With this important caveat squarely in view, the alliance-building literature nevertheless proceeds from the observation that the challenges long leveled against the "morality of the settler project" by Indigenous movements have produced a "particular historical juncture," wherein not insignificant segments of the settler population are prepared to work with and alongside Indigenous Peoples (Bell 2014, 7–8; see also Cherry 2024; Swain 2022) and in some cases, to work directly against the state. That said, not all alliances are alike, nor are their tactics or terrains of struggle identical.

One of the most important insights of this literature is that alliances are often microcosms in which broader relations of power—such as ableism, cisheterosexism, colonial chauvinism, and white supremacism—are reproduced *and* contested. Davis (2010, 5) notes that the contributors to *Alliances* describe three distinct ways in which settler-Indigenous alliances can be broadly characterized: (1) partnerships of relative mutual respect; (2) settler paternalism, whereby non-Indigenous participants or organizations seek to impose an agenda; or (3) a commitment to upholding Indigenous leadership. Some of these tendencies are likely a consequence of the motivating factors that bring various individuals, communities, and organizations into the process of alliance building. A major strength of the alliance-building literature is that it tends to be methodologically rooted in dialogue with grassroots actors and, thereby, has more ready insight into the multiplicity of their motivations. At times, people with somewhat jaggedly fitted commitments like those struggling for self-determination and those appealing to the state for recognition of human/civil rights can collaborate in temporary alliances striving toward clear and relatively short-term shared goals. This was the case for the alliances that forced the province of Ontario to open the Ipperwash Inquiry. As Davis, O'Donnell, and Shpuniarsky record (2007, 103–19), the Coalition for a Public Inquiry into the Death of Dudley George made the terms of their alliance quite explicit in their "Statement of Unity." Whereas, for Indigenous members of the Coalition the fundamental issue was "one of sovereignty," for settlers "there was a responsibility to address this clear violation of human and civil rights of Aboriginal people" (103). The authors gloss these distinct motivations as useful for enabling the Coalition to act as "an accessible doorway for non-Aboriginal social justice groups and the broader public to come on board" (112). However, little is done to interrogate how congruent these underlying political commitments ultimately are beyond the limited goal of establishing an inquiry.

At other times, even relatively long-standing relationships of solidarity and mutual aid can flounder if actions deemed necessary or tactical under certain conditions are unacceptable to a sufficient number of participants. Lucille Marr (2001, 81) tracks one such instance with the Mennonite Central Committee of Ontario's decision to back away from endorsing the formation of the Union of Ontario Indians. This was deemed "too political for the constituency to handle at this time," even though many Mennonite communities were engaged in long-standing efforts of direct and material support to resurgent Indigenous movements (see Wallace 2013). It's because of these incongruities in motivating commitments and in the ever-present power differentials that scholars like Davis, O'Donnell, and Shpuniarsky (2010, 114) emphasize that this work is always "risky for all parties involved."

While the alliance-building literature initially positioned itself as primarily interested in movements, there is an unmistakable current of methodological individualism that runs through and seems increasingly to feed many of its predominating concerns. Avril Bell (2014, 173–74) notes in her study of settler and Indigenous identities that after having understood how these identities are produced through the "legal and political processes" of state building, she focuses most "directly on the responses and responsibilities of settler subjects *as individual actors.*" As such, in much of the most recent scholarship—and, as I show in the next section, in grassroots political discourses as well—the collective work of alliance building is increasingly read through and even overshadowed by a concentration on the individuated figure of the ally. Displacing a prior interpretation of alliances as emerging through the articulation of collective movements and/or civil organizations, the increasing focus on allies implies that alliances can be understood as an aggregation of otherwise discrete individual actors.

Perhaps most troublingly, this focus also signals a shift in the theory of change undergirding much of the alliance-building literature. Above, I note that scholars studying settler-Indigenous alliances have long been attentive to the reproduction of broader power relations within coalition spaces. As I contend more fully below, however, the shift in emphasis toward a theory of change premised on individuated allies and allyship *reifies* the social relations that shape settler rule, eliding how they might be overcome *through* the collective work of alliance building itself.

The dominant application of the ally framework is premised on a conceptual definition of allyship as a phenomenon that occurs across at least two degrees of foundational separation—experienced, again, at the level of the individual. Kevin FitzMaurice (2010) evinces this in his contribution to the *Alliances* volume:

> The term "ally" suggests a relationship across difference. In its basic form, to be an ally is to align oneself and to work cooperatively and collaboratively with a group other than one's own . . . a relationship across not only difference, but differences in power and colonial standing. (352–53)[1]

Allies, as rendered in this formulation, are *definitionally* outsiders, differentiated in both a demographic sense but also in terms of being thought of most often as outside a given struggle. In some instances, allies are presumed to be fully apart from the struggle itself and from the regime of power with which it contends. However, for those who do seek to position allies in relation to contested regimes of power, allies are understood to be separated from those with whom they ally themselves by the fact of their relatively privileged social location. As Andrea Sullivan-Clarke (2020, 182) makes clear in her critique of ally talk, this presumption of privilege was not particularly reflective of the actual social makeup of groups—like Veterans Standing with Standing Rock or Black Lives Matter—who organized to stand beside Oceti Sakowin water defenders.[2] The dyadic political relationship assumed by allyship discourse obscures both the multiple and co-constitutive forms of power that exist within and between any and all groups, *as well as* how alliances are generative of their own form of collective power that can be oriented with relative autonomy against the dominant regime.

Consequently, much of this scholarship increasingly fixates *not* on the political struggles of alliances to achieve actual reconciliatory or anticolonial ends but rather on the individual struggles that allies themselves face while striving to act in solidarity. Davis, O'Donnell, and Shpuniarsky (2007) presage this tendency in their very first article where rather than emphasizing solidarity as work through which all can be beneficially transformed, they stress that being an ally "means being open to being transformed, to risk being *hurt* at a *personal* level" (emphasis mine, 110). This fixation on the affective responses of allies resonates with criticism that Cornel West offered of dominant theories of white allyship during the Black-led uprisings in the summer of 2020 following the murder of George Floyd. West notes that the "genius" of white supremacist societies is to make "every issue revolve around white fears, insecurities, and anxieties rather than Black suffering, Indigenous peoples' suffering, trans suffering—no matter what colour." He continues: "It's that self-indulgent, narcissistic move—no matter how sophisticated, no matter how 'progressive' . . . that we have to accent here." He argues that we ought to be striving to think not about ally-ship but about "solidarity *across the board*" (Harvard Book Store 2020). The alliance-building literature presumes that all would-be allies supporting Indigenous movements do so from a position *best* characterized by forms of privilege they seek to attenuate—often to their own chagrin and for largely moral/ethical reasons. I will show that this presumption both seriously lim-its the scope of what the allyship framework deems politically possible and obscures the potential to link collective liberation struggles across a variety of social locations.

What's in an Ally's Toolkit Anyway?

In recent years, there has been a veritable explosion of toolkits designed to educate and incite positive solidarity across any number of political strug-gles (Campt 2018; "Men as Allies Toolkit"; "LGBT Ally Toolkit"; "Raise Your Voice"). To the degree that these toolkits receive scholarly attention at all, I suspect that many scholarly readers would interpret them as a very elemen-tary or merely introductory tool for political education. Toolkits are likely to be treated as efforts to translate theories or commitments that are pre-sumed to be more complex or perhaps more politically charged than many scholars or activists might assume to be acceptable to their imagined lay reader. By contrast, my interest in toolkits emerges from a desire to study them as texts of political theory. I contend that ally toolkits stand as the intellectual products of typically nonelite actors laboring to develop a the-ory of change and spur political action under conditions not fully of their own making. In essence, I am insisting on taking nonelite actors seriously both as political agents and theorists of their own actions.

As such, I compose an activist archive of five ally toolkits designed pri-marily for a readership of would-be settler allies in the Canadian context. My role here mixes curator and researcher and is therefore open to critique for perhaps having presupposed my argument through the selection of materials. Archives writ large, however, are never neutral things; they are always at once products and processes of power. Power sets the agenda of what is or is not to be preserved, thereby acting as a throttle on which voices are likely to be available to posterity. Activist archives are often inchoate cumulations of material that individual activists and/or collectives acquire and/or produce in the course of organizing. These include the minutes of meetings, communication threads, press releases, books, zines, pamphlets, posters, banners, chants/slogans, stencils and art gear, props, and equip-ment used in demonstrations, etc. While I provide more details for each ally toolkit where pertinent, as an overview it may assist the reader to know that they are authored in number of distinct ways. Each is a relatively short document, designed for easy distribution and consumption. One is single authored, another is authored by a labor union federation, with yet another written by a professional association subcommittee; while two are produced by NGOs. Further, in all but one case, there is clear evidence that these toolkits were either primarily authored by, or at least were composed in close dialogue with, Indigenous persons. The outlier here is the Canadian Building Trades Union's (CBTU) toolkit, for which I was unable to locate information pertaining to authorship.

Each of these toolkits were selected based on having a relatively wide distribution among various community and civil society groups since publication and can thereby be considered significant contributions to a developing public discourse and political theory of allyship. For example, Lynn Gehl's "Ally Bill of Responsibility" has been hosted online by the Unist'ot'en Camp, the University of Windsor's Aboriginal Education Centre, and the Sexual Assault Centre of Edmonton. *Build Together: Indigenous Allyship,* produced by the Canadian Building Trades Union, has been shared by the International Union of Painters and Allied Trades. The BC Association of Social Workers' (BCASW) "Towards a New Relationship" has been shared by the Creative City Network of Canada, the Kettle and Stony Point First Nation, and a variety of social worker colleges and associations. The "Treaty 7 Indigenous Ally Toolkit," authored jointly by the Calgary Foundation and the Montréal Indigenous Community Network, has been shared by the Indigenous Rights and Resource Governance Group, Forward Housing, and the Alberta Teachers of English as a Second Language. Finally, and likely the most widely shared document, is the "Indigenous Ally Toolkit" authored by the Montréal Urban Aboriginal Community Strategy Network (the same group that co-authored the Treaty 7 document). This toolkit has been featured in several CBC news stories and has been shared by the Canadian Medical Association, the BC Museums Association, and the Centre for Community Organizations. In each case, these are just a few of the civil society organizations publicly sharing these toolkits, which is to say nothing of their distribution through more informal/community-based networks. Indeed, these toolkits were ultimately selected because each was shared across at least one network of activists with which I have connections. This broad circulation should evidence that these documents are of significance both on their own terms as theoretical texts but also for the clear scope of traveling they have done between and within community groups. The broad distribution of these toolkits likely indicates a greater degree of social purchase than paywalled academic writing.

While there is little by way of complete consensus across even this relatively small sample of toolkits, they are unified in their intention to offer guidance around how settlers can work as allies to Indigenous Peoples. In what remains of this section, I discuss common themes surfacing across most of the documents. These include: the importance of language and speech acts; discussions of what I call "ally affect"; and descriptions of allyship as motivated by universal, liberal humanist principles.

Perhaps unsurprisingly, given that these toolkits strive to be as broadly accessible as possible, there's a pervading interest in language across many of them. In three of the toolkits, this interest appears in the most explicit form possible with the inclusion of a lexicon or glossary of terms. Something of a spectrum of specificity emerges across these glossaries. At the most abstracted end is the CBTU's toolkit, which offers snapshot definitions of nine keywords meant to give the reader the most broadly applicable language for discussing Indigenous-related issues (e.g., Indigenous, Aboriginal, Métis, Privilege). All the CBTU's keywords are in English (Canada's Building Trades Union 2018, 8). By contrast, the Calgary Foundation's toolkit provides slightly more extensive definitions than the CBTU document, but they thematically center on the six Indigenous nations whose territories are covered by Treaty 7. Additionally, the Calgary Foundation toolkit includes both forms of greetings and names for the "landscape now known as Calgary" in Blackfoot, Cree, Îyâxe Nakoda, and Tsuut'ina ("Treaty 7" 2019, 1). The Montréal Urban Aboriginal Community Strategy Network toolkit strikes something of a balance between these approaches, offering a dozen keywords of which three are specific to the territories on which Montréal is situated. Like the glossary in the Calgary Foundation's toolkit, this one includes a (smaller) number of words in both Anishinaabemowin and Kanien'kéha to situate the reader in the territories of and around Montréal ("Indigenous Ally Toolkit" 2019, 4).

This spectrum of specificity is likely the result of at least two factors. First, the amount of Indigenous involvement in designing the toolkit itself, which is evidenced as being considerable in both the Calgary and Montréal toolkits. Second, the likely geographical dispersion of the toolkit's intended readership. That is, the CBTU toolkit may be more generic because it imagines readers drawn from member-trade unions spread across the entirety of what's presently known as Canada. It is therefore difficult for the CBTU to highlight specific Indigenous nations or languages without excluding others. Interestingly, then, the CBTU toolkit—reflecting the organization of the institution from which it originates—reconstitutes the precise problem of methodological nationalism that alliance building and allyship literatures intended to bypass. This also reveals some of the political possibilities opened by deliberately place-based approaches to political struggle, showing the tensions of scale endemic to anticolonial mobilizing.

The politics of language bear further consideration here. Most notably, there is a clear effort across these toolkits to give readers a contemporary vocabulary. They often explain that much of the received language is not merely antiquated but is also deeply implicated in the reproduction of white supremacist epistemologies. Perhaps because of the brevity required by the toolkit format, some of the contemporary realities of ongoing colonization are obscured in favor of a more sanitized language. This was made most apparent around the usage of the term "Indian," which the CBTU toolkit (2018) describes as an "*outdated term* which should be avoided . . . although it is still used in *some* legal settings" (emphasis mine, 8). The Montréal toolkit is somewhat more forceful on this matter, correctly listing "Indian" alongside other racial slurs used against Indigenous Peoples as "terms that are not okay for you [a settler] to say" ("Indigenous Ally Toolkit" 2019, 4). In neither case, however, do these toolkits confront the fact that in Canada today "Indian" is both a racial slur *and* a constitutional term of art. Or, to put the matter more bluntly, far from being "outdated," the ongoing nature of Canada's system of colonial apartheid means that while "Indian" is undoubtedly a racial slur when used against Indigenous Peoples, it is a form of racism embedded in the very constitutional and legislative foundations of the Canadian state. Indeed, in the case of the Calgary Foundation toolkit, there's a strange obfuscation of the Indian Act's role in advancing, maintaining, and regularizing colonial apartheid. The toolkit suggests that "*although* the Indian Act was enacted in 1876, Indigenous people have only recently begun to obtain the same rights as other people in Canada" (emphasis mine, "Treaty 7" 2019, 4). The use of "although" is inexplicable here, as it seems to suggest that the relationship between the Indian Act and the social marginalization of Indigenous Peoples is unlikely or incidental. It implies that the Indian Act might have been meant to alleviate such marginalization, rather than the actuality whereby the Act regularized colonial apartheid through law. To be meaningfully antiracist in such a context clearly demands something more than merely better language.

The importance of language—or, more precisely, of speech acts—manifests in another way across these three toolkits, as well as in the document produced by the BCASW. Territorial acknowledgments are treated here as significant acts of allyship, asserting that they contribute toward reconciliation in and of themselves. Indeed, discussion of such acknowledgments is given considerable space in both the Calgary toolkit, where the topic takes up one-sixth of the total space, and even more so in the CBTU toolkit where it accounts for nearly a third of the entire document. Described as a "simple way" to show "commitment to Indigenous allyship" (Canada's Building Trades Union 2018, 5), across all these toolkits there is emphasis on the fact that territorial acknowledgments should never be merely pro forma. Rather, they ought to be opportunities for those who give them and those who encounter them to "form deeper connections and grow their knowledge of the original people of the land" and, further, they should "come from a personal place" ("Treaty 7" 2019, 2). The intended value of such acknowledgments, then, is twofold: to show respect for Indigenous Peoples' relationships with the surrounding lands and to invite settlers into a process of self-education. There is, however, no sustained emphasis within the toolkits on the *political* work that land acknowledgments can do—under certain conditions—by revealing that settler rule is seriously contested by ongoing assertions of Indigenous jurisdictions. Territorial acknowledgments, while treated as deeply significant by these toolkits, also have their political edges sanitized into being about recognition and consciousness *for the settler*—typically individuated—rather than about advancing an explicitly political program of land back. This observation echoes long-standing Indigenous critiques of such acknowledgments (Rudder 2019; Vowel 2016).

Another major theme suffusing these toolkits is attention to what I call "ally affect." There is a focus throughout these toolkits—which mirrors trends in the scholarship noted above—on the emotional orientation and comportment that settlers ought to have toward their role as "allies." Across these toolkits, the necessity of settlers refusing guilt as the motivating or animating force of their allyship with Indigenous Peoples is among the most consistently and directly addressed questions about ally affect. In Lynn Gehl's (2012) "Ally Bill of Responsibilities," she urges would-be allies to "not act out of guilt, but rather out of a genuine interest in challenging the larger oppressive power structures." The importance placed on ally affect echoes throughout many of the other toolkits. For instance, the CBTU toolkit stresses that part of "learning to be an ally" means understanding both complicity and the privilege that it produces but it "*doesn't* mean dwelling on feelings of guilt." Instead, allies ought to be "challenging ourselves to do better" (2019, 1–2). Similarly, the Montréal toolkit makes clear that guilt "should not be the main reason" for supporting Indigenous Peoples. The toolkit asserts that while it "is completely normal" to "grapple with these feelings of guilt" as one educates themselves about colonialism, emphasis must always remain on "the steps and actions" being taken to make allyship meaningful, rather than seeking absolution ("Indigenous Ally Toolkit" 2019, 5).

Many of the toolkits reviewed presume guilt as the reflexive emotional state animating or at least initiating the work of would-be allies. I want to emphasize that this can be usefully read as a diagnostic of the sorts of interactions that are likely occurring with many would-be allies. In short, toolkits can double as barometers of, or responses to, actual problems/dynamics stymying movements. And, by extension, these dynamics might also indicate something about the likely composition of those movements at present, particularly the sorts of social locations occupied by guilt-ridden, would-be allies. As such, the toolkits place considerable emphasis on the importance of self-reflection as itself an act of allyship. Arguing for standpoint epistemology, or an appreciation of one's positionality, Gehl's (2012) sixth responsibility asserts that allies can come to better understand "the larger oppressive power structures that serve to hold certain groups and people down" by "critically reflecting on their own experiences with oppressive power structures." Gehl suggests that by "reflecting on their subjectivity"—by which I infer she means how one's social location shapes their relationship with dominant regimes of power—allies can "ensure critical thought." Other toolkits follow a parallel course. The BCASW makes clear that the very impetus for their putting together a toolkit in the first place was to "encourage and facilitate reflexivity and dialogue about reconciliation" in the wake of the Truth and Reconciliation Commission's 2015 Calls to Action (Indigenous Women's Working Group 2016, 2—3). The Calgary Foundation's toolkit places a similar emphasis on self-reflection as allyship. Whereas the BCASW's account has a distinctly individualist bent to it, the Calgary Foundation toolkit stresses that self-reflection must also be coupled to a practice of "regularly debriefing with community members" ("Treaty 7" 2019, 5). It's important to note that in all cases, self-reflection is characterized not merely as a necessary component of or precondition for allyship but rather as a key enactment of the responsibilities of being an ally. Even as they continue to assert that actions speak louder than words, the overriding stress placed on self-reflection *as praxis* says something quite significant about the relatively limited scope of anticipated political activity underpinning the theory of allyship developed in and through these toolkits. Moreover, the priority placed on self-reflexivity implies a causal direction between thought/consciousness and action/being that may rest on shaky epistemological and political grounds.

Finally, having attempted to uproot some of the more problematic ways in which ally affect manifests itself within movements, evincing motivations amongst would-be allies that are often more egocentric than they are concerned with solidarity, these toolkits attempt to reground the commitments of would-be allies in appeals to universal, liberal humanism. In the Calgary Foundation toolkit, this attempt is made with jarring directness when it reminds the reader that "Indigenous people are grandparents, parents, children, & siblings. They are doctors, teachers, social workers, entrepreneurs and artists—they are human beings" ("Treaty 7" 2019, 5). This passage is jarring *not* because it says anything even remotely controversial or radical. Quite the opposite; it ought to be jarring because it reveals the prevailing conditions of a social order in and through which Indigenous Peoples are so thoroughly and systematically dehumanized that it is necessary to make such an assertion *at all*. Again, the content of the toolkits can be seen as a diagnostic of just how far anticolonial work still has to go. Beyond this vital groundwork, however, both the Calgary Foundation and the Montréal toolkits assert that one of the guiding principles for allies is recognition of the fact that "every person has a basic right to human dignity, respect, and equal access to resources" (ibid., 3). Moreover, both toolkits argue that allyship is ultimately aimed at making this principle a reality ("Indigenous Ally Toolkit" 2019, 2). The claim, then, is that the need for allyship emerges consequent to the recognition by the would-be ally that they have a *shared* or *universal* status in common with those with whom they ally themselves *as a result of them all being, simply, humans.* Moreover, the claim implies that this shared status or commonality imposes an ethical and moral obligation on the would-be ally to call for some form of minimal equality.

In several instances these toolkits are quite direct about the mechanisms through which equalization is to take place. Dealing specifically with allyship in the workplace, the CBTU's toolkit (2018, 3) is perhaps the most explicit when it cites the "Canadian Human Rights Act or the comparable Provincial Human Rights Act[s]" as the ultimate authority for backstopping discriminatory practices. As is the case for much *liberal* political theory, these toolkits tend to conceive of the state as standing outside of and above social relations of domination, exploitation, and discrimination, imagining that the state might intervene to ensure the alleviation of those conditions should they arise. Such occasions are thereby treated as incidental rather than inevitable within, or as a consequence of, the very social order of which the state is simultaneously a manifestation and the primary mechanism for social reproduction (see Brown 1995; Simpson 2016).

According to these toolkits, the work of the ally, then, is primarily to advocate. The CBTU and the BCASW stress this, writing that the basic definition of an ally is one who "supports and *advocates* for others" (emphasis mine, Canada's Building Trades Union 2018, 1). As such, the toolkits aim to enable readers to "*advocate* for systemic change at a local, community, and societal levels" (emphasis mine, Indigenous Women's Working Group 2016, 3). That is, the toolkits considered here strive to facilitate allies in seeing their capacity to appeal to authorities that are supposed to be legitimately constituted with the power to intervene wherever social antagonisms happen to arise. Such legitimacy is something that, especially in a colonial situation, can hardly be assumed.

"Ally," Another Word for Having Too Much to Lose?

How then are the texts reviewed discursively constructing the ally as a political subject? Put differently: not only how is the ally imagined as an ideal type but also who is actually being implicitly constructed as and called upon to be a would-be ally within this theory of change? The fairest answer, implied by the texts themselves, is that they are theorizing a *generic ally*. That is, I take it that in both the scholarship and the ally toolkits, the desire is to understand the ally as a political relationship that is capacious enough to not be predetermined in terms of its specific content. I suspect that the toolkit authors, in particular, would answer that they are not engaged in a process of interpellation—or, conversely, that their interpellative work aims at universality—and that *anyone* can *potentially* become an ally of the sort they have theorized.

I want to suggest here that by considering the type of work that is asked of would-be allies—the political horizon of allyship—we can see that these toolkits actually imply a rather specific conceptualization of their imagined ally. The effort to step outside of or to get beyond the particularities of real, granular questions about how various interests, commitments, political institutions, and structures of power articulate with one another ultimately risks reproducing the very abstractions that alliance building and allyship, as practices and analytics, were meant to challenge. The toolkits reveal some of this when they venture into enumerating practical steps that can be taken as acts of allyship. For instance, expanding upon the process of self-reflection, the Calgary Foundation's toolkit encourages would-be allies to ask themselves whether their interest in allyship stems "from the fact that the issue will meet quotas or increase chances of any funding?" In short, it prompts inquiry into whether there is a business and/or financial motive behind their allyship. Moreover, as an active step, the same toolkit pushes its readers to hire Indigenous Peoples ("Treaty 7" 2019, 5). Both are potentially quite important acts, as they can stymie the extractive and performative elements of reconciliation as a "carnival" put on by state actors or private interests (see James 2012; George 2017). They can also transfer very real resources to Indigenous persons—and, by extension, their families/communities—who have been historically excluded from workplaces and economic life writ large as a consequence of Canada's apartheid laws. At the same time, though, in a relatively short list of recommended tangible acts of allyship—in a toolkit that is designed precisely to encourage action—these suggestions represent a type of action that is not open to everyone equally. Instead of a *generic* ally, then, the distinct impression is of an ally who might be described as a member of the *professional* and/or *managerial* sectors—part of the petite bourgeoisie. Moreover, given what we know about the co-constitution of these class hierarchies in Canada through racializing and gendering regimes, this may also reveal the implicit whiteness and male-ness of how the ally is being constructed as an imagined political subject (Statistics Canada 2023).

Tellingly, this imagining of the would-be ally as a very specific social actor is most apparent *precisely* where the toolkits intend to be most universal. In the already quoted passage from the Calgary Foundation's toolkit, where the reader is implored to see Indigenous persons as human beings, that human-ity is established, in part, through an appeal to the fact that Indigenous persons are "doctors, teachers, social workers, entrepreneurs, and artists" ("Treaty 7" 2019, 5). Given the negative portrayal of Indigenous persons in media, popular culture, and public discourse writ large, there is good sense in emphasizing that they in fact occupy every rung of social life. However, con-structing an appeal to basic humanity through a group's proximity to profes-sional class-based respectability is not without political consequences. The most immediate of which seems to be an appeal that would-be allies recog-nize the need to support Indigenous persons through a shared commonality of class position—which is always-already constructed through regimes of ableism, cisheteropatriarchy, and white supremacy. Something significant is left unsaid by the fact that the Indigenous person as service worker, as land defender, unemployed, displaced and/or dispossessed is not considered a via-ble representative of the "human being" as a universal subject. The discon-nect lies in the imagined readership for whom this appeal is presumably being constructed so as to overcome prejudices of petite bourgeois respectability.

The scholarly literature on alliance building also reflects this tendency for calls to allyship to implicitly construct their subjects from a very spe-cific social strata. This was evidenced above, in the second section, where I discussed how the alliance-building literature turned toward the theory of allyship as an aggregation of individuated moral or ethical projects, rather than as a collective political struggle. To enunciate one's political self in pri-marily individualized terms implies an assumption about the relative social power of the would-be ally. The tendency to interpellate allies of a specific social strata also appears to shape the type of decolonizing work pursued by settlers themselves, as evidenced through Carolyn Stirling's interviews. Stirling (2014) notes that there is a clear bifurcation in terms of how the settlers she interviews—many of whom are of white-collar professions, par-ticularly within various levels of the education sector—think of allyship in decolonizing work:

Interestingly land was seldom mentioned by the participants in this study despite many of them living close to and/or being involved in land disputes . . . for the participants in this study the focus of decolonization is on decolonizing their minds and restoring Indigenous languages and cultures. (389)

This is a striking division in the sorts of labor that would-be allies are emphasizing. A clear preference emerges among Stirling's interlocutors to engage in the vital—though, compared to other anticolonial work, less likely to be stigmatized or criminalized—intellectual and cultural work of decolonizing language and correcting the historical record. This work is absolutely crucial, but the stark division in uptake may speak to the specific articulation of this type of decolonizing work with the *professional* incentives/disincentives already guiding those would-be allies. In which case, the toolkits' earlier question about the personal/financial gains derived from allyship makes good sense as an issue to guard against, even as it still reveals the relatively narrow and rarefied social strata of those imagined as would-be allies.

We could also consider Avril Bell's work (2014) theorizing allyship. Grounding her account of settler allyship in what she describes as Levinasian ethics, Bell writes that the relationship between self (here: settler) and Other (Indigenous peoples) "is not reciprocal, but one of 'radical generosity' . . . It is the movement of a self who doesn't 'have time' for self-concern." Bell insists that her turn to ethics intends to "provoke and incite us to better forms of political engagement," by forcing our commitments to reorient to a starting place of radical alterity, "while stopping short of providing any prescriptions" for specific political actions (Bell 2014, 179−80). This is certainly a laudable and unambiguous commitment toward "the Other," even at the imagined expense of oneself. It might, however, be worthwhile to ask: Under what social conditions is it reasonable to ground a political program in the *expectation* that its partisans act with no self-concern? (see Mensah and Williams 2017). A standard answer suggests it is only under conditions of relative affluence that it becomes possible to orient one's politics toward "the Other" (see Inglehart 1977). And to a certain extent, something important is grasped here: most apparently, that these texts *likely are* (though perhaps unintentionally) interpellating relatively affluent settlers as would-be allies. But, if that is the case, the subject being constructed here cannot really be claimed as a generic ally.

Testing the theory of allyship developed across these toolkits and the alliance-building literature against a clear limit case may be instructive in seeing where its ethical grounding breaks down politically. To my mind, it is difficult to sustain as a political argument the claim that a person living in conditions of severe destitution, such as entrenched houselessness or displacement, can be called upon and expected to act as an ally, *inasmuch as that is presumed to mean that they must act with* no *self-concern.* That many such marginalized people *do,* in fact, sustain relationships of deep and reciprocal solidarity with Indigenous Peoples is not proof positive of the theory of allyship. Rather, it is a consequence of materially rooted and far more expansive social relations of solidarity than are captured in the concept of allyship.

The problem of an ethics-first approach lies in the ways in which it replicates a basic conceit at the core of the theory of allyship; that is, the theory's radically dyadic vision. It reduces the political to relations between allies (as definitionally well-to-do) and those to whom they are allied (as definitionally disadvantaged). This is to say that the theory of allyship strips away a broader social context, filled with an uneven topography of *relative*—in the dual sense of being both in proportion and interconnected—social power. The unevenness of the social system is productive of contradictions that can, if deliberately politicized, offer fruitful bases for building solidarity. In short, because it abstracts its subjects from the bundle of contradictory relations in which they live textured social existences, the political program implied by allyship lacks a *social* theory. That is, a theory of political activity as always-already situated within and necessarily responsive to a differentially shared social totality (Grant and Snelgrove 2023).[3]

A more fulsome answer, I believe, insists on the importance of this wider social context—shaped and produced within a global system—when developing a theory of solidarity that is more robust than the account of allyship we have received here. One of the strengths of such an approach is that it prompts us to consider not what can be asked of the affluent or comfortable, those with a considerable stake within the presently dominant social order. Instead, it invites a focus on what is already being built or envisioned by and among the *global masses* who have been dispossessed, displaced, and rendered or pushed increasingly toward destitution within the social conditions produced by settler imperialism. Importantly, this is *not* an invitation to replace one ideal subject with another that is somehow considered more morally pure as a consequence of suffering. Nor does it totally foreclose the possibility of any particular alliances *a priori.* Rather, it incites a concrete method of inquiry by which we can approach our obligations to one another.

At the panel talk featuring Cornel West in the summer of 2020 referenced above, Keeanga-Yamahtta Taylor suggested that "this whole 'ally' thing has to go . . . I'm not interested in 'allies.'" Her reason presages the concerns that I have attempted to theorize here; she asserts that the framework of allyship rests on the presumption that "over here in 'our' America, everything's *great*—we just need improve 'your' America." The reality, Taylor insists, is that America—though I would extend her argument further to incorporate the world system of settler imperialism—"is a country of suffering." Even as the distribution and intensity of that suffering is radically uneven along lines of ability, class, colonial/national status, gender, race, etc., Taylor is emphatic that "we have to move this conversation beyond 'allyship,' to talk about what is actually happening . . . and what are the strategies, and tactics, and politics, and understandings of history that are necessary to transform it so that all of our lives can improve" (Harvard Book Store 2020). In short, what are the actual social conditions within and through which political coalitions for radical transformative change are already forming?

In a recent dialogue with Ruth Wilson Gilmore, Nick Estes makes several similar points. Endorsing Gilmore's call to return to a conception of differentiated but united struggle against a "common antagonist," Estes notes that "the horizon of struggle used to be freedom and liberation. Now the horizon of struggle is how do the perpetrators of violence and oppression recognize my injury or recognize my suffering? It's become an individualized project." He notes that getting back to liberation struggles is, in many ways, also about getting back to basics: asking fundamental questions about the conditions under which more and more people increasingly struggle to survive and then striving collectively to meet those needs (Estes, Gilmore, and Loperena 2021, 263–64). Concretely, we might return to my proposed limit case, empowered to ask not how we can expect people experiencing entrenched houselessness or displacement to become allies who act without self-concern, but rather how can the conditions they face be understood as differentiated outcomes of the shared social relations that are constitutive of settler rule? This question is more than theoretical, as it enables us to develop political programs in which self-concern is not set aside but rather fulfilled and addressed *through* its articulation *with* Indigenous sovereignty and *against* the dispossessive regimes of proprietorship that have historically been used to incentivize collaboration with regimes of settler rule. Ultimately, this social theory of anticolonial action transforms how the self is even enunciated, *not* merely in ideational terms but also in its very material dependencies on others. Rather than focusing on interpellating professional and managerial types as the imagined would-be allies whose allyship is thought to be constituted through a negation, we can instead begin thinking about this type of liberatory work as enabling a greater degree of *presence* among those who have much to gain *with* one another.

Conclusion

I am far from the first voice, or even the most forceful, to express a degree of skepticism as to whether discourses of allyship offer a sufficiently robust account of the sort of *thick* relationships necessary to engage in political struggles in and against settler rule (Dhillon 2019; Estes et al. 2021). More-over, the critique of allyship that I have developed here is not meant to be from some point of removal or scholarly distance. Rather, it is informed by and immanent to the various intellectual and praxis-based tendencies *within* movements.

Jodi Dean (2019, 18) asserts that the discourse of allyship, ultimately, is not about solidarity but "is a matter of the *self . . .* of the *individual* who stands alone, and of this single individual taking on a struggle that properly belongs to another. *It's as if struggles were possessions.*" Dean's antipathy toward allyship as today's predominating discursive/theoretical frame for political relationships rests on her opposition to its egocentricity: "Ally-ship is a disposition, a confrontation not with the state or capitalist power but with one's own discomfort." The discussion that I have staged in this article with both the alliance-building literature and my activist archive of ally toolkits from the Canadian context has shown that allyship is primar-ily about the self only if that self is conceived as an *ideational and moral project* that is divorced from material needs and the relational context in which that self is necessarily situated. As shown in the fourth section, the attempt to theorize the ally as a generic subject has more often functioned to strip away the actually existing social relations and material conditions through which political solidarities can, and historically have been, made and remade. Real self-concern, regard for oneself as a subject produced through and situated within social relations (which always encompasses how one relates with the more-than-human world), necessitates constantly grappling with how one's interests articulate—link up with and express themselves—with those of others. As emphasized in the oft-cited quote that is typically ascribed to Lilla Watson but that she insists on attribut-ing collectively to Aboriginal activists in Queensland in the 1970s: "If you have come here to help me, you are wasting your time. But if you have come because your liberation is bound up with mine, then let us work together" (quoted in Barker 2021, 124).

Crucially, this is not to claim that merely adopting a relational concep-tion of the self is a panacea for overcoming settler rule or its imperial mode of living. As Starblanket and Stark (2018) show, such a claim would simply reproduce the idealism that it critiques. Rather, what I'm suggesting is that a social theory of political solidarity enables us to see past the dyadic struc-ture superimposed by the frame of the ally/allied relationship and to con-front the reality that undoing settler rule is a question of articulation *all the way down.* We cannot settle for recomposing unjust or colonial settler-Indigenous relations *into* a deepening or widening of their articulation with other relations that are themselves reliant upon distinct forms of exploita-tion and domination. Settler imperialism is a world system, and what might appear as greater degrees of inclusion achieved in one place often produce deepening processes of dispossession and exploitation elsewhere. Ultimately, a political program that is about liberation instead of advantage must be responsible to the totality of these relationships. This likely necessitates a politics thicker and more durable than allyship, in which the liberation of each becomes the condition for the liberation of all.

PHIL HENDERSON is a postdoctoral fellow in political science at the University of Toronto.

Acknowledgments

I'd like to acknowledge the helpful and encouraging feedback received from my three anonymous reviewers. As well as the significant encouragement from many mentors and colleagues including: Heidi Stark, Rita Dhamoon, John Borrows, Michael Asch, Kevin Bruyneel, the Global Marxisms reading group, Stacie Swain, Brydon Kramer, Shianna McAllister, Daniel Sherwin, and Bradley Clement. I have also learned much from my students. I'd also like to dedicate this article to the memory of Catherine Wallace. Her toolkit was never metaphorical; rather, it was put tirelessly towards the work of collective liberation. Catherine Wallace ¡presente!

References

Aazhoodenaang, Enjibaajig. 2022. *Our Long Struggle for Home: The Ipperwash Story.* Vancouver: On Point Press.

Asch, Michael. 2014. *On Being Here to Stay: Treaties and Aboriginal Rights in Canada.* Toronto: University of Toronto Press.

Barker, Joanne. 2021. *Red Scare: The State's Indigenous Terrorist.* Berkeley: University of California Press.

Barrera, Jorge. 2021. "RCMP Arrest 14, Clear Road on Wet'suwet'en Territory in Ongoing Dispute over Land Rights, Pipeline." CBC News, November 18. https://www.cbc.ca/news/canada/british-columbia/rcmp-wet-suwet-en-pipeline-resistance-1.6254245.

Bell, Avril. 2014. *Relating Indigenous and Settler Identities: Beyond Domination.* London: Palgrave Macmillan.

Bhatia, Amar. 2013. "We Are All Here to Stay? Indigeneity, Migration, and Decolonizing the Treaty Right to Be Here." *Windsor Yearbook of Access to Justice* 31, no. 1: 39–64.

Bishop, Anne. 2015 [1994]. *Becoming an Ally: Breaking the Cycle of Oppression in People.* 3rd ed. Halifax: Fernwood Publishing.

———. 2005. *Beyond Token Change: Breaking the Cycle of Oppression in Institutions.* Halifax: Fernwood Publishing.

Brown, Wendy. 1995. "Rights and Losses." In *States of Injury: Power and Freedom in Late Modernity*. Princeton, N.J.: Princeton University Press.

Campt, David W. 2018. *The White Ally Toolkit Workbook*. I AM Publications.

Canada's Building Trades Unions. February 2018. *Build Together: Indigenous Allyship*. Build Together. http://www.buildtogether.ca.

Cherry, Keith. 2024. "'The Kids Don't Want Reconciliation, They Want Land Back': Thinking about Decolonization and Settler Solidarity after the Death of Reconciliation." *Contemporary Political Theory*. https://link.springer.com/article/10.1057/s41296-024-00684-2.

Coulthard, Glen Sean. 2014. *Red Skin, White Masks: Rejecting the Colonial Politics of Recognition*. Minneapolis: University of Minnesota Press, 2014.

Davis, Lynne. 2010. "Introduction." In *Alliances: Re/Envisioning Indigenous-non-Indigenous Relationships*, edited by Lynne Davis, 1–12. Toronto: University of Toronto Press.

Davis, Lynne, Vivian O'Donnell, and Heather Shpuniarsky. 2007. "Aboriginal-Social Justice Alliances: Understanding the Landscape of Relationships through the Coalition for a Public Inquiry into Ipperwash." *International Journal of Canadian Studies* 36: 95–119.

Davis, Lynne, and Heather Yanique Shpuniarsky. 2010. "The Spirit of Relationships: What We Have Learned about Indigenous/Non-Indigenous Alliances and Coalitions." In *Alliances: Re/Envisioning Indigenous-non-Indigenous Relationships*, edited by Lynne Davis, 334–48. Toronto: University of Toronto Press.

Dean, Jodi. 2019. *Comrade: An Essay on Political Belonging*. London: Verso.

Desai, Chandni. 2021. "Disrupting Settler-Colonial Capitalism: Indigenous Intifadas and Resurgent Solidarity from Turtle Island to Palestine." *Journal of Palestine Studies* 50, no. 2: 43–66.

Dhamoon, Rita Kaur. 2021. "Relational Othering: Critiquing Dominance, Critiquing the Margins." *Politics, Groups, and Identities* 9, no. 5: 873–92.

Dhillon, Jaskiran. 2019. "Notes on Becoming a Comrade: Indigenous Women, Leadership, and Movement(s) for Decolonization." *American Indian Culture and Research Journal* 43, no. 3: 41–54.

Epp, Roger. 2008. *We Are All Treaty People: Prairie Essays*. Edmonton: University of Alberta Press.

Estes, Nick, Ruth Wilson Gilmore, and Christopher Loperena. 2021. "United in Struggle: As Racial Capitalism Rages, Movements for Indigenous Sovereignty and Abolition Offer Visions of Freedom on Stolen Land." *NACLA Report on the Americas* 53, no. 3: 255–67.

Federici, Silvia. 2014 [2004]. *Caliban and the Witch: Women, The Body and Primitive Accumulation*. Brooklyn: Autonomedia..

FitzMaurice, Kevin. 2010. "Are White People Obsolete? Indigenous Knowledge and the Colonizing Ally in Canada." In *Alliances: Re/Envisioning Indigenous-non-Indigenous Relationships*, edited by Lynne Davis, 352–53. Toronto: University of Toronto Press.

Gehl, Lynn. 2012. "Ally Bill of Responsibilities." Accessed January 30, 2025. https://www.lynngehl.com/ally-bill-of-responsibilities.html

George, Rachel. 2017. "Inclusion is Just the Canadian Word for Assimilation: Self-Determination and the Reconciliation Paradigm in Canada." In *Surviving Canada: Indigenous Peoples Celebrate 150 Years of Betrayal*, edited by Kiera Ladner and Myra Tait, 49–62. Winnipeg: Arbeiter Ring Publishing.

Grant, John, and Corey Snelgrove. 2023. "Returning to Totality: Settler Colonialism, Decolonization, and Struggles for Freedom." *Philosophy and Social Criticism*. https://journals.sagepub.com/doi/pdf/10.1177/01914537231219935

Green, Joyce. 2001. "Canaries in the Mines of Citizenship: Indian Women in Canada." 34, no. 4: 715–38.

Grossman, Zoltán. 2017. *Unlikely Alliances: Native Nations and White Communities Join to Defend Rural Lands*. Seattle: University of Washington Press.

Hall, Stuart. 2019a. "Race, Articulation, and Societies Structured in Dominance [1980]." In *Essential Essay, Volume 1*, edited by David Morley, 172–221. Durham, N.C.: Duke University Press.

———. 2019b. "Gramsci's Relevance for the Study of Race and Ethnicity." In *Essential Essay, Volume 2*, edited by David Morley, 21–55. Durham, N.C.: Duke University Press.

Harris, Cheryl I. 1993. "Whiteness as Property." *Harvard Law Review* 106, no. 8: 1707–91.

Harvard Book Store. 2020. "Where Do We Go From Here: A Fundraiser for Black Lives." YouTube, July 13. https://www.youtube.com/watch?v=Er2jE4B9kDA&list=PLzAJnbl3TW7PMssHaaUzTkiue5KvcT6WC&index=24.

Henderson, Phil. 2024. "Federalism and Settler Imperialism: Racial Regimes, Whiteness, and Conquest in Canadian Constitutionalism," *Canadian Journal of Political Science* 57, no. 2: 466–87.

———. Forthcoming. *On the Shores of Anger: Canadian Colonialism and Settler Resentment*. Halifax: Fernwood Publishing.

Horne, Gerald. 2014. *The Counter-Revolution of 1776: Slave Resistance and the Origins of the United States of America*. New York: New York University Press.

———. 2018. *The Apocalypse of Settler Colonialism: The Roots of Slavery, White Supremacy, and Capitalism in Seventeenth-Century North America and the Caribbean*. New York: Monthly Review Press.

———. 2020. *The Dawning of the Apocalypse: The Roots of Slavery, White Supremacy, Settler Colonialism, and Capitalism in the Long Sixteenth Century*. New York: Monthly Review Press.

"Indigenous Ally Toolkit." 2019. Montréal Urban Aboriginal Strategy Network. Accessed December 23, 2021. http://reseaumtlnetwork.com/resources/

Indigenous Women's Working Group. 2016. *Towards a New Relationship: Tool Kit for Reconciliation/Decolonization of Social Work Practice at the Individual, Workplace, and Community Level*. Vancouver: British Columbia Association of Social Workers.

Inglehart, Ronald. 1977. *The Silent Revolution: Changing Values and Political Styles Among Western Publics*. Princeton, N.J.: Princeton University Press.

James, Matt. 2012. "A Carnival of Truth? Knowledge, Ignorance and the Canadian Truth and Reconciliation Commission." *International Journal of Transitional Justice* 6, no. 2: 182–204.

Ladner, Kiera L. 2017. "Taking the Field: 50 Years of Indigenous Politics in the *CJPS*," *Canadian Journal of Political Science* 50, no. 1: 163–79.

Lethabo King, Tiffany. 2019. *The Black Shoals: Offshore Formations of Black and Native Studies*. Durham, N.C.: Duke University Press.

"LGBT Ally Toolkit." n.d. Amnesty International. Accessed December 16, 2021. www.amnestyusa.org/lgbt .

Linebaugh, Peter. 2014. *Stop, Thief! The Commons, Enclosures, and Resistance.* Oakland: PM Press.

Lowe, Lisa. 2015. *The Intimacies of Four Continents.* Durham: Duke University Press.

Mackey, Eva. 2016. *Unsettled Expectations: Uncertainty, Land and Settler Decolonization.* Halifax: Fernwood Publishing.

Macpherson, C. B., ed. 1978. *Property: Mainstream and Critical Positions.* Toronto: University of Toronto Press.

Marr, Lucille. 2001. "Breaking Down Barriers: MCC Ontario and Ontario Native Communities, 1967–1999." *Journal of Mennonite Studies* 19:78–91.

Mays, Kyle T. 2021. *An Afro-Indigenous History of the United States.* Boston: Beacon.

"Men as Allies Toolkit: Standing Up for Women." n.d. Women's Fund Rhodes Island. Accessed December 16, 2021. www.wfri.org.

Mensah, Joseph, and Christopher J Williams. 2017. *Boomerang Ethics: How Racism Affects Us All.* Halifax: Fernwood Publishing.

Mills, C. Wright. 1956. *The Power Elite.* Oxford: Oxford University Press.

Monaghan, Jeffery. 2013. "Mounties in the Frontier: Circulations, Anxieties, and Myths of Settler Colonial Policing in Canada." *Journal of Canadian Studies* 47, no. 1: 122–48.

Morden, Michael. 2014. "Across the Barricades: Non-Indigenous Mobilization and Settler Colonialism in Canada." *Canadian Political Science Review* 8, no. 1: 43–62.

Moreton-Robinson, Aileen. 2015. *The White Possessive: Property, Power, and Indigenous Sovereignty.* Minneapolis: University of Minnesota Press.

Morin, Brandi. 2021. "'No One is Going to Believe You': When the RCMP Abuses Indigenous Women and Girls." *Al Jazeera*, December 29. https://www .aljazeera.com/features/longform/2021/12/29/no-one-will-believe-you -when-the-rcmp-abuses-indigenous-girls.

Mowatt, Morgan, Matthew Wildcat, and Gina Starblanket. 2024. "Indigenous Sovereignty and Political Science: Building an Indigenous Politics Subfield." *Annual Review of Political Science* 27: 301–316.

"Raise Your Voice: A Trans Ally Toolkit." Nd. American Civil Liberties Union. Accessed December 16, 2021. www.aclu-mo.org/trans.

Regan, Paulette. 2010. *Unsettling the Settler Within: Indian Residential Schools, Truth Telling, and Reconciliation in Canada.* Vancouver: UBC Press.

Rudder, Kiara. 2019. "Hayden King and others question the effectiveness of land acknowledgements." *The Eyeopener*, January 29. https://theeyeopener .com/2019/01/hayden-king-and-others-question-the-effectiveness-of -land-acknowledgemenets/

Rutherford, Scott. 2020. *Canada's Other Red Scare: Indigenous Protest and Colonial Encounters during the Global Sixties.* Montréal: McGill-Queen's University Press.

Simpson, Audra. 2016. "The State is a Man: Theresa Spence, Loretta Saunders and the Gender of Settler Sovereignty." *Theory & Event* 19, no. 4: 136–62.

Simpson, Leanne Betasamosake. 2017. *As We Have Always Done: Indigenous Freedom through Radical Resistance.* Minneapolis: University of Minnesota Press.

Smith, Linda Tuhiwai. 2012. *Decolonizing Methodologies: Research and Indigenous Peoples*, 2nd ed. London: Zed Books.

Starblanket, Gina, and Dallas Hunt. 2018. "How the Death of Colten Boushie Became Recast as the Story of a Knight Protecting His Castle." *Globe and Mail*, February 13.

Starblanket, Gina, and Heidi Kiiwetinepinesiik Stark. 2018. "Towards a Relational Paradigm—Four Points for Consideration: Knowledge, Gender, Land, and Modernity." In *Resurgence and Reconciliation: Indigenous-Settler Relations and Earth Teachings.* Edited by Michael Asch, John Borrows, and James Tully. Toronto: University of Toronto Press. 175–208.

Stark, Heidi Kiiwetinepinesiik. 2016. "Criminal Empire: The Making of the Savage in a Lawless Land." *Theory and Event* 19, no. 4. https://muse.jhu.edu/article/633282.

Statistics Canada. 2023. "Racialized Canadians Are Less Likely to Find as Good Jobs as Their Non-racialized and Non-Indigenous Counterparts Early in Their Careers." Statistics Canada. https://www150.statcan.gc.ca/n1/daily-quotidien/230118/dq230118b-eng.htm.

Stirling, Carolyn. 2014. "Decolonize This—Settler Decolonization and Unsettling Colonialism: Insights from Critical Ethnographies with Indigenous and Allied Educator-Activists in Aotearoa/New Zealand, the United States of America and Canada." Ph.D. diss., State University at New York-Buffalo.

Sullivan-Clarke, Andrea. 2020. "Decolonizing 'Allyship' for Indian Country: Lessons from #NODAPL," *Hypatia* 35: 178–89.

Swain, Stacie. 2022. "Cracking the Settler Colonial Concrete: Theorizing Engagements with Indigenous Resurgence through the Politics Below." In *Democratic Multiplicity: Perceiving, Enacting, and Integrating Democratic Diversity.* Edited by James Tully, Keith Cherry, Donna Forman, Jeanne Morefield, Joshua Nichols, Pablo Ouzel, David Owen, and Oliver Schmidtke, 234–58. Cambridge: Cambridge University Press.

Tabar, Linda, and Chandni Desai. 2017. "Decolonizing is a Global Project: From Palestine to the Americas." *Decolonization: Indigeneity, Education & Society* 6, no. 1: i–xix.

Táíwò, Olúfémi O. 2022. *Elite Capture: How the Powerful Took Over Identity Politics (and Everything Else).* London: Pluto Press.

Taylor, Keeanga-Yamahtta. 2019. *Race for Profit: How Banks and the Real Estate Industry Undermined Black Homeownership.* Chapel Hill: University of North Carolina Press.

"Treaty 7 Indigenous Ally Toolkit." Autumn 2019. Calgary Foundation and Montréal Indigenous Community Network. www.calgaryfoundation.org

Vowel, Chelsea. 2016. "Beyond Territorial Acknowledgements." https://apihtawikosisan.com/2016/09/beyond-territorial-acknowledgments/

Wallace, Rick. 2013. *Merging Fires: Grassroots Peacebuilding between Indigenous and Non-Indigenous Peoples.* Halifax: Fernwood Publishing.

Whitaker, Reg, Gregory S. Kealey, and Andrew Parnaby. 2012. *Secret Service: Political Policing in Canada from the Fenians to Fortress America.* Toronto: University of Toronto Press.

Notes

1. FitzMaurice's account here, like many others within this literature, owes a debt to Anne Bishop's earlier work on allyship—which they are largely applying to the context of settler-Indigenous relations. There is an interesting tendency to cite merely the first of Bishop's two major works: *Becoming an Ally.* As Bishop herself notes, on its own this text is overly focused on allyship as an individuated process of unlearning harmful beliefs and actions (Bishop 2015, 3). Her second companion book is *Beyond Token Change,* the subtitle of which indicates important moves in her thinking: *Breaking the Cycle of Oppression in Institutions.* While still, to my mind, somewhat constrained, the relative paucity of citations to this text, speaks to the in-built limitations of the theory of allyship undergirding the literature.

2. I'd like to thank one of my anonymous reviewers for suggesting this material, and an anonymous *NAIS* board member for making the important observation that the solidarity between Standing Rock water defenders and BLM remains an enduring two-way form of solidaristic practice.

3. Grant and Snelgrove (2023) suggest that the utility of thinking about a social totality is that it aims to "overcome the restrictions produced by treating these [social] positions in isolation, and to register those moments of turbulence experienced by subjects operating within systemic or structural constraints . . . totality thinking is defined by an effort to trace systematically obscured connections and a refusal to fetishize the particular . . . [it is an] effort to overcome nominalist thinking that treats structures, subjects, and political standpoints as individual and separate from one another."

CORRINNE T. SULLIVAN, SIBYL DIVER, JESSICA K. WEIR, CAROLYN SMITH, *and* BETH PIATOTE

So You Care About Indigenous Scholars? Claiming the Academy as Indigenous Place by Creating Comic Art Across Difference

Abstract

University campuses are located within the homelands and lifeworlds of Indigenous Peoples, and often host Indigenous faculty, staff, and students from multiple Indigenous nations. Yet many Indigenous scholars continue to experience higher education as an extractive force and carry additional loads that extend far beyond the intense pressure that all academics experience to excel in a hierarchical setting. We examine how a year-long solidarity collective of Indigenous and allied scholars and artists created four comic art posters centering the experiences of Indigenous scholars in the academy. The *So You Care About Indigenous Scholars?* posters, titled "Extraction Zombies," "Pass the Ball," "The S.S. Academy," and "Indigenous Land," are an arts-based intervention using humor and irony to grow critical consciousness toward Indigenizing and decolonizing the academy. Following Patricia Hill Collins's flexible solidarity thesis (2020), we discuss our experiences building an intentional and contingent alliance, where differently positioned individuals came together for a common cause of Indigenizing the academy. We show how our positionalities informed, charged, and constrained the project, and how making mistakes and learning through doing is part of working across difference. In becoming "a group going together, shifting camp together," our collective both visualized and materialized a different kind of academic collaboration, unsettling our academic institutions—beyond making space for Indigenous scholars we demonstrate that Indigenous leadership is already present in the academy and claim the academy itself as Indigenous place.

HEREIN WE SHOW how and why we formed a yearlong solidarity collective to develop a poster series about the experiences of Indigenous scholars with the extractive academy, experiences which we find are rarely noticed by our colleagues. We use the term "extractive academy spaces" as a catch-all phrase describing university spaces that primarily value contributions from Indigenous people for academic self-interest. We share our process of working differently from this norm as an act of resistance to the harm we have experienced and/or witnessed. As Indigenous (Corrinne, Carolyn, and Beth) and non-Indigenous (Sibyl and Jess) scholars, we detail how our individual positionalities informed, charged, and constrained our contributions. Our collective both visualized and materialized a different kind of academic collaboration—not just in the form of the posters but in our collaborative process. Our resistance work claims the academy as Indigenous place. Our experience was not straightforward: it held surprises and, as always, remains exposed to colonial-imperial privilege reasserting its authority. We share our collaboration and learning therein as a contribution to the growing community of practice that is unsettling places of learning and research in higher education (Smith et al. 2020a; Smith, Tuck, and Yang 2019), and make the argument for building critical consciousness, both within ourselves and within the academy.

The comic art poster series that forms our focus in this discussion is called *So You Care About Indigenous Scholars?* and comprises individual posters titled "Indigenous Land," "Extraction Zombies," "Pass the Ball," and "The S.S. Academy."[1] The posters are rich with teachable moments about uncovering and overturning colonial-imperial privilege (e.g., figure 1). They were created with the intention of celebrating and demonstrating Indigenous Peoples' ongoing survival, resistance, and resurgence in the academy and beyond and are designed to support a more just academy through humor and irony. In quite different ways, we drew on our individual and collective experiences to contribute content. Artist/writer duo Nicole Burton and Hugh Goldring from Ad Astra Comix (now with Petroglyph Studios) transformed these contributions into comic art through a collaborative process. Our motivations in making the posters, and how we did so as a collective of Indigenous and non-Indigenous academics, offer important insights such as learning and making informed judgments about when and where to work alongside each other, as well as determinations around when to step up and when to step back. This was possible due to our shared interest in decolonizing and Indigenizing the academy through cultivating respectful and culturally-safe spaces—spaces that are needed for negotiating more just relationships. This is not an issue that affects only Indigenous Peoples. This is a way for all of us in the academy to contribute to restoration and repair.

We begin by acknowledging we are all here now together. We affirm that "there is not a university [. . .] that is not built on what was once native land" (Gould, qtd. in Justice 2004, 101). Writing out of North America and Australia, we recognize that these lands remain Indigenous lands despite colonization. Powerfully, university campuses are within the homelands and lifeworlds of Indigenous Peoples whose creation stories now encapsulate colonization and rework its destructive forces in these places of learning (Leddy et al. 2023; Trudgett, Page, and Sullivan 2017; Smith et al. 2020a). Indigenous faculty, staff, and students from multiple nations are also here—part of the academy. Indigenous people contribute their expert knowledge as part of contemporary and changing knowledge systems that inform and form rigorous academic methodologies (Leddy et al. 2023; Harriden 2023; Page et al. 2017; Smith et al. 2016; Smith 2013). Each of the Indigenous scholars in this collective nurtures diverse intercultural communities in the academy, even though they experience the ongoing colonial histories and legacies of their respective universities in different ways.

Through our collaboration in making comic art posters using flexible solidarity, we reveal that Indigenous leadership is already here in the academy and that university campuses are inherently Indigenous places given that they are built upon Indigenous lands. We offer ways to rework the extractive academy by powerfully illustrating the violence of current practices upheld in university institutions. In sharing our intercultural collaboration, we reaffirm the critical importance of establishing respectful relations that center Indigenous scholars while holding non-Indigenous scholars accountable to sharing resources and power with Indigenous colleagues. We offer this example of working together in solidarity to others to highlight that it is possible to work differently, to work better.

Collaborative Approach and Background

Positionality has been critical to our collaborative, intercultural, and intersectional approach toward Indigenizing the academy, with our respective positionalities influencing the possibilities, responsibilities, capacities, and worldviews expressed in our comic art posters (e.g., O'Sullivan et al. 2016; Walter and Anderson 2013). We contribute these posters in solidarity with other social justice movements and are in staunch support of the Black Lives Matter movement. We see the distinct experiences of Indigenous scholars intersecting with the experiences of Black scholars and other underrepresented communities who are also resisting colonized spaces of the academy. At the same time, Indigenous scholars have distinct concerns and experiences with the academy, including particular knowledge

FIGURE 1. "The S.S. Academy," *So You Care About Indigenous Scholars?* poster series (Smith et al. 2020b).

and experience with Indigenous governance structures and educational philosophies that are specific to Indigenous lands and peoples (Gaudry and Lorenz 2018). Our analysis here centers on how the different positionalities of Indigenous and non-Indigenous people co-shape our intellectual and artistic collaboration toward claiming Indigenous space in the academy. Our biographies introduce our positionalities, including on which side of the Pacific Ocean we live.

For our non-Indigenous coauthors, the academy is primarily a system that recognizes and respects our/their Western culture, law, and heritage.

By contrast, Indigenous colleagues often experience an academy in which we/they are not heard equally and are also denied equal opportunities to be heard (Bedard 2018; Cote-Meek 2014; Gaudry and Lorenz 2018; Kwaymullina 2016, 440).

As Indigenous studies scholars have documented, the racialized logics of the Doctrine of Discovery, and its domestic expression as Manifest Destiny (North America) and *terra nullius* (Australia), has built and sustained notions of white supremacy in higher education and research (Asmar and Page 2018; Bunda, Zipin, and Brennan 2012; Wildcat et al. 2014; Fredericks 2009; Nakata 2007; Moreton-Robinson 2015). Imperialism and colonization have made the academy a space of exclusion, shutting out Indigenous Peoples and their expert knowledge, as well as facilitating the theft of Indigenous lands (Anderson et al. 2019; Lee and Ahtone 2020). Indigenous scholars who tough it out in the academy experience daily macro and micro aggressions about their place and authority in the university system. Even in the work intended to build more respectful knowledge and power relations, colonial power asymmetries risk the misappropriation and misuse of Indigenous knowledge systems (Anderson et al. 2019; Arsenault et al. 2019; see also figure 2). For example, instead of engaging with Indigenous scholarship on its own terms, it is easier for the academy to "other" Indigenous knowledge as cultural, local, exotic, mysterious and/or existing in the past (Smith et al. 2016).

Without structural and systemic change, universities re-create and perpetuate material-discursive practices of marginalization, which is why solidarity work is so important within university departments and the academy broadly. Significantly, debates on decolonial academic practice highlight different views around whether resistance work is about forming diverse political communities, or if this work can only be undertaken by Indigenous people when non-Indigenous people recognize that their role within the resistance movement must be more than using their privilege to speak up (Tuck and Yang 2012). Patricia Hill Collins's flexible solidarity thesis articulates how differently positioned individuals come together for a common cause, whether they have experienced oppression and discrimination and/ or hold a commitment to social justice (2020). This is compared with ideological solidarity in which unity requires submission and uniformity. In our collective, we aligned with flexible solidarity for this project, while appreciating that this decision to form an intentional alliance is contextual and contingent (e.g., Clifford 2001).

As we discuss below, the Indigenous scholars who co-created this collaboration engaged with non-Indigenous scholars both by choice and necessity. Collectively, we remained aware of the risk of experiencing yet more of the

FIGURE 2. A detail from "Extraction Zombies," *So You Care About Indigenous Scholars?* poster series (Smith et al. 2020c).

academy's structural racism and everyday aggressions through our intercultural and collaborative efforts and the trend of non-Indigenous scholars dominating collaborative intercultural research with Indigenous Peoples (de Leeuw and Hunt 2018). In forming this intentional alliance, however, we held a shared interest in finding modes of collaboration that could respect our different roles and responsibilities, while always centering Indigenous voices and leadership. We worked dynamically and in collaboration as "a group going together, shifting camp together" (Smith et al. 2020a, 941). As shared here, the existing relationships, and the trust built and demonstrated, were essential in the rest of the work becoming possible.

Briefly, the relational history of this collaboration began around 2010, when Carolyn, Beth, and Sibyl initially met through the University of California (UC) Berkeley Native American community that supports research on Indigenous matters and community building. Carolyn and Sibyl then spent ten years working together through the Karuk Tribe-UC Berkeley collaborative, a group of Indigenous and non-Indigenous partners that facilitate eco-cultural restoration in the mid-Klamath (Smith, Diver, and Reed 2023). Carolyn and Sibyl met Jess after reading her book in a formative seminar with Kim TallBear, when Sibyl and Cleo Woefle-Erskine invited Jess to Berkeley together with the Joseph Meyers Center in 2014 (Weir 2009). This transnational connection built on existing relations between mentors in both continents and has been sustained through ongoing scholarly collaboration and friendships (Weir et al. 2019). The connection with Ad Astra Comix/Petroglyph Studios founders Hugh Goldring and Nicole Burton occurred at an Anishinaabe nibi (water) gathering hosted by Aimee Craft and colleagues, and a decolonizing water project workshop that followed. At these events, Sibyl befriended Canadians Hugh and Nicole, and in 2018 they stayed with Sibyl to attend a Bay Area book fair (in California), while also guest teaching in Sibyl's environmental justice course about their arts-based collaborations with Indigenous activists and presenting at Stanford's inaugural environmental justice symposium, now a yearly tradition.

Among these connections, the posters were conceptualized when Jess emailed Sibyl to explore a transnational writing project on critical and respectful allyship during Hugh and Nicole's serendipitous visit to the Bay Area in 2018. This initial conversation launched multiple discussions among us, together with colleagues and mentors. In 2019, Corrinne was introduced to Jess by a mutual colleague at a geography conference. They discovered their shared commitment to working for a more just academy through flexible solidarity, and subsequently found that their respective academic departments were neighbors on their university campus in Sydney. The two-day workshop, travel, and the posters were funded by Jess and Sibyl through their general research funds, with some of Jess's travel from Australia to the United States coinciding, and cofunded, with other academic commitments.

Through a preworkshop online discussion, we agreed to each write vignettes about our experiences with violences exerted through and within the extractive academy, as well as what we thought and did in response. These were recommended as preparatory work by writer/artist duo Hugh and Nicole. Both Indigenous and non-Indigenous scholars prepared these reflections, engaging with the problem through our respective positionalities. We shared with each other online in the week before the in-person, two-day workshop held on Muwekma Ohlone territory at Stanford University, which broke the ice between the participants, and helped build trust among a transnational group given that some individuals had not previously met.[2]

Choosing to Rework the Extractive Academy

Indigenous scholars prioritize leveraging the Western academy for positive change because it is such an influential place for knowledge production, culturemaking, and education (Coates, Trudgett, and Page 2020; Nakata 2007). In this, the scholarship on decolonizing and Indigenizing the academy very clearly affirms that Indigenous voices must be centered in matters that are of importance to them (Bodkin-Andrews, Page, and Trudgett 2018). The literature also affirms that Indigenous peoples should be in leadership positions: having survived long histories of marginalization and discrimination, Indigenous people are the ones who have experienced, and thus can identify, structural racism; they hold the necessary skill and experience to make positive change. When leading and being included in mutually respectful and beneficial decision-making spaces, Indigenous people are well positioned to contribute strategies toward alternative pathways for decolonizing institutions in part by foregrounding their own knowledge systems and governance practices (Coates, Trudgett, and Page 2024; Trudgett, Page, and Coates 2022).

Indigenous peoples' research, educational approaches, and priorities are shaped by Indigenous understandings about being with the land and others in animate relation—an ethical interbeing relationality that is reflected within Indigenous governance systems and place-based cultures (Anderson et al. 2019; Kovach 2015; Louis 2007; Martin and Mirraboopa 2003; Smith 2012; Wilson 2008). Indigenous and non-Indigenous scholars can bring such relationality, Indigenous protocols, and Indigenous governance systems into academic knowledge production and research practice (Wilson 2008, Whyte, Brewer and Johnson 2016, Arsenault et al. 2018, Craft 2017; Smith et al. 2016). This includes the potential for *two-eyed seeing,* which means to learn from one eye with the strengths of Indigenous knowledges and ways of knowing, and from the other eye with the strengths of Western knowledges and ways of knowing, to gain new perspectives and to create new knowledges. *Two-eyed seeing* builds on Mi'kmaw Elder Albert Marshall's *Etuaptmumk* concept (Arsenault et al. 2018; Denny and Fanning 2016). Forging a path of respectful relations requires attending to the specific cultures, histories, and futures of Indigenous peoples that arise, in part, from present-day places of learning. This reflexive and relational approach is important for all who now benefit from living on Indigenous lands because it demonstrates respect for Indigenous people and a willingness to learn about and through difference.[3]

In our experience, Indigenous scholars are often asked to explain the significance of their work, the validity of their methods, and the reasoning behind their priorities at a level that exceeds the rationale white scholars are required to present when legitimizing their work. As a collective, we observe that Indigenous scholars carry this greater burden in all spheres, including grant applications, conference presentations, manuscript submissions, and so on. Such extra work takes up valuable time and space and signals that imperial and colonial privilege is commonplace. What is the source of this inequity? Is it because Indigenous principles and positionalities are different and unfamiliar to the Western academy? As we contemplate the reasons underlying uneven treatment of Indigenous and non-Indigenous scholars, we consider how the additional labor for legitimacy performed by Indigenous scholars often requires appealing to the sympathy and care of non-Indigenous people holding positions of authority to judge the value of people and ideas. This is not just about Indigenous scholars taking on emotional labor, it is also the performance and reproduction of pain and trauma enacted through a lifetime of discriminatory experiences, which can be compounded by systemic and structural racism experienced by family members and ancestors. Such concerns were raised at our poster workshop. As one Indigenous scholar said, "I wish we could get points for being polite. We have to pack so much down without exploding." Another Indigenous collaborator summed up the irony of how these uneven power dynamics are expressed in and among our differentiated selves in the academy and how we must address this: "We keep saying sorry that we are sharing this really horrible experience with you, because I had to live through it and deal with it. It's a way of self-silencing. This is a no sorry space, we are not sorry here."

So, what do non-Indigenous scholars do once they understand how far they really are from realizing the restoration and repair needed in universities and the importance of centering Indigenous voices? And what does it mean for Indigenous scholars to collaborate with non-Indigenous scholars within discriminatory power structures, where societal structures convey social privilege to some and not others? There was considerable clarity in the collective about non-Indigenous peoples needing to hear, listen to, and heed Indigenous Peoples. But, for non-Indigenous scholars, just listening is not enough—it is about building meaningful relationships with Indigenous colleagues, as critical to understanding when and how to take action.

Native Hawaiian scholar Renee Pualani Louis affirms the importance of working in relationship; she states, "It implies that all parts of the research process are related from inspiration to expiration . . . It's about displaying characteristics of humility, generosity and patience with the process and accepting decisions of the Indigenous people in regard to the treatment of any knowledge shared" (2007, 133).

As a collective we agree. Relationships must come first. Relationships must be valued as the center of the knowledge, learning, and research (Wilson 2008). At the two-day workshop, through the process of respectfully getting to know each other, the non-Indigenous collaborators gained a better sense of how and when to speak in the collective. This work (learning to listen in a new way) is deeply reflexive, especially around balancing power, valuing each other, deliberating, and honoring everyone's respective lives. It is about learning one's place within a set of relationships by centering issues of positionality and Indigenous leadership throughout. This departs, for example, from more limited research negotiations around benefit distribution, where the ethical attention of non-Indigenous allied scholars often lies. Such ethical considerations need to be brought into academic institutions, departments, and sites of structural racism that configure the professional and personal experiences of Indigenous scholars. Yet, as a collective a deeper relational accountability to engagement across difference is argued as necessary, emphasizing a set of ethics that extends beyond outputs and outcomes.

We named the poster series *So You Care About Indigenous Scholars?* because this title foregrounds the importance of accountability among academics to respond in solidarity to Indigenous people facing structural racism in the academy, including deeper actions that align with the meaning of land acknowledgments that are now more common on campus. We posted the following four comic art posters online for free download:

- **Indigenous Land** (Figure 3) emphasizes that the university campus always was, always will be Indigenous land, and a place of Indigenous teaching (Sullivan et al. 2020).
- **Extraction Zombies** (Figure 2) highlights the tokenism and minority tax experienced by many Indigenous scholars, perhaps in your university department? (Smith 2020c)
- **Pass the Ball** (Figure 4) expresses frustration about non-Native scholars occupying the fields of Native knowledge, university spaces, and refusing to "pass the ball" or recognize Native scholars as experts in these very fields—and imagines a win for the team when Native scholars are included, valued, and what might be achieved together when non-Natives share the ball (power and control) (Piatote, Sullivan et al. 2020).
- **The S.S. Academy** (Figure 1) depicts micro and macro aggressions experienced by Indigenous scholars, who are working in all corners of the academy but are not always appreciated for their merits (Smith et al. 2020b).

FIGURE 3. A detail from "Indigenous Land," *So You Care About Indigenous Scholars?* poster series (Sullivan et al. 2020).

Collaborating through Our Relations, Revealings, and Missteps: Jess and Sibyl Reflect

Our collaborative effort to critique and rework the extractive academy was initially proposed by the non-Indigenous collaborators as a new approach to critically engage with allyship and the act of being accomplices, through the comic art of Ad Astra Comix/Petroglyph Studios. The Indigenous scholars within this collective valued the potential of this approach, and their involvement prompted a critical shift in the project to center the experiences of Indigenous scholars. The strength of existing relationships made this transition possible and relatively smooth, even though we were building new relationships through the collective. Our experiences through this process show how making mistakes and learning through doing is part of working across difference in flexible solidarity.

As non-Indigenous scholars interested in critically interrogating questions of allyship, Sibyl and Jess initially brainstormed a collaborative project around creating comic posters to explore how non-Indigenous allies can be more helpful and materially involved as accomplices for Indigenizing the academy, rather than opportunists who perpetuate extractive power dynamics. Our imagined audience included motivated non-Indigenous scholars who may have little opportunity to collaborate directly with Indigenous scholars. The illustrations would center on the unhelpful and, at times, abusive comments made by non-Indigenous scholars in work corridors and fieldwork locales, whether with good intentions or not. The initial project would emphasize the importance of establishing different models of academic practice and then invite critical commentary by Indigenous scholars. Jess and Sibyl imagined a publication they could initiate, where Indigenous collaborators would make candid interventions at any point in the text. And so, the "decolonial posters for the departmental water cooler" collaboration was conceived—with the understanding that it was not possible without Indigenous participation. Yet, this is where forming the collaboration *almost* failed, before it had even begun.

In wanting to avoid draining capacity or "bothering" Indigenous colleagues, Jess and Sibyl initially proposed designing as much of the project as they could on their own, at least to create a framework for colleagues to work with, something fun and impactful that would not take Indigenous colleagues away from their primary commitments. As non-Indigenous collaborators, Jess and Sibyl also saw their approach of initiating the project, then inviting Indigenous colleagues to contribute as desired, to be useful work that revealed their serious intentions and capacity, and an attempt to follow teachings they had received on not approaching Indigenous scholars or communities empty handed or without having done their homework. Through previous work, they were familiar with the layers of responsibilities and heavy workloads carried by Indigenous scholars and leaders and did not want to add to this burden. Indigenous scholars have often requested that non-Indigenous scholars educate themselves and each other about power asymmetries and knowledge discrimination in the academy (Bodkin-Andrews and Carlson 2013; Bodkin-Andrews et al. 2018). Yet, by almost cutting off the ability to co-create the project with Indigenous leadership from the beginning, Jess and Sibyl had done too much and taken a serious misstep in their planning.

Luckily, Indigenous collaborators on the project told them as much. The workshop was about centering Indigenous scholars. This required Indigenous collaborators and contributions to be centered from the start. Sibyl and Jess had underestimated how important this work was to Corrinne, Beth, and Carolyn, as individuals who were open to working in a meaningful, intercultural collaboration. Sibyl and Jess retraced their steps and reflected on the initial project approach, reinforced by educational and professional environments that center individuality and separateness in the extractive academy.

Fortunately, there was enough trust through existing relationships for Indigenous collaborators Corrinne, Beth, and Carolyn to course correct the project, a reflection of their generosity in this space and the importance of preexisting relationships. As one Indigenous collaborator told Sibyl and Jess, "I would not have responded if you were not my friend." This Indigenous collaborator talked about this in the debrief the day after the poster workshop:

> I know you well enough that you would not take advantage of our stories, narratives and our time. I know you, your work and your intentions. It was fine. As it was presented, it wasn't necessarily Indigenous-led. But I wouldn't feel that way with other folks. With other folks it would have to be generated with an Indigenous partner. But it was also this wild and crazy thing—like catnip to me. A creative outlet. Knowing you and the layout of your plan, it was flexible enough that it could turn into something with an Indigenous focus. The framework was there, but within that there was a lot of room. I so appreciated the step back by our allies, Jess and Sibyl, because it was something that I could voice when I had something to say. And stepping back when I didn't have anything to say. I didn't feel put upon to open my veins, to do a dance.

In response to the invitation, one Indigenous collaborator raised the issue directly, where their decision of whether to be involved or not depended on whether Jess and Sibyl heard, in that moment, what they were saying: that is, critically questioning who can speak, and how, on these matters. Such feedback about how one has played into colonial/imperial privilege can be very confronting and challenging to receive; but such discussions of speaking position should always occur and remain open to (re)negotiation. This practice is inherent to understanding and being transparent about what is exactly occurring in the ongoing intercessions of relationships. In our experience, it is productive for non-Indigenous scholars to identify this part of their practice and sit with the discomfort. Compared to the experiences Indigenous scholars face in extractive academy spaces, the feeling of being temporarily uncomfortable after making a mistake, owning it, and then doing something about it, is not too much to ask.

Regular back and forth conversations between Indigenous scholars and accomplices established the dialogical relationality we needed to determine what was and was not appropriate or possible in our collaboration. Critically, collective members maintained self-awareness around their relationality being mediated by colonial privilege at all times. After expressing the long quote above, a nervous laugh escaped from the Indigenous collaborator, who then said: "Hear that," and immediately, another Indigenous collaborator responded and confirmed what was heard. "She said it in a 'ha, ha, ha' way. That power is still there. There is still that inherent power dynamic in the relationship." It was quite clear that although much conversation and negotiation had taken place, and there had been some redistribution of power, Indigenous colleagues remained wary.

Authentic Collaboration Toward Flexible Solidarity

It was an exercise of agency and bodily sovereignty when Indigenous collaborators shared their views with non-Indigenous colleagues about the unequal power relationships in the collaboration. These exchanges ultimately necessitated the rethinking of the project and involved transparent conversations about what we/they did and how we/they did it. For a collaboration to be possible, the non-Indigenous collaborators needed to decouple themselves from their inherent power, and Indigenous collaborators needed to see the orientation of the project to center their leadership. In moving toward flexible solidarity, Indigenous collaborators were able to express themselves more freely than in other spaces, could ask direct questions without offending, and could put challenges forward that effectively depressed the power differential with non-Indigenous scholars. As a collective, we then could all share our own truths without judgment, or without unspoken repercussions. As this Indigenous collaborator said:

> I don't say safe spaces very often, but it felt like a safe space. I wasn't sure what to expect, but I felt comfortable. I didn't feel those awkward first encounters that you have when you first meet people. Having the vignettes posted online ahead of time took the edge off a little bit.

And this is also why we deliberately do not always pinpoint who is speaking in this paper. There are ramifications for sharing our stories in academia. As one Indigenous collaborator said:

> We are already in a precarious position, we are already rendered as different, mysterious. Knowing that they [the vignettes] are not going to be weaponised against us. There's a lot of reflexivity involved in that.

With the realignment to an Indigenous-led project, the workshop was transformed with new purpose. The Indigenous scholars in the collaboration shaped and informed the process and defined the content for posters that are very clearly about their experiences. This involved making all the key decisions with the artists about the scripts and illustrations. Non-Indigenous collaborators continued to organize the workshop, including organizing online meetings prior to and afterward, and note-taking throughout. Our time together in February was immensely valuable, and for non-Indigenous collaborators, the raw workshop notes facilitated the continuous referencing of in-person connections in the co-creation of poster dialogue and concepts.

Significantly, our different positionalities were strikingly obvious from the vignettes we wrote prior to the workshop. First, and broadly, they were written as either Indigenous recipients of and resisters to colonial and imperial violence, or non-Indigenous witnesses and inadvertent perpetrators of this violence. Second, non-Indigenous narratives reflected on a particularly striking moment in time that they had witnessed, as compared to the cacophony of moments that arose from the Indigenous scholars' narratives. Indigenous scholars wrote about very recent personal-material interactions in departmental corridors, meeting rooms, and other locales within the academy. These were narrated as an everyday theme of existence and unavoidable reality. Such reflections documented how those violences were predominately unnoticed, misunderstood, downplayed, and/or tokenized by non-Indigenous colleagues. Thus, the narratives of collaborators also shared the toll of living with this violence among the whole group, as well as the labor and energy involved in changing the status quo of ongoing racialized violence in the academy. Sharing the narratives of racialized violence experienced by the Indigenous collaborators made it more clear to the non-Indigenous collaborators why the workshop was prioritized by Indigenous collaborators, despite organizing missteps, and why Indigenous scholars would lead the development of the posters notwithstanding their already overcommitted schedules. While we are colleagues, reading similar academic scholarship and working in similar places, we have vastly different situated positions and lived realities in the academy. Indigenous scholars must negotiate structural and systemic exclusion from the academy while dealing with extractive relationships seeking to exploit their Indigenous positionality (Anderson et al. 2019; Kwaymullina 2016, 438).

Workshop logistics were organized around respecting relational ethics. The workshop began with a land acknowledgment, chant (an *oli* in the Native Hawaiian tradition), and welcome provided at different times on the first morning by Gabi and Ma'ili, both part of the Indigenous community at Stanford and student collaborators of Sibyl's. Their joining us was invaluable, both for their friendship and for the contribution they made in creating the space for us to work in a good way—by invoking the feeling of the place and helping us take the time to feel where we were, to be present. They also invoked the good relationships that the Stanford Native community has extended to so many visitors coming to the campus, including non-Indigenous researchers striving to work in solidarity with Indigenous Peoples. The land acknowledgment is critical to being together on better terms and gaining the confidence to work across difference in decolonizing work, supporting resistance and self-preservation. To do what you know is right, in and among the academic violences that operate otherwise, is transformative. It sets different terms of engagement and counters, to give just one example, colonial and imperial violences represented in the streets and buildings of Stanford. This includes decolonizing initiatives led by Native students at Stanford, such as the renaming of buildings and dormitories named after Junipero Serra, a primary founder of the Franciscan missions that exploited and sought to assimilate Indigenous Peoples throughout California.

Around the workshop table, we got to know each other more through reflecting together about the vignettes and how they might be illustrated—speaking and listening according to our different positions and co-creating the direction of our collaboration. Indigenous scholars in the group led the discussion by expanding on their experiences, with non-Indigenous collaborators asking for clarification at times and accepting challenges that were posed. On multiple occasions Indigenous scholars would, with humor and authority, make sure the discussion did not move into centering non-Indigenous experiences. For non-Indigenous participants, being included in such an extraordinary and candid discussion, one that offered real-time critical commentary on their language and behavior, provided a unique and privileged learning experience about the extent of their own reflexivity, or, sometimes, the lack thereof. "I thought it would be more about me," one non-Indigenous collaborator jokingly announced at our postcollaboration debrief the following day, with the group breaking into laughter. Tips could also be candidly traded between non-Indigenous participants, including this comment offered with good humor, "I am pretty sure that it is not a good idea to expect Indigenous people to reassure you for your uncertainty about what to do."

In line with relational ethics of respect and reciprocity (Diver and Higgins 2014), all aspects of the workshop's organization were collaborative and each task understood as valuable. For example, providing and sharing food is not just essential; it is part of social/cultural ceremony, and it is also an important focus of social interaction. However, the labor and care involved in providing and serving food is not as respected in the academy, as it is in Indigenous-led settings. Also, documenting and taking notes can be denigrated in the academy as secretarial: it is part of the patriarchy, because it is "women's work." Yet this work, too, is essential, and it is also a central skill of ethnographic research. These and other essential parts of workshop organizing labor supported those who were taking the intellectual leadership for content and decision-making. Although non-Indigenous participants sometimes described themselves as "stage crew," they were appreciated for playing a convening and supportive role that offered a sense of mutual sharing, valuing, and belonging. Service takes time, effort, and practice and involves skills that non-Indigenous people can take on, enabling frontline work that is often being conducted by Indigenous scholars and leaders. It is also work that can be shared between Indigenous and non-Indigenous colleagues, where sharing labor facilitates the process of getting to know each other: time for laughing and joking around and building reciprocal relations.

While understanding that structures and processes of privilege are still at work, typical differentials of power in the academy were dispersed. The group centered Indigenous practices of knowing, being, and doing in the workshop space. The obvious contrast between our workshop and a conventional or commonly encountered academic workshop could not have been starker. One Indigenous coauthor reflected on the outcomes of the shifts in practices of our workshop:

> Everyone is laughing and talking, there is no violence to us that is being done at that moment. To think of that—freedom. At the same time, we cannot leave the table. We need our allies and accomplices to do this emotional labor too. There is a clear need to shoulder the dual responsibilities of the academy.

Laughter, coupled with the weight of what was at stake, provided a rich timbre of intention and commitment and contributed to the development of a collaborative method made possible by mutually holding trust within the group. We were all together doing the work of change—shifting to a better academy and creating comic art posters to help others to also see this alternative pathway as a reality. Indigenous scholars Corrinne, Beth, and Carolyn reflected on how much is at stake in what we might achieve in these forums, not just for the next generation of Indigenous scholars coming through but for their own Indigenous communities and for a more just society. Sometimes non-Indigenous colleagues advise overburdened Indigenous colleagues with the recommendation, "'You just need to say no." However Indigenous scholars explain, "But you can't say no. But there is no willingness for people to understand this." Many Indigenous scholars feel a deep sense of accountability and responsibility to their families and communities. This commitment continues into the academic space, although is rarely recognized by colleagues, nor is it accounted for or included as part of academic service (Asmar and Page 2018).

The collaboration continued after the workshop through the pandemic of COVID-19, when we met on Zoom from our different continents. Our task was to fine tune those precise moments that expressed the extractive academy for a broad Indigenous and non-Indigenous scholarly audience, without overindulging or privileging the non-Indigenous audience. We also had to share our individual experiences and positionalities in a way that would honor and speak to the diversity of Indigenous Peoples engaging with the academy.

Originating from transcripts of the workshop dialogue, the series title *So You Care About Indigenous Scholars?* emphasizes the workshop's original intent to expand learning opportunities for non-Indigenous people, as well as the incisive wit and openness of Indigenous collaborators responding to the frustrations of working in academic institutions that tokenize Indigenous Peoples. This learning opportunity arises through witnessing real and personal moments of structural racism and daily micro and macro aggressions that organize the experiences of many Indigenous scholars, as well as the overall milieu for academic learning. These posters do not depict the experiences of allied scholars, even though they were copresent and working for change as part of being a group shifting camp together. Further, while Jess and Sibyl believed they were clued into violences occurring in their respective universities, both remain astounded at the reach and impact of the extractive academy for Indigenous scholars and the emotional load that Indigenous colleagues carry as part of being in the university. This extends far beyond the intense pressure that all academics experience when attempting to excel in a deeply hierarchical setting.

As a transnational undertaking, the collaboration sought to represent distinct Indigenous nations and cultures, while also recognizing the signals that Indigenous people use to recognize each other globally, including through visual representation. For example, as an Indigenous yet non-Haudenosaunee person, one collaborator wondered if it was inappropriate to use lacrosse, a highly recognized Indigenous sport originating from Haudenosaunee peoples, as the visual representation for the comic art poster "Pass the Ball." Authors had to weigh the cultural specificity of the sport against its power to communicate multifaceted Indigenous knowledges and practices across international borders. We also had to translate different terms and cultural understandings that are unique to our own continents and find a language that was legible to all.

We invite you to engage with the posters and track their meaning through the storytelling and artwork. Here, we take a moment to reflect on "Pass the Ball," one poster that formed quickly on the morning of the first day. Other posters required more time and emerged after deeper trust and clarity had been built (figure 4). "Pass the Ball" reflects the everyday tussle for power that Indigenous scholars experience in academic meetings, on projects, committees, and so on. The inspiration for "Pass the Ball" came from specific experiences of working with non-Indigenous colleagues in linguistics departments who resist the idea that Indigenous people who are not linguists have rights to, ownership of, and competence *with their own languages.* It felt important to ground the analogy in a game with widely recognized Indigenous origins. The message to these non-Indigenous linguists who do not want to make room for Indigenous knowledges and relationships to language is "pass the ball—and by the way, it's our ball. And our field. And our game."

FIGURE 4. A detail from "Pass the Ball," *So You Care About Indigenous Scholars?* poster series (Piatote et al. 2020).

Perhaps the "Pass the Ball" vignette was a testing of the waters for the collaboration? If the non-Indigenous workshop collaborators could really listen to the message and understand the meaning, possibly they were ready to go deeper into the transgressions of the academy and recognize how they too might be complicit in (or unable to see) the everyday violences present in the academy.

Positionality, Collaboration, and Allyship

The collaborative and creative experience described throughout this piece helped articulate and acknowledge, for all of us, the structural racism that is ongoing in our home institutions. We recognize the importance of laying this bare for a broader audience—an audience who is then invited to engage with these problems through the posters. As one Indigenous collaborator reflected, "white people think western institutions are theirs because they are in them." Nonetheless, she continued:

> If we want to work in a relationship with non-Indigenous people, then we need to value their opinions, their voices. It is an important voice, because it is part of the story, it just should not be centered when it comes to the Indigenous experience . . . I want to co-exist in this space, I value what my [non-Indigenous] colleagues bring as well.

Some Indigenous scholars want to work with non-Indigenous scholars, while others do not; our analysis does not intend any disrespect toward the latter.

We recognize that the decision to collaborate is not a given and remains contingent upon contextual conditions. In reflecting on our choice to engage in a collaborative project, we recall the disturbing reality that some non-Indigenous scholars (and university students) are not aware that Indigenous Peoples continue to exist and are making important contributions in the academy. To work across Indigenous/non-Indigenous difference in flexible solidarity is our act of resistance to this disappearing act. At the same time, it is clear from this example that there is an incredible amount of teaching labor provided by Indigenous scholars, who may not wish to spend their time and energy on collaborative projects. For many Indigenous scholars, the choice of whether to collaborate in this way is made on a case-by-case basis and influenced by their relationships with collaborators, what is being offered, the purpose or possible outcomes of the collaboration, and life circumstances. Indeed, this is also true when Indigenous scholars are approached by Indigenous colleagues with an invitation to join a collaboration.

Through the posters, and documented here, we challenge our colleagues to think about what it means for our campuses to be situated on Indigenous lands and to benefit from genocide and from the occupation of land, as both Indigenous and non-Indigenous scholars. In this, there needs to be both critical and material engagement in understanding the roles of an ally or an accomplice. Fundamentally, allies do not get to name themselves as allies—it is simply not enough to self-identify and name yourself as such. The term "allyship" is a verb, therefore, being an ally is not an identity; it is about being present and taking continuing action.

In the academy, Indigenous scholars make this judgment (of who they deem to be allies or not) and provide this label with legitimacy. Allyship toward reparation and repair is not about non-Indigenous scholars acting alone, nor deciding what is or isn't important; allyship is about non-Indigenous scholars working as part of the whole, in collaborative and reciprocal relationships with Indigenous scholars. Consider these reflections by Indigenous collaborators:

> There are allies and then there are allies. Anyone can put on the allied t-shirt, earrings, but an accomplice is someone with skin in the game. They need to say "I will sit down. I will give up power." They will be there when the ship goes down.

Another Indigenous collaborator added to the above quote, "I don't need you to show up if you are not showing up." Indigenous scholars in the collective have experienced many iterations of non-Indigenous people identifying their privilege and then not doing anything about it; for instance, one of the Indigenous collaborators remarked, "It irritates me no end the excuses people make for not doing better. The sun has set, you don't get to do that anymore."

The Indigenous scholars noted some of the comments they have heard from their non-Indigenous colleagues, such as, "I don't want to be a bother," or "I don't know what to do because I might make a mistake." One Indigenous collaborator countered, "I would rather you make the mistake. It's about recognizing and trying and learning." Clearly, collaborative efforts should still minimize the load for Indigenous scholars by first reading the work of Indigenous scholars, attending their presentations, events, and so on—and continuing to do so over an academic career (Page, Trudgett, and Bodkin-Andrews 2019). As one Indigenous collaborator said:

> If you are that interested and want to be invested, you need to go and learn. Do the work before you come into the space, and not expect Indigenous people to do it for you. If you are that person, you are not here yet. You are not yet an ally.

The humility and vulnerability to perceive and be open to criticisms about colonial and imperial privilege is undermined by the extractive academy within which most of us are groomed for an individualistic model of career building and expected to become experts in our field. Instead, we want to work differently. This is a project about us all learning in relationship, where everyone takes a risk. As one of the Ad Astra/Petroglyph Studios artists pointed out and asked openly: "What are you as a settler risking? Is decolonization more than a collection of professional opportunities to you?"

We have received a lot of feedback from Indigenous scholars appreciating how these posters acknowledge their experiences without shying away from the racial injustices that occur at all levels of the academy. Colleagues and strangers wrote emails or social media posts saying, "I feel seen," and "this is literally my life." Some viewers expressed their responses as "laughing/ crying," enjoying moments of dark humor, such as the "biting back" that becomes possible when posters called out the "extraction zombies" lurking in university hallways and sought a cure. In the longer term, we are using the posters as a teaching tool and are encouraged to hear others confirming the value of this collaborative effort. As one colleague said, "It's kind of a little sad that I can look at specific lines on them and say, 'Yep, that's happened to me,' but we need to make sure our students don't fall into the same struggles that we've faced!"

Conclusion

Through our collaboration in making comic art posters through flexible solidarity, we began with the established understanding that Indigenous leadership is a current reality in the academy and that campuses are situated on Indigenous lands. We offered ways to rework the extractive academy and powerfully illustrated the violence of current practices upheld in university institutions. By both visualizing and materializing a different kind of academic collaboration, we are unsettling our academic institutions—not only making space for Indigenous scholars but claiming the academy itself as Indigenous place. Throughout our intercultural collaboration, we reaffirm the critical importance of establishing respectful relations that center Indigenous scholars and ensure the accountability of non-Indigenous scholars in sharing resources and power with Indigenous colleagues. It is possible to work differently; it is just a matter of meaningfully challenging and transforming our approaches to doing the work.

CORRINNE T. SULLIVAN Wiradjuri Nation (Australia) is professor of geography and urban studies at Western Sydney University.

SIBYL DIVER is a lecturer in the Earth Systems Program at Stanford University.

JESSICA K. WEIR is associate professor at the Institute for Culture and Society at Western Sydney University.

CAROLYN SMITH (enrolled member-descendant of the Karuk Tribe) is assistant professor in the Department of Anthropology at University of California, Berkeley.

BETH PIATOTE is Nez Perce from Chief Joseph's Band, and is an enrolled member of the Colville Confederated Tribes. Beth is associate professor in the Department of Comparative Literature at the University of California Berkeley.

Acknowledgments

We acknowledge colleagues involved in early discussions but were logistically unable to join this collaboration—Kim TallBear, Kyle Whyte, and Bhiamie Williamson. We also thank the Native American Cultural Center at Stanford, including Ma'ili Yee and Gabi Saiz, for their warm welcome and for helping to create the space for us to work together in a good way. Thank you to the Center for Human Rights and International Justice at Stanford, especially Penelope Van Tuyl and Jessie Brunner, for hosting our group and for your wonderful kitchen. Thank you to Ad Adstra Comix/Petroglyph Studios founders, Nicole Burton and Hugh Goldring, for hearing the stories and realizing our vision in a beautiful set of posters to share with others. Finally, we acknowledge our ancestors, Elders, and teachers who are guiding us in this work.

References

Anderson, Kim, Elena Flores Ruiz, Georgina Tuari Stewart, and Madina Tlostanova. "What can Indigenous Feminist Knowledges and Practices Bring to Indigenizing the Academy?" *Journal of World Philosophies* 4, no. 1 (2019): 121–55.

Arsenault, Rachel, Carrie Bourassa, Sybil Diver, Deborah McGregor, and Aaron Witham. 2019. "Including Indigenous Knowledge Systems in Environmental Assessments: Restructuring the Process." *Global Environmental Politics* 19, no. 3:120–32. https://doi.org/10.1162/glep_a_00519.

Arsenault, Rachel, Sibyl Diver, Deborah McGregor, Aaron Witham, and Carrie Bourassa. 2018. "Shifting the Framework of Canadian Water Governance through Indigenous Research Methods: Acknowledging the Past with an Eye on the Future." *Water* 10, no. 1: 49. https://doi.org/10.3390/w10010049.

Asmar, Christine, and Susan Page. 2018. "Pigeonholed, Peripheral or Pioneering? Findings from a National Study of Indigenous Australian Academics in the Disciplines." *Studies in Higher Education* 43, no. 9: 1679–91.

Bedard, Beth. 2013. "Resistance: Traditional Knowledge and Environmental Assessment among the Esketemc Canadian First Nation Community." Ph.D. diss., Durham University.

Bodkin-Andrews, Gawaian., and Carlson, Bronwyn. 2013. "Racism, Aboriginal and Torres Strait Islander Identities, and Higher Education: Reviewing the Burden of Epistemological and Other Racisms." In *Seeding Success in Indigenous Australian Higher Education*, edited by R. G. Craven and J. Mooney, 29–54. Bingley, U.K.: Emerald Group Publishing Limited.

Bodkin-Andrews, Gawaian, Susan Page, and Michelle Trudgett. 2018. "Shaming the Silences: Indigenous Graduate Attributes and the Privileging of Aboriginal and Torres Strait Islander Voices." *Critical Studies in Education,* 1–18.

Bunda, Tracey, Lew Zipin, and Marie Brennan. 2012. "Negotiating University 'Equity' from Indigenous Standpoints: A Shaky Bridge." *International Journal of Inclusive Education* 16, no. 9: 941–57.

Clifford, James. 2001. "Indigenous Articulations." *Contemporary Pacific* 13 (2001): 468–90, http://dx.doi.org/10.3917/mult.030.0037.

Coates, Stacey K., Michelle Trudgett, and Susan Page. 2020. "Indigenous Higher Education Sector: The Evolution of Recognised Indigenous Leaders within Australian Universities." *Australian Journal of Indigenous Education,* 1–7. https://doi.org/10.1017/jie.2019.30

Coates, Stacey K., Michelle Trudgett, Susan Page. 2024. "A Model of Senior Indigenous Leadership in Australian Higher Education: An Indigenous Academic Perspective." *Journal of Leadership Education,* https://doi.org/10.1108/JOLE -03-2024-0047.

Collins, Patricia Hill. 2020. "The New Politics of Community Revisited." *The Pluralist* 15, no. 1: 54–73. https://doi.org/10.5406/pluralist.15.1.0054.

Cote-Meek, Sheila. 2014. *Colonized classrooms: Racism, Trauma and Resistance in Post-secondary Education.* Halifax: Fernwood Publishing, 2014.

Craft, Aimee. 2017. "Giving and Receiving Life from Anishinaabe Nibi Inaakonigewin (Our Water Law) Research." *Methodological Challenges in Nature-Culture and Environmental History Research*, edited by J. Thorpe, S. Rutherford, and L. Anders Sandberg, 105–19. New York: Routledge. https://ssrn.com/abstract=3428778.

De Leeuw, Sarah, and Sarah Hunt. 2018. "Unsettling Decolonizing Geographies." *Geography Compass* 12, no. 7: e12376.

Denny Shelley K., and M. Fanning Lucia. 2016. "A Mi'kmaw Perspective on Advancing Salmon Governance in Nova Scotia, Canada: Setting the Stage for Collaborative Co-existence. *The International Indigenous Policy Journal* 7, no. 3: 4.

Diver, Sibyl W., and Margot Higgins. 2014. "Giving Back Through Collaborative Research: Towards a Practice of Dynamic Reciprocity." *Journal of Research Practice* 10, no. 2.

Fredericks, Bronwyn. L. 2009. "The Epistemology That Maintains White Race Privilege, Power and Control of Indigenous Studies and Indigenous Peoples' Participation in Universities." *Australian Critical Race and Whiteness Studies Association eJournal 5,* no. 1: 1–12.

Gaudry, Adam, and Danielle Lorenz. 2018. "Indigenization as Inclusion, Reconciliation, and Decolonization: Navigating the Different Visions for Indigenizing the Academy." *AlterNative* 14, no. 3: 218–27.

Harriden, Kate. 2023. "Working with Indigenous Science(s) Frameworks and Methods: Challenging the Ontological Hegemony of 'Western' Science and the Axiological Biases of Its Practitioners." *Methodological Innovations* 16, no. 2: 201–14.

Justice, Daniel. 2004. "Seeing (and Reading) Red: Indian Outlaws in the Ivory Tower." In *Indigenizing the Academy: Transforming Scholarship and Empowering Communities*, edited by D. Mihesuah and A. Wilson, 100–123. Lincoln: University of Nebraska Press.

Kovach, Margaret. 2015. Emerging from the Margins: Indigenous Methodologies. In *Research as Resistance: Revisiting Critical, Indigenous, and Anti-oppressive Approaches*, edited by S. Strega and L. Brown, 43–64. 2nd ed. Toronto: Canadian Scholars' Press.

Kwaymullina, Ambelin. 2016. "Research, Ethics and Indigenous Peoples: An Australian Indigenous Perspective on Three Threshold Considerations for Respectful Engagement." *AlterNative: An International Journal of Indigenous Peoples* 12, no. 4: 437–49.

Leddy, Lianne, Brittany Luby, Kimberley McLeod, Emma Stelter, and Kim Anderson. 2023. "Refusing Confederation: Indigenous Feminist Performance as a Tool for Colonial Reckoning and Community (Re)Building," *NAIS: Journal of the Native American and Indigenous Studies Association* 10, no. 2 (Fall 2023): 5–35.

Lee, Robert. and Tristan Ahtone. 2020. "Land-Grab Universities." *High Country News*, March 30.

Louis, Renee. P. 2007. "Can You Hear us Now? Voices from the Margin: Using Indigenous Methodologies in Geographic Research." *Geographical Research* 45, no. 2: 130—39.

Martin, Karen, and Booran Mirraboopa. 2003. "Ways of Knowing, Being and Doing: A Theoretical Framework and Methods for Indigenous and Indigenist Re-search." *Journal of Australian Studies* 27, no. 76: 203—14.

Moreton-Robinson, Aileen. 2015. *The White Possessive: Property, Power, and Indigenous Sovereignty*. Minneapolis: University of Minnesota Press.

Nakata, Martin. 2007. *Discipling the Savages, Savaging the Disciplines,* Canberra: Aboriginal Studies Press.

O'Sullivan, Sandy, Barbara Hill, Maree Bernoth, and Susan Mlcek. "Indigenous Approaches to Research." 2016. *Nursing and Midwifery Research: Methods and Appraisal for Evidence-based Practice 5e*, 257—76. Elsevier.

Page, Susan, Michelle Trudgett, and Gawain Bodkin-Andrews. 2019. "Creating a Degree-Focused Pedagogical Framework to Guide Indigenous Graduate Attribute Curriculum Development." *Higher Education* 78, no. 1: 1—15.

Piatote, Beth, Corrinne Sullivan, Carolyn Smith, Sibyl Diver, Jessica Weir, Nicole Burton, and Hugh Goldring. "Pass the Ball: So You Care about Indigenous Scholars? Poster Series." 2020. https://www.petroglyphstudios.org/posters.

Smith, Carolyn, Diver Sibyl, and Ron Reed. 2023. Advancing Indigenous Futures with Two-eyed Seeing: Strategies for Restoration and Repair through Collaborative Research. *Environment and Planning F* 2(1—2): 121—143.

Smith, Carolyn, Corrinne Sullivan, Beth Piatote, Sibyl Diver, Jessica Weir, Nicole Burton, and Hugh Goldring. "The SS Academy: So You Care About Indigenous Scholars? Poster Series." 2020b. https://www.petroglyphstudios.org/posters.

Smith, Carolyn, Corrinne Sullivan, Beth Piatote, Sibyl Diver, Jessica Weir, Nicole Burton, and Hugh Goldring. 2020c. "Extraction Zombies: So You Care About Indigenous Scholars? Poster Series." https://www.petroglyphstudios.org/posters.

Smith, Linda Tuhiwai, Maxwell Te Kahautu, Puke Haupai, and Pou Temara. 2016. "Indigenous Knowledge, Methodology and Mayhem: What Is the Role of Methodology in Producing Indigenous Insights? A Discussion from Matauranga Maori." *Knowledge Cultures* 4, no. 3: 131.

Smith, Aunty Shaa, Neeyan Smith, Sarah Wright, Paul Hodge, and Lara Daley. 2020a. "Yandaarra Is Living Protocol." *Social & Cultural Geography* 21, no. 7: 940—961.

Smith, Linda Tuhiwai. 2013. Decolonizing Methodologies: Research and Indigenous Peoples. London: Zed Books.

Smith, Linda Tuhiwai, Eve Tuck, and Wayne K. Yang. 2019. *Indigenous and Decolonizing Studies in Education*. New York: Routledge.

"So You Care About Indigenous Scholars?" Comic Series Posted by Petroglyph Studios, accessed December 1, 2024, https://www.petroglyphstudios.org/posters

"So You Care About Indigenous Scholars?" Seminar, Posted by the Institute of Culture and Society—Seminar Series, Western Sydney University, May 20 2021. Video. https://westernsydney.edu.au/ics/events/ics_seminar_series /past_ics_seminars/seminars_in_2021/ics_seminar_series_-_C_Sullivan _B_Piatote,_S_Diver_and_J_Weir

Corrinne Sullivan, Beth Piatote, Sibyl Diver, Jessica Weir, Carolyn Smith, Nicole Burton, and Hugh Goldring. 2020. "Indigenous Land: So You Care About Indigenous Scholars? Poster Series."

Trudgett, Michelle, Susan Page, and Corrinne Sullivan. 2017. "Past, Present and Future: Acknowledging Indigenous Achievement and Aspiration in Higher Education." *HERDSA Review of Higher Education* 4:29–51.

Trudgett, Michelle, Susan Page, and Stacey K Coates. 2022. "Great Expectations: Senior Indigenous Leadership Positions in Higher Education." *Journal of Higher Education Policy and Management* 44, no.1. http://doi.org/10.1080 /1360080X.2021.2003013.

Tuck, Eve, and K. Wayne Yang. 2012. *Decolonization Is Not a Metaphor: Decolonization: Indigeneity, Education & Society* 1, no. 1: 1–40.

Walter, Maggie, and Chris Andersen. *Indigenous Statistics: A Quantitative Research Methodology.* London: Taylor & Francis, 2013.

Weir, Jess K. 2009 *Murray River Country: An Ecological Dialogue with Traditional Owners.* Canberra: Aboriginal Studies Press.

Weir, Jess K., Cleo Woelfle-Erskine, Sibyl Diver, Sharon Fuller, and Margot Higgins. 2019. "Doctoral Fieldwork with and Without Indigenous Communities in Settler-Colonial Societies." *ACME: An International Journal for Critical Geographies* 18, no. 6: 1300–20.

Whyte, Kyle. P., Joseph P. Brewer, and Jay T. Johnson. 2016. "Weaving Indigenous Science, Protocols and Sustainability Science." *Sustainability Science* 11:25–32. http://link.springer.com/article/10.1007%2Fs11625-015-0296-6.

Wildcat, Matthew, Mandee McDonald, Stephanie Irlbacher-Fox, and Glen Coulthard. "Learning from the Land: Indigenous Land Based Pedagogy and Decolonization." *Decolonization: Indigeneity, Education & Society* 3, no. 3 (2014).

Wilson, Shawn. 2008. *Research Is Ceremony: Indigenous Research Methods.* Halifax: Fernwood Publishing.

Notes

1. They are free to download and share under a Creative Commons attribution noncommercial no derivatives 4.0 international licence. See the Petroglyph Studios website https://www.petroglyphstudios.org/posters. (Artist collaborators were formerly with Ad Astra Comix.)

2. Our workshop was held on February 10–11, 2020, Stanford University, California, with the posters released on social media in October 2020.

3. See additional discussion among authors at this May 20, 2022 Institute for Culture and Society seminar: https://westernsydney.edu.au/ics /events/ics_seminar_series/past_ics_seminars/seminars_in_2021/ics _seminar_series_-_C_Sullivan_B_Piatote,_S_Diver_and_J_Weir.

SARAH PLOSKER *and* CATHY MATTES

Indigenous Beadwork as a Method of Teaching Linear Algebra

Abstract

In this work, the authors describe efforts aimed at Indigenizing a second-year linear algebra course at a small liberal arts university in Manitoba, Canada. This is done through an assignment, part hands-on and part written work, that explores the connection between Indigenous beadwork and linear algebra. Our collaboration was perhaps unconventional: Sarah, the first author, is a mathematics professor; while Cathy, the second author, is an associate professor in art history. However, we both had similar goals of putting theory into practice and making positive changes to student learning outcomes in a culturally appropriate way. We situate our work in the context of the current scholarly literature, adding to the important ongoing dialogue on Indigenization of course content and reflecting on the process and outcomes. This transformation of the course curriculum represented an applied approach to immerse Indigenous knowledge and pedagogy into a mathematics classroom. We hope that it may serve as an example of how other educators, particularly in science, technology, engineering, and mathematics (STEM), can integrate Indigenous knowledge-centered pedagogy into their classroom.

FOLLOWING THE RELEASE of the Truth and Reconciliation Commission of Canada's *Calls to Action* (2015), the authors collaborated to create, implement, and assess the impact of an Indigenous beadwork assignment in a second-year undergraduate linear algebra course taught by Sarah Plosker at Brandon University, a small, liberal arts university in southwestern Manitoba, Canada. The idea behind the creation of the course assignment was to see if learning Indigenous beadwork is useful in developing students' understanding of linear algebra. We felt it was an important first step in aligning our math curriculum with the Truth and Reconciliation Commission of Canada's *Calls to Action*. The assignment itself was in part a hands-on activity, followed by reflective written work asking students to connect the mathematical concepts from class with what they learned about beadwork in several in-person beading events.

The main contribution of this work is to provide an example of how mathematics instructors can cultivate cultural relevance in their classroom, putting theory into practice by using beadwork to Indigenize university education. We describe the entire experience in this work from start to finish. This includes a "pre-project" phase when the authors met and built a trusting relationship. We describe in detail the motivations behind the project, which were threefold: first, we hoped the pedagogical approach would be engaging to the students and, in turn, increase learning; second, we wanted to respond to the Truth and Reconciliation Commission of Canada's *Calls to Action,* as stated above; finally, the project was meant to be a meaningful response to a series of racialized events that took place locally. We situate our work within the larger body of literature, provide a detailed description of our methodology, our experiences, and the specific outcomes of the students' assigned work, which overall, we found to be positive. We conclude with a reflection on the project as a whole, lessons learned, and potential future development if we were to repeat the project in the future.

Local context played a role in how we approached this project. Yet, the themes raised here offer insights beyond the local level. Culturally responsive teaching is becoming a worldwide phenomenon; matters of indigeneity and identity are taken up in the Indigenous studies discourse in and beyond Canada. A project such as this can show openness and cultural sharing; it can also build trust and provide affirmation for Indigenous students who may be wrestling with their sense of self or apprehensive about disclosing their Indigenous identity, as it makes them vulnerable to stereotypes and potential racism. While not meant to be a precise guide to other instructors wishing to do something similar in their classroom, it may serve to spark some ideas on how to implement a similar project in one's own classroom, adapting it to the local context.

In what follows, we begin the conversation by providing some professional details about ourselves, our university, and detailing our motivation for the project.

Project Background

Brandon University (BU) has campuses on Treaty 1 and Treaty 2 lands, and we are a gathering place for people from many backgrounds and around the world. In this way, we carry on the Indigenous customs of our homes in Brandon. We acknowledge Brandon is on shared territory between the Dakota Oyate, the Anishinaabeg, and the National Homeland of the Red River Métis. Today, many other Indigenous people call Brandon their home, including the Ininew, Anisininewuk, Denesuline, and Inuit (Brandon University, 2025).

Brandon University was founded in 1899 as a Baptist college and became a university in 1967. The Science Building, which housed chemistry, physics, botany, zoology, geology, geography, mathematics and computer science, and psychology, was officially opened in 1972. The Arts and Library Building was officially opened in 1961, and an Aboriginal art minor was created in 1993.[1] In 2019–2020, BU had just over 3,000 students, over 300 faculty members, five faculties (Arts, Education, Graduate Studies, Health Studies, Science), and a School of Music. At present, the Department of Visual and Aboriginal Art is one of the longest-running fine arts programs in Canada that offers regular Indigenous studio and art history courses. It is one of the only programs in Canada that offers accredited degree majors and minors in Indigenous art, and the only one that requires all its students to take two Indigenous art history courses, regardless of their major within fine arts.

The university's mission is to "promote excellence in teaching, research, creation and scholarship. We educate our students so that they can make a meaningful difference as engaged citizens and leaders. We defend academic freedom and responsibility. We create and disseminate new knowledge. *We embrace cultural diversity and are particularly committed to the education of First Nations, Metis and Inuit people.* We share our expertise and resources with the greater community" (Brandon University 2020; emphasis added). The university's mandate, and specific emphasis on cultural diversity and commitment to Indigenous Peoples, is important in the context of the current conversation. Our commitment to this mission helped in the launch of the project and is described further below. Thirteen percent of BU students identify as Indigenous (Brandon University, 2025). This number is understood by many to be a low estimate, as students do not always self-identify, for various reasons, on their entrance application to BU. The Indigenous Peoples' Centre on campus offers academic support, transition support (assistance locating, e.g., housing, dentists), cultural/spiritual support (cultural events, beading club), and personal and social support (e.g., movie night, soup lunch).

The importance of relationship-building with an Indigenous partner such as an Elder, Knowledge Keeper, community member, or in this case, an Indigenous academic professor, in creating a project such as this cannot be overstated; it is the foundation of a reciprocal collaboration and is an important factor in culturally responsive education. For historical (and continuing) reasons of colonial exploitation and extractivism, Indigenous persons can be skeptical of others calling upon them for their assistance and expertise. There is no formulaic way of forging such relationships, but in general, time, caring, and emphasis on two-way communication are the key components. The collaborative project followed a year of the authors' time directed at forming a respectful, trusting, and collegial relationship.

The course was aimed at math and computer science majors, and as such the enrollment is typically small (eight students were enrolled the semester of the study). The beadwork assignment represented an Indigenous pedagogical approach to teaching some of the linear algebra concepts from class. Students were asked to: (1) attend a beading session in class, hosted by Cathy; (2) attend a follow-up beading session, open to the community, at the Indigenous Peoples' Center on campus; and (3) write a short description of how beadwork fits in with topics covered in the math course (roughly two to three paragraphs; no more than a page long). Collaborators Sarah and Cathy collected data including observations/field notes at in-person beading events both inside and outside the classroom, followed by a qualitative analysis of the written work of the students.

We note three main reasons for initiating this project. Firstly, the project was conceived as a response to the Truth and Reconciliation Commission of Canada's *Calls to Action* (2015). As part of the Indian Residential Schools Settlement Agreement in 2007, the Truth and Reconciliation Commission of Canada was established to facilitate reconciliation among former students, their families, their communities, and all Canadians (Truth and Reconciliation Canada Commission of Canada 2024). The TRC published ninety-four *"calls to action"*—actionable items meant to redress the legacy of residential schools and advance the process of Canadian reconciliation (Truth and Reconciliation Commission of Canada: Calls to Action 2015). Our project was an attempt to integrate culturally appropriate topics into the course curriculum. We believe there was a disconnect between our university's mission statement and the student body, and the lack of any Indigenization of course content in mathematics at the university. We wanted to actively respond to the TRC *Calls to Action.*

The second main motivation for the collaboration was as a response to a series of "white pride" events and security risks at the University in December 2017, some of which were reported by the media (Laychuk 2017). Both authors attended a Sharing Circle as the situation unfolded and discussed actions we personally could take going forward. A Sharing Circle is just what it sounds like: participants sit in a circle as equals, and a sharing stick is passed around. Only the person with the stick is allowed to talk, and everyone else listens. It is a great way to air grievances, look for solutions, and connect with each other. Sharing Circles can be highly emotional events, often involving people sharing very personal stories. There may be laughter, crying, and hugging. The fact that Sarah participated in the Sharing Circle led Cathy to trust that Sarah's intentions were genuine, and this helped pave the way to a trusting, respectful relationship.

Finally, the third reason for initiating the project was the potential for further learning. As teachers, it soon becomes obvious that not everyone learns best by reading from a textbook. Given our student body, we wanted to create a course assignment based on the Four Rs of First Nations and Higher Education: Respect, Relevance, Reciprocity, and Responsibility (Kirkness and Barnhardt 1991). In particular, an assignment such as this would bring relevance to the theoretical aspects we were learning in the course. Mathematical concepts are often quite theoretical, and being able to work things out with one's hands can be useful in solidifying core concepts.

Research Context

In recent years, there has been much interest in Indigenizing course content in mathematics, as well as blending arts and mathematics in higher education in Canada. This can be seen both in the academic literature as well as recent relevant national and international conference presentations.

Recent Canadian Mathematical Society Meetings have included sessions on diversity, arts, Indigenization and reconciliation, and the relation between these matters and mathematics (Canadian Mathematical Society 2019; Canadian Mathematical Society 2020). These special sessions included a diverse set of talks from mathematics educators across Canada and the U.S., with topics ranging from the impact of course design, inclusive and experiential teaching, active and collaborative learning in mathematics courses, mathematical storytelling, and more. Interest in blending arts and mathematics can also be seen in the United States. Past Joint Mathematics Meetings (an annual mathematics conference held in the States) have had special sessions on mathematics and mathematics education in fiber arts, and now feature an annual mathematical art exhibition (Jensen 2017; American Mathematical Society 2020). While these represent significant contributions to the topic of Indigenizing math education content and/or linking math and art, educators would have to be physically present at the talks to participate; only talk titles and abstracts are available online. There are no video recordings, transcripts, conference proceedings, or other written resources resulting from these talks, thus limiting their accessibility and usage.

An impressive amount of research into mathematical aspects of Indigenous design has been discussed by Edward Doolittle (2017), including geometric transformations with respect to the unified syllabics and birch bark biting, symmetry and groupings in West Coast art and totem poles, quill boxes, pueblo pottery, and the geometry, design, and embedded sequences and series in star blankets. This work was referenced in a slideshow given as a presentation by Doolittle at a teachers' conference in Saskatchewan in 2017; however, at the time of publication it appears to have been taken down, a truly unfortunate limitation of digital work.

Research by Gwen Fisher and Blake Mellor (2007) explores group theory (a particular area of mathematics) via the symmetries of clusters of beads woven together. They also explore various patterns and geometric objects, including the sphere, prisms, and pyramids. Later, Fisher and Mellor (2012) focus on flat beading, called angle weaves. This is achieved using mathematical tiling theory (in mathematical terms, "tilings of the plane"). Their works are academic in nature, offering deep mathematical results rather than being experiential math education projects. Many different types of fiber arts are discussed in their connection to mathematics in Sarah-Marie Belcastro and Carolyn Yackel's (2007) edited collection, including quilts, crochet, knitting, cross-stitch, knots, cables, braids, and embroidery, particularly with respect to their connection to geometry and graph theory, among other areas of mathematics. The book focuses on the relationship between mathematics and the fiber arts and offers methods of introducing the relevant mathematics into the classroom, though it does not specifically involve Indigenous fiber art.

On the topic of Indigenous education, Adam Gaudry and Danielle Lorenz (2018) conducted a study based on an anonymous survey of Indigenous academics and their allies. Their work identifies and differentiates three different types of Indigenization happening in the institutional practice of Canadian academia: Indigenous inclusion, reconciliation Indigenization, and decolonial Indigenization. Specifically, they focus on policy and praxis in the Canadian academy, and their intervention is better suited toward administrators than educators. Elsewhere, Karen Ragoonaden and Lyle Mueller (2017) conducted a study using student interviews in a general first-year university course at University of British Columbia's Okanagan campus. Their work explored culturally responsive pedagogy and success in first-year university courses and programs. Their work showed the importance of circles of learning, peer mentoring, and the student-instructor relationship; it is perhaps the most relevant of the body of literature cited here regarding the impact of culturally responsive pedagogy in university education.

Indigenization efforts in science and mathematics are happening within Canada, the U.S., and internationally. Saiqa Azam and Karen Goodnough (2018) reflected on a self-study of Indigenizing science education in a science methods course within the University Education Program at a university in Newfoundland (in Atlantic Canada). In the study, Azam used a talking circle to learn about and build relationships with the students. The study has some crossover with our project in terms of Indigenizing the curriculum and creating a more inclusive, culturally relevant learning experience for the students. With respect to Indigenization of mathematics in Saskatchewan, Canada, Shana Graham (2015) discussed various approaches to the goal of linking tipis and mathematics, which evolved into a meta-analysis of their experience relating Indigenous ways of knowing with mathematics. Denise Mirich and Laurie Cavey (2015) described mathematics lessons that took the form of moccasin-making to teach the mathematical topics of measurement and area in an elementary school class at a school on a reserve in the U.S. Much like the project described herein, the works of Graham and Mirich and Cavey describe specific projects taken on by math educators to Indigenize course content. More generally, Glen Aikenhead (2017) analyzes "taken-for-granted notions about school Mathematics" and explores measures to help enhance school mathematics "in a way that simultaneously promotes both academic achievement and reconciliation" (73).

On an international level, the mathematics education of Indigenous Mapuche People of Chile is explored by Huencho Ramos (2015), with the idea of implementing culturally relevant teaching activities into mathematics education. Ramos took a qualitative approach to this goal, including a five-step process of not only identifying the ethnomathematics knowledge of the Mapuche people but also analyzing how this knowledge is transferred by way of kimches (wise people) in Mapuche communities. Elsewhere, Tony Trinick, et al. (2015) describes a project exploring the revitalization of cultural knowledge through mathematics education in New Zealand. This article identifies particular challenges in implementation, including a lack of local experts, which meant that teachers had to rely on books and other resources. This, in turn, took much time and effort. Also in New Zealand, Robin Averill et al. (2009) describe three models for culturally responsive teaching in mathematics teacher education. The studies considered the perceptions of preservice and early career teachers in incorporating cultural approaches to mathematics into their teaching. In their work, Averill et al. list conditions that they feel are necessary for effective culturally responsive teaching in mathematics, many of which align with the approach we took to our project, including deep mathematical understanding (in terms of Sarah's teaching and expectations from the students), cultural knowledge (in terms of Cathy's classroom visit), and opportunities for flexibility of approach (in terms of students' assignment writeups). These works all indicate, implicitly or explicitly, that creating a space for culturally relevant mathematics education in one's classroom is no easy task, but at the same time, it is important to attempt to do so and to reflect on or evaluate the process.

Indigenous perspectives on mathematical geometry and space are considered within the context of Papua New Guinea and Australia by Kay Owens (2014). The study found that three principles—language structures, reference lines and points, and measures of space—can be used by teachers to create geometry lesson plans rooted in culture. Eleanor Abrams et al. (2013) discussed the gap in mathematics and science achievements in public schooling in Australia and the U.S., and in U.S. STEM careers. Using a wide variety of sources, they cite the need to create culturally responsive curricula and culturally relevant learning opportunities in K—12 mathematics and science. Our project aims to do precisely this within the university setting.

With Sarah being a mathematician and Cathy an Indigenous art historian, we felt the need to disseminate our work as there is a notable gap in resources for those outside of critical Indigenous studies. Our project put pedagogies from the different fields of mathematics and Indigenous art into conversation with one another. Although our literature review shows that there are some studies that have engaged in similar questions, there has been a long-standing gap in culturally relevant pedagogical interventions in STEM fields, and we believe our work contributes to this small but growing body of scholarship. Filling the gap in the literature is particularly necessary in light of the Truth and Reconciliation Commission of Canada's *Calls to Action*, specifically Call 10.3, which concerns the need for development of culturally appropriate curricula; the latter portion of Call 62.2, which identifies the need for necessary funding to postsecondary institutions to educate teachers on how to *integrate Indigenous knowledge and teaching methods into classrooms* (emphasis added); and Call 63.3, which highlights the importance of building student capacity for intercultural understanding, empathy, and mutual respect. This latter call also emphasizes the need to fulfill the general spirit of Indigenization: integrating Indigenous knowledge, history, and teaching and learning methods into the classroom.

Our project is a grounded example that was done in relation to local context and people. Culturally relevant learning and Indigenization of course curriculum is of growing global importance, and there is a clear need to document research of this kind. Our aim herein is to contribute to this growing but still vastly underrepresented body of literature, and to exemplify change from the bottom up.

Indigenizing Mathematics Through Beadwork

An entire class (one hour and twenty minutes) in the second week of the semester was devoted to beadwork. Sarah wanted the students to learn about beadwork early in the semester so she could make reference to various techniques as they were learning mathematical concepts throughout the course. Cathy and her research assistant (RA) came to class and had a large display of beaded items to show the students. Cathy gave a brief history of beading, descriptions of her own beadwork, and instructions on how to make beaded earrings. Students did hands-on work with the beads, starting their own pair of earrings using "brick stitch," while Cathy and her RA gave instructions to the class and helped students one-on-one.

FIGURE 1. Examples of earrings of the same style as for the assignment.

Figure 1 shows examples of the style of earring that the students worked on: a main triangle shape with colored diamonds in the center of the triangle and strands of beads dangling from the main triangle, using three different colors. Beaded brick stitch earrings are made using a needle and thread. Individuals start with four beads of the same color on the thread and then make a "bridge" by stringing the needle through the third and fourth beads. Pulling the thread tight, this changes the line of four beads into a 2x2 square of beads. In linear algebraic terms, this is a linear transformation from the four-dimensional real vector space R^4 to the set of 2x2 matrices M_2 (figure 2).

At this point, only one color of bead has been used, so if we look at the 2x2 square we made, it is symmetric in that you can rotate it or flip it over, and it looks the same (this corresponds, for example, to all the letters in figure 2 being "w," i.e., if all four beads were white). When working with only one color, some mistakes are not critical. However, if we have different color beads, like in figure 3, then we cannot rotate or flip without changing the pattern.

$$\begin{pmatrix} b \\ w \\ g \\ r \end{pmatrix} \rightarrow \begin{pmatrix} w & g \\ b & r \end{pmatrix}$$

FIGURE 2. A general four-dimensional vector being transformed into a 2x2 matrix. Image by Sarah Plosker.

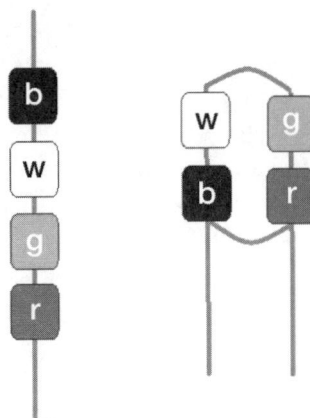

FIGURE 3. Four beads (b, w, g, r) forming a column on the left, which then, by threading the needle through the beads in a certain way, becomes a square with two beads in the first row (w, g) and two beads in the second row (b, r). Compare with the mathematical visualization of figure 2.

After placing the initial four beads of the earring, we start adding a second color of bead, and later, a third color, so one must be very careful to orient the needle and thread through the beads in the correct direction, otherwise the pattern that emerges from the colors (a diamond shape inside a larger triangle) will not appear correctly. This is a great way to see explicitly what types of matrices are invariant (i.e., they don't change) under the different geometric transformations of reflection, rotation, etc. At any point in making the earrings, if you make a mistake you can carefully undo it by threading the needle through the beads in the opposite direction. This is, to a mathematician, an invertible function. Many mathematical concepts can be conveyed by this hands-on activity, which brings to life what some students may consider rather stale theoretical content.

Our analysis used qualitative inquiry methods. In the classroom, we relied on observations of the students. Both authors as well as the RA made mental observations of the students' behavior (this was not difficult to do, given the small number of students) and discussed our thoughts on several occasions soon after the classroom visit. It was not possible to write field notes during the event as we were all actively involved (with Cathy and her RA doing the presentation and helping students, and Sarah taking part in the beading as well as walking around to observe students). Field notes, as such, were written down after the fact; our discussions of our observations and subsequent reflections were recorded with as much accuracy as possible. Participating in this study was voluntary; students submitted a consent form permitting to the use of their written work and observational data.

For the written assignment, both authors read through the submissions separately and then met to discuss the submissions together, reviewing key features of each students' work. Some questions we asked ourselves to guide our analysis were: Did the student clearly articulate the connections they noticed between the beadwork and course content, as well as their other academic experiences? Did the student relate this connection to their interests in an introspective way? Did the students personalize the assignment writeup in any way?

Cathy noted several thoughts on Indigenous knowledge sharing in this circumstance: she really appreciated when some of the students started to make diagrams on the chalkboard or drew diagrams on paper. This activity showed they were engaged, and collaboration is a key aspect of culturally responsive learning—it also showed active learning strategies that play a key role in Indigenous learning and ways of knowing. Indigenous teachers like Cathy are used to having those we teach follow our specific directions, as that's a pedagogy for how Indigenous knowledge is transmitted. The most difficult way of doing something is shown first, so that an easier way can be found for each individual after—there is no "easiest way" of doing something as it is highly tied to the individual. The rationale for showing the most difficult way of doing something first is that you will never find an easier way unless you've learned the way of the knowledge-sharer first. Teaching techniques in math are typically one of two methods: start with a simple/low dimensional example and then expand into more difficult examples and a general technique; or start with the general theorem and then offer a simple example bringing the high-level theorem down to earth.

The second important thought Cathy noted is regarding the teacher as a learner during the class. This follows Indigenous culturally responsive teaching models, being student-centered and eschewing conventional (Western/Euro-centric) educational practice. This is also quite common with Indigenous knowledge transmission: educators usually place themselves in the position of student, which can be tricky at times. Cathy appreciated Sarah's willingness to do so. (During the class when Cathy and her RA were presenting, Sarah sat at the desks with the students, facing the front of the classroom.) Cathy finds she is usually challenged when she invites other beadworkers to teach and to learn from them alongside her students, even though she has beaded for most of her adult life. While it can be challenging as a teacher to not share or interject one's own thoughts, it is important to show respect to a special guest, especially given the fact that in this case, the teacher (Sarah) was white, and the guests (Cathy and her RA) were Indigenous.

The class visit was a condensed learning activity: normally fine arts students taking a course on Indigenous art would have multiple lessons prior to making something like earrings. Sorting bags with multiple colors of beads is often a preliminary lesson in patience. In contrast, due to time constraints, we skipped straight to students making earrings for this project. Many students made mistakes, and some had to start over multiple times. Some students got out of their desks and started drawing diagrams together on one of the chalkboards in the classroom; they were trying to get a clearer picture of how the thread was going through the beads to produce the desired outcome. Other students kept to themselves, quietly working away with extreme focus. Some students had to make the mistakes themselves, as they did not believe Cathy when she explained that if they moved the thread in a certain way, they would undo everything. Sarah notes that this desire of students to check for themselves is somewhat akin to a proof by construction, or reading a mathematical result and trying to prove it oneself rather than reading the proof that the author provides. Students did not let their frustrations defeat them, and they remained excited throughout the lesson.

The style in which Cathy and her RA conducted their class visit was very much couched in Indigenous pedagogies and ways of knowing, being, and doing. While each Indigenous knowledge and pedagogy system is unique, they are distinct from the Eurocentric (Western) system currently in place. Cathy promoted a deep connection to student learning through an experiential approach, valuing shared themes and similarities in Indigenous knowledge systems in her pedagogy by promoting cultural appreciation and connectedness. It was in no way a formal lecture delivered to the class; rather, it was a respectful discussion and hands-on activity meant to foster inclusive and transformative learning. The classroom visit was reminiscent of the "trans-systemic" synthesis between Indigenous and Eurocentric knowledge systems discussed in Battiste-Henderson (2021)— the idea of attempting to weave differences and similarities into an overarching method of comprehending.

Beyond our observations of the event, the major data collected in this study consisted of students' written assignments. We discuss these outcomes in the next section.

Student Assignment Outcomes

As stated in the previous section, Sarah wanted the students to learn about beadwork early on, so that she could reference various techniques as they were learning mathematical concepts throughout the semester. The idea was that the students would be able to then visualize the beadwork as they learned the corresponding mathematical theories. In particular, the first steps of the "brick stitch" transform a line of four beads into a 2x2 square of beads (two rows of two beads per row, one stacked below the other). This is an example of a "linear transformation" in mathematics. Students often struggle with the rigorous manner in which linear transformations are taught. The brick stich allowed for a concrete visual example of the abstract notion of a linear transformation. When discussing the mathematical notion of dimension, Sarah made reference to the fact that the earrings were supposed to lay flat and pointed out that some mistakes in the beadwork meant that the two-dimensional objects became three-dimensional (so, for example, a triangle in the beadwork pattern accidentally became a pyramid). Mistakes were "invertible" (a property of certain linear operations)—if you traced your steps backward carefully, you could undo the mistake you made. These are just some examples of how Sarah subsequently wove the beadwork demonstration into her pedagogy.

For the written work, Sarah notes that the "no right answer" written reflection style of the assignment was a stumbling block for some students, since it was so different from their usual math homework. Most of the students approached Sarah after class or during office hours, in some cases multiple times throughout the semester, to discuss what to write for the assignment. Sarah managed these discussions similarly to inquiries regarding typical math problems: by relating the question to topics from class, drawing on the students' knowledge from other courses (e.g., the prerequisites), discussing possible approaches, and ultimately leaving it up to the student to decide in the end how to "solve" the problem. The written work reflected the students' personalities and ways of thinking, with some writeups being more in the style of a journal entry, while others were written more like a mathematical textbook—one writeup distilled the student's knowledge of beadwork gained through the beadwork activities into a step-by-step algorithm (many math and computer science students think in terms of algorithms and flowcharts). Each student's work was distinct, but most, if not all, mathematical connections made in class or during discussions outside of class were touched on by at least one student.

We describe and give examples from the written work below. We note that the depth of the written work varied; in some cases, it was rather surface level, and in other cases it was quite deep, introspective, and thoughtful. We also note that the written work reflected the students' personalities, and to some degree, whether the student attended a lunch hour or evening beading session at the Indigenous Peoples' Center (students were asked to

attend a follow-up beading activity at the IPC on campus at their convenience during the semester; beading events were held weekly at the IPC at
this time). In the evening, the beading events were open to the entire community; grandmothers and artists attended, and there was more interaction, whereas lunch- hour sessions tended to be more serious, with students
and faculty members working on specific projects. The context and atmo-
sphere of the two types of sessions were quite different.

One student was absent for the beadwork and did not attend the follow-up at the IPC, and as such, that student's work was written rather
generically and stood out from the others' written work as lacking intro-
spection as well as connections between the beadwork and mathematical
knowledge. Another student wrote interesting individual sentences, but
both Cathy and Sarah would have liked to have seen additional detail. For
example, "The beading session at the Indigenous People's Center . . . was
really more amazing and interesting than the classroom setting." Cathy and
Sarah both read this in a positive way, in that it affirmed the importance of
the follow-up session at the IPC, but the student did not provide details as
to why. Similarly, in the student's mathematical discussion, they stated that
the beadwork "fits in the matrix representation where you can choose the
colors for rows and columns" but did not go into more mathematical detail
on matrix representations or provide mathematical examples.

Some students explained the linear transformation from the four-
dimensional real vector space R^4 to the set of 2x2 matrices M_2 as illustrated
in figure 2. They went on to explain how certain geometric operations like
rotations or flips may or may not change the pattern, depending on exactly
what operation is performed, and how many distinct colors are used. Because
of symmetry, some mistakes at this stage are not noticeable. However, as
we continued with the brick stitch pattern in the classroom demonstration, mistakes become more apparent. They mentioned invertible functions
and the connection to carefully undoing a mistake by threading the needle
through the beads in the opposite direction.

Additional mathematical insights can be gleaned from this activity,
which offers a dynamic way of engaging with otherwise theoretical content.
Several students went into detail about the dimensions involved in beadwork (i.e., putting the thread through the wrong bead produced a pyramid
instead of a triangle). One student discussed how this related to the notions
of one-to-one and onto functions between spaces of different dimensions
(these functions are ways of transforming one thing to another in some nice
mathematical way). These types of functions were not discussed explicitly
in this manner in class, so students' analysis extended beyond simply par-
roting class discussions.

One student had a strong computer science background, so their written work reflected their discussions with Sarah regarding planning in advance where each bead will be placed, versus the "painterly style" of beadwork that does not involve preplanning. The student stated that "free-handing a piece can be rewarding but may not end up how you would like," and explained how a computer program could be helpful "by printing out line by line a series of spaces and stars." This would help artists avoid gaps of space where a whole bead doesn't quite fit. The student's work indicated that they had thought a lot about the intersection of the topics of beading and mathematical programming in computer science, and the authors particularly enjoyed reading their concluding remarks: "At the end of the day a mathematician orders numbers into lines to solve for unknowns in an equation, while an artist places beads onto a string to create something beautiful. Both are simply looking to display rows of information in useful and meaningful ways." The authors note that a matrix displays useful information to a mathematician in the same way that a particular beaded design displays meaning to an artist.

Mathematicians are often rather concrete and like to do things in a logical order. One student, who may have been frustrated by the lack of rigidity in the "rules" for beading earrings, wrote out an algorithm in an attempt to provide greater mathematical rigor to the project, almost like a formula for how to make earrings: step one, step two, step three, etc. The student thought of each successive bead that was put on the thread as being labeled 1, 2, 3, . . . and then would provide instructions such as "Put needle through beads 5+2n and 6+2n through same side as it exits previous sub-step," where n is the number of desired rows in the "bridge" of the earring. For example, if the bridge was two rows, then this step would indicate to put the needle through beads 9 and 10, in the hole that the needle just exited in the previous step. The student indicated that they wanted to create this algorithm to avoid continually asking for instructions. The student also identified some similarities between math and beading, including the idea that if you make a big mistake, then "erase everything (or cut the thread) and start fresh again." Sarah enjoyed this student's writeup as it gave a great deal of insight into a mathematician's mind and the potential differences in the ways that a typical math or art student might learn or approach a problem.

One student's writeup stood out as being incredibly introspective; it was written as though it were a journal or diary entry. Cathy notes that this parallels Indigenous ways of thinking and storytelling: the student wrote as though they were telling a story. The work contained a great deal of self-reflection and comedy (e.g., MATH as "Mental Abuse Towards Humans"). The student described their struggles with beading, their frustrations while making mistakes, and the stress of not quite fully understanding. The student noted the connection with learning math, in particular to their time in twelfth-grade math in high school, and summarized quite nicely, "In dealing with a complex and intricate art form, whether it be beading, or Linear Algebra, it's very easy to get overwhelmed in just how many different ways there are to mess up. All it takes however, is a few deep breaths and a positive self-affirmation or two to gently nudge yourself back on the right path." We appreciate the student's honesty and vulnerability in sharing their feelings and note the similarities in the psychology behind solving mathematical problems and working with an artistic medium such as beadwork—neither is easy, and often how we work through the obstacles we face is what determines success.

Lessons Learned

In this collaborative project, we aimed to explore whether learning Indigenous beadwork is useful in students' understanding of linear algebra. Incorporating Indigenous ways of learning can help break free from the traditional "chalk talk" that is all too common in academia. Not everyone learns in the same way—typical math courses that are taught straight from the textbook may not be useful for many students. Kinesthetic learning, including tactile, conversation-based, and visual learning (as well as teaching) is more conducive to Indigenous learning and teaching. Indeed, Kovach (2010) writes about the Conversation Method as an Indigenous research methodology that is applicable here, since it reflects Cathy's approach to teaching beadwork: conversation based, without any written instructions. Indigenous scholars such as Simpson (2017) discuss Indigenous knowledge transmission as kinetic and based on relationship-making; a number of the students mentioned positive interactions and building relationships with other beaders at the Indigenous Peoples' Center in the follow-up in-person event.

As a first attempt at such an exercise, we believe the project was extremely successful and have a number of ideas for minor revisions to the project in future iterations. To further blur the divide between art and math, "crits" in studio art courses allow students to obtain feedback on their work and submit their work twice for review by the professor. Allowing students a second attempt, after some initial feedback, would be highly beneficial for the students, as most math and computer science students are not used to this type of assignment. In particular, many students were not used to discussing themselves or their thoughts, feelings, and opinions; many were not used to writing any sort of descriptive essay, even a rather short one.

After the semester ended, Danny Luecke (math and math education faculty member at Turtle Mountain Community College, a tribal college in North Dakota) proposed several interesting connections to linear algebra topics that Sarah did not think of during the project (personal comm., 2024). For example, beading on a stretchy material to demonstrate scaling by pulling and stretching (scaling a vector simply means multiplying each component of the vector by a number; for example, to visualize scaling the vector by two we could stretch a string of beads so that it becomes twice as long as it originally was). This led Sarah to reflect on other topics, such as adding vectors, which could be done by combining two strings of beads so that the first bead in each of the two strings sits next to each other, the second beads sit next to each other, and so on. The concept of a vector space can be very abstract to a student. One way to visualize a vector space might be to think of the string itself, with its infinite possibilities of combinations of beads that can be put onto it. Besides these missed opportunities, our work did not touch on comparing different beading styles (brick, peyote, lazy, etc.) and beading on different surfaces (leggings, moccasins, bonnet, earrings). Such work would likely lead to different interesting mathematical connections but would be beyond the scope of this article.

Conclusion

We have presented a collaborative project whereby the authors created an Indigenous beadwork assignment in an undergraduate mathematics course (specifically, Linear Algebra II). Important insights are drawn from the process of the project, including historical and local context, background motivation, and relationship building, as well as the outcomes of the assignment, including classroom activities, beadwork sessions at the Indigenous Peoples' Center (IPC) on campus, and students' written work. The data collected for this research project included observations by the authors and an RA at the in-person event, as well as a qualitative analysis of the students' written component of the assignment. We also reflected on what went well in the project and things we would change about the project in the future.

The main objectives of this collaboration were to integrate culturally appropriate topics into the course curriculum in an Indigenization and reconciliation effort—to actively respond to the *Calls to Action* set forth by the Truth and Reconciliation Commission of Canada—and to explore the degree to which Indigenous beadwork helps with students' understanding of abstract concepts of linear algebra. The impetus for the project came from a series of events that took place locally, leading the authors to meet at a Sharing Circle and ultimately create this project.

Our work puts theory into practice and can be used as a real-world example for other educators wanting to know how to implement culturally responsive teaching "in the field." A project such as this allows educators to push students out of their comfort zone and gives them permission to think about math in a way that they had probably never thought about before. Our work shows how Indigenous beadwork can contribute to culturally relevant mathematics learning, and helps to advance the growing body of work related to culturally relevant STEM learning discussed in the literature.[2]

At the time of writing, **SARAH PLOSKER** was an associate professor in mathematics and held a Canada Research Chair (CRC) in quantum information theory at Brandon University. She is now a professor and Canada Research Chair at Brandon University. She is originally from Regina and started at the university in 2013.

At the time of writing, **CATHY MATTES** was an associate professor of art history at Brandon University (2002–2021). She is now an associate professor in history at the University of Winnipeg. She is Southwest Manitoba Métis, and has been beading since she was twenty, when she learned from her auntie Jean Baron Ward.

References

Abrams, Eleanor, Peter C. Taylor, and Chen Guo. 2013. "Contextualizing Culturally Relevant Science and Mathematics Teaching for Indigenous Learning." *International Journal of Science and Mathematics Education* 11, no. 1: 1–21. https://doi.org/10.1007/s10763-012-9388-2.

Aikenhead, Glen S. 2017. "Enhancing School Mathematics Culturally: A Path of Reconciliation." *Canadian Journal of Science, Mathematics and Technology Education,* 17, no. 2: 73–140. http://dx.doi.org/10.1080/14926156.2017.1308043.

The American Mathematical Society. n.d. "Meet Us at the Joint Mathematics Meetings 2020 (JMM 2020), in Denver, CO, USA." Accessed online March 18, 2020. https://www.mdpi.com/about/announcements/1711.

Averill, Robin, Dayle Anderson, Helen Easton, Peter T. Maro, Denise Smith, and Anne Hynds. 2009. "Culturally Responsive Teaching of Mathematics: Three Models from Linked Studies." *Journal for Research in Mathematics Education,* 157–86. https://doi.org/10.2307/40539330.

Azam, Shazia, and Karen Goodnough. 2018. "Learning Together about Culturally Relevant Science Teacher Education: Indigenizing a Science Methods Course." *International Journal of Innovation in Science and Mathematics Education* 26, no. 2: 74–88.

Battiste, Marie, and James Henderson (Sa'ke'j) Youngblood. 2021. "Indigenous and Trans-Systemic Knowledge Systems (ΔᵇdΔg∇ὸⁿ ˋᵤᵒᵀ∇dg∇ ◁ᵇd ᵎ₹◁ᵖⁿⁿ⁺ⁿ∪⌐ ˋᵤᵒᵀ∇dg∇ ⁿ⁺ⁿ∪ᶜⁿ)." *Engaged Scholar Journal* 7, no. 1: i—xix. https://doi.org/10.15402/esj.v7i1.70768.

Belcastro, Sarah-Marie, and Carolyn Yackel, eds. 2007. *Making Mathematics with Needlework: Ten Papers and Ten Projects.* New York: CRC Press. https://doi.org/10.1201/b10652.

Brandon University. n.d. "About BU" and "Historical Sketch." Accessed online March 19, 2020. https://www.brandonu.ca/president/.

Brandon University. n.d. "Indigenous Peoples' Center." Accessed online January 15, 2025. https://www.brandonu.ca/ipc.

Brandon University. n.d. "Land Acknowledgement." Accessed online January 15, 2025. https://www.brandonu.ca/ipc/land-acknowledgement/.

Chow, Alice, and Andrew McEachern. n.d. *The Art of Mathematics.* The Canadian Mathematical Society. Accessed online December 1, 2019. https://cms.math.ca/Events/winter19/sessions_scientific.

The Canadian Mathematical Society. n.d. "Teaching Strategies for Increasing Diversity in Math" and "The Art of Mathematics." Accessed online December 1, 2019. https://cms.math.ca/Events/winter19/sessions_scientific

Canadian Mathematical Society. n.d. "Indigenization and Reconciliation in Mathematics." *The Canadian Mathematical Society.* Accessed online March 1, 2020. https://summer19.cms.math.ca/index.php/education-sessions/.

Doolittle, Edward. 2017. "Transformations, Symmetry, and the Starblanket: The Mathematics of Indigenous Design." Saskatchewan Teachers' Federation. Accessed online December 14, 2019. https://www.stf.sk.ca/sites/default/files/transformations_symmetry_starblanket.pdf.

Fisher, Gwen L., and Bih-Yaw Mellor. 2012. "Using Tiling Theory to Generate Angle Weaves with Beads." *Journal of Mathematics and the Arts* 6, no. 4: 141—58. https://doi.org/10.1080/17513472.2012.736935.

Fisher, Gwen L., and Bih-Yaw Mellor. 2007. "Three-Dimensional Finite Point Groups and the Symmetry of Beaded Beads." *Journal of Mathematics and the Arts* 1, no. 2: 85—96. https://doi.org/10.1080/17513470701416264.

Gaudry, Adam, and Danielle. Lorenz. 2018. "Indigenization as Inclusion, Reconciliation, and Decolonization: Navigating the Different Visions for Indigenizing the Canadian Academy." *AlterNative* 14, no. 3: 218—227. https://doi.org/10.1177/1177180118785382.

Graham, Suzanne R. W. 2015. "Indigenization of Mathematics Curriculum: An Evolving Experience." In *Proceedings of the Eighth International Mathematics Education and Society Conference,* edited by S. Mukhopadhyay and B. Greer, 1: 170—75.

Huencho Ramos, Andrea. 2015. "Mapuche Ethnomathematics: Mathematical Learning's Promotion from Cultural Knowledge." In *Proceedings of the Eighth International Mathematics Education and Society Conference,* edited by S. Mukhopadhyay and B. Greer, 1:176—80.

Jensen, Sara. 2017. "Mathematical Knitting." Carthage College. Accessed online February 24, 2020. http://sarajensen.org/knitting.html.

Kovach, Margaret. 2010. "Conversation Method in Indigenous Research." *First Peoples Child & Family Review* 5, no. 1: 40–48. https://doi.org/10.7202/1069060ar.

Laychuk, Ryan. 2017. "Brandon University Students Alarmed by 'Horrifying' Posters, Stickers Promoting White Supremacy." *CBC News,* December 6. https://www.cbc.ca/news/canada/manitoba/brandon-university-posters-1.4434556.

Luecke, Danny (Turtle Mountain Community College), message to authors, July 9, 2024.

Mirich, Daniel L., and Cavey, Laurie O. 2015. "Lacing Together Mathematics and Culture." *Mathematics Teaching in the Middle School* 21, no. 1: 16–24. https://doi.org/10.5951/mathteacmiddscho.21.1.0016.

Owens, Kay. 2014. "Diversifying Our Perspectives on Mathematics about Space and Geometry: An Ecocultural Approach." *International Journal of Science and Mathematics Education* 12, no. 4: 941–74. https://doi.org/10.1007/s10763-013-9441-9.

Ragoonaden, Karen, and Mueller, Lisa. 2017. "Culturally Responsive Pedagogy: Indigenizing Curriculum." *Canadian Journal of Higher Education* 47, no. 2: 22–46. https://doi.org/10.47678/cjhe.v47i2.187963.

Simpson, Leanne Betasamosake. 2017. *As We Have Always Done: Indigenous Freedom through Radical Resistance.* Minneapolis: University of Minnesota Press.

Truth and Reconciliation Commission of Canada. n.d. Crown-Indigenous Relations and Northern Affairs Canada. Accessed online August 5, 2024. https://www.rcaanc-irnac.gc.ca/eng/1450124405592/1529106060525

Truth and Reconciliation Commission of Canada. 2015. *Final Report of the Truth and Reconciliation Commission of Canada: Summary: Honouring the Truth, Reconciling for the Future.* Accessed online January 15, 2020. https://publications.gc.ca/collections/collection_2015/trc/IR4-7-2015-eng.pdf.

Trinick, Tony, Tamsin Meaney, and Uenuku Fairhall. 2015. "Finding the Way: Cultural Revival through Mathematics Education." In *Proceedings of the Eighth International Mathematics Education and Society Conference,* University of Auckland, edited by S. Mukhopadhyay and B. Greer, 1:224–30.

Kirkness, Verna J., and Barnhardt, Ray. 1991. "First Nations and Higher Education: The Four R's—Respect, Relevance, Reciprocity, Responsibility." *Journal of American Indian Education,* 1–15.

Notes

The project was approved by Brandon University's Research in Ethics Committee (BUREC) and Sarah received a certificate of completion of the Tri-Council Policy Statement: Ethical Conduct for Research Involving Humans (TCPS) Course on Research Ethics (CORE) tutorial.

1. Please see https://www.brandonu.ca/president/about-bu/ for more information on the university. We provide only a short overview here.

2. For more information about the project, see https://www.brandonu.ca/research-connection/article/beadwork-and-linear-algebra/ or contact Sarah at ploskers@brandonu.ca.

CATHLEEN D. CAHILL

Representation Matters: Narrating Native Women's Lives in Children's Educational History Texts

Super SHEroes of History: Indigenous Peoples: Women Who Made a Difference
by Katrina M. Phillips
Scholastic Children's Press, 2003

Deb Haaland: First Native American Cabinet Secretary
by Jill Doerfler and Matthew Martinez
Gateway Biographies series, Lerner Publishing Group, 2023

My Name is LaMoosh
by Linda Meanus
Oregon State University Press, 2023

REPRESENTATION MATTERS! As we have recently seen in discussions around the film *Killers of the Flower Moon,* this is true about which characters we center and whose stories we tell as well as who is telling them. We are also living in a moment in which the stakes of whose history is available—even in children's books—are high and can result in librarians and teachers potentially losing their jobs over which stories they include in their lessons and libraries.

These high stakes will likely not come as a surprise to scholars of colonialism who know that there is a long history of suppressing Native histories and denigrating Indigenous pasts while replacing them with nationalist histories. In boarding schools, government teachers told Native children to forget their histories and learn those of the colonizers, thus leading to scenarios where Native children put on pageants that depicted the first Thanksgiving, playing both Pilgrims and Indians.[1]

Indigenous people have also written back and insisted on self-representation. From the development of the Cherokee syllabary, to Simon Pokagon's birchbark book, *The Red Man's Rebuke,* at the 1893 Chicago World's Fair, to the many autobiographies and memoirs written by Native people, including Charles Eastman (Ohiyesa), Gertrude Bonnin (Zitkala-Ša) and Luther Standing Bear, Native people have offered their perspectives (along with critiques of non-Native representations) and sought to correct the record. While many of these authors aimed their books at non-Native audiences in the moment of their writing, the texts have come to be important historical documents that have preserved Native voices from the past for current and future generations.

The books considered in this review are part of an ongoing genealogy of works that introduce broad audiences to history from Indigenous perspectives while simultaneously entering Native voices into the historical record. They each go about this in slightly different iterations, but all focus on Native women.

Katrina Phillips (citizen of the Red Cliff Band of Lake Superior Ojibwe) comes to children's literature after writing scholarly books and articles focused on representation, self-representation, and sovereignty. She has also engaged with public history and with tribal and community histories and programs. Her turn to children's books is perhaps a logical outcome of those engagements.

Here she embarks on a project that highlights the stories of multiple Native women in history through Scholastic's Super SHEroes of History series. Phillips chose to feature women who were leaders in their communities. These women "resisted foreign influence, preserved Indigenous traditions or went into U.S. politics" and "most of them had to overcome many obstacles . . . but they were still able to achieve things that made a difference to their communities and the times in which they lived" (5).

This short chapter book is aimed at readers ages eight through ten in grade levels three through five. The bulk of the book comprises eight chapters that explore the lives of four Native women from the seventeenth, nineteenth, twentieth, and twenty-first centuries. Each woman—Pocahontas (Powhatan), Lozen (Chiricahau Apache), Mary Golda Ross (Cherokee), and Deb Haaland (Laguna Pueblo)—receives a biographical chapter, which is followed by a contextual one. For example, the book opens with a biographical chapter on Pocahontas, which is followed by a chapter on Virginia in the 1600s.

Eight more mini-biographies of other Indigenous "SHEroes" are also included. Seven of the twelve women Phillips has chosen are from the twentieth and twenty-first centuries, including Mary Golda Ross, a Cherokee rocket scientist, and U.S. Poet Laureate Joy Harjo (Muskogee). Those choices may help students connect with modern women while also emphasizing the ongoing presence of Indigenous nations in the present. Phillips also includes stories of women who fought for their nations' sovereignty, like Lozen, the Apache woman who defied gender roles to fight against the U.S. military, or Queen Lili'uokalani of Hawai'i who resisted annexation by the U.S. She draws from tribal oral histories when writing the biographies, telling her readers, "Historical accounts can vary a lot depending on whose point of view they are told from."

The book is brightly illustrated with historical drawings and photographs, both black and white and color (some have been colorized). The layout is collage-like with color blocks and boxes that offer further information or questions for readers to consider. It also contains a timeline, a map, and a glossary with twenty-four terms that have been highlighted throughout the text.

Although merely an introduction to Indigenous women's stories, Phillip's book is an important starting point. Some of these women, like Pocahontas, may be familiar through pop culture portrayals such as the eponymous 1995 Disney movie, but most of the others will likely be new to their audience. And indeed, that audience is wide. The Scholastic series also explores the experiences of women in the civil rights movement, female global activists, and women of the ancient world. The Scholastic brand has an extremely broad reach. According to their website, they are the "world's largest publisher and distributor of children's books" through their well-known school book fairs. They are currently in "115,000 schools, reaching 3.8 million educators, 54 million students, and 78 million parents/caregivers domestically."[2]

Jill Doerfler (White Earth) and Matthew J. Martinez (Ohkay Owingeh) delve deeper into Deb Haaland's history in *Deb Haaland: First Native American Cabinet Secretary,* which is part of the Gateway Biographies series published by the Lerner Publishing Group in Minneapolis, Minnesota. Both scholars have brought their academic backgrounds into engagement with their nations' systems of governance. Doerfler has expressed her "commitment to bridging scholarly efforts with the practical needs of American Indian peoples, communities, and nations."[3] She worked closely with the White Earth Nation during its constitutional reform efforts leading to the ratification of the nation's new constitution in 2009.[4] Martinez has also engaged with tribal governance, serving as first lieutenant Governor of Ohkay Owingeh Pueblo.

Additionally, he has also worked to educate people about Native cultures and histories through a variety of mediums ranging from college classrooms, to documentary films, to his current work protecting historical landscapes as executive director of the Mesa Prieta Petroglyph Project.

Perhaps inspired by their own work in governance, the authors tell the story of Haaland, an historic Native politician. In 2018, New Mexicans elected Haaland to represent their state in the U.S. House of Representatives. She shared the honor of being the first Native woman elected to Congress with Kansas Representative Sharice Davids (Ho-Chunk), who also won her seat that year. In 2021, Haaland became the first Native person to serve as a cabinet member when President Joseph R. Biden nominated her as secretary of the interior. This is an important first as the Interior Department is the office in the Executive branch that has had the responsibility of liaising with tribal governments since 1824.

Aimed at young readers with a reading level of fifth grade, the biography is forty-eight pages long (inclusive of back matter).[5] It tells Haaland's story as a life of service and political engagement fully anchored in her Pueblo community and family. The book is brightly illustrated with color photographs of Haaland, New Mexico, and sites of Indigenous activism.

Doerfler and Martinez do not shy away from the difficult issues that Native women and communities have faced. Instead, they illustrate how Haaland's Indigenous identity and community connections led her to address pressing issues including the violence and sexual assault of Native women, the trauma of the boarding school experiences, and environmental concerns in her public work.

The authors ground Haaland in place and in her Kʼawaika (the Keres language name for Laguna) identity. They describe her childhood, education, early career, and then focus on her work as secretary of the interior. The daughter of military parents, Haaland returned to Laguna Pueblo each summer to live with her maternal grandparents. They played an important role in shaping her perspective. Haaland's maternal grandparents were both removed from their families by the federal government and sent to boarding schools. They shared their stories with Haaland and her knowledge of how that difficult history led her to implement the Federal Boarding School Initiative. Similarly, the authors describe how Secretary Haaland has decisively moved to address the tragedy of Missing and Murdered Indigenous Women (MMIW) by forming the Missing and Murdered Unit (MMU) in the Bureau of Indian Affairs Office of Justice Services as one of her first actions as secretary of the interior. She recognized the roots of that violence in the history of sexualizing and denigrating Indigenous women and so tasked her employees in the Interior Department with identifying the sites on federal land in the United States that include the sexualized slur for Native women ("squ*w") and assigning them different names.

While the historic nature of Haaland's career is focused on her position in federal governance, Doerfler and Martinez also highlight her work in tribal governance, a reminder that while she is a citizen of the United States, she is also a citizen of Laguna Pueblo. Before she served in the U.S. Congress or the Cabinet, she worked for her pueblo, being the first chairwoman elected to the Laguna Development Corporation Board of Directors. In that role, she "supervised operations for the second-largest tribal gaming business in New Mexico" (20). She also served as tribal administrator for San Felipe Pueblo. Additionally, they also reveal her engagement with New Mexico State politics when she ran for lieutenant governor and then served as chair of the state's Democratic Party.

In Doerfler and Martinez's hands, Haaland's story is a civics lesson about service to community, to country, and to nation(s). It illustrates different levels and sites of governance and offers all children—but especially Indigenous children—a role model for civic engagement. In some ways it is a familiar political story of hard work and rising in the ranks, but in so many other ways it is not. When the politician is a Native woman the picture changes, as does the focus of the governmental department she leads. Doerfler and Martinez recognize this, as does Haaland. They open with a discussion of Haaland's symbolic clothing choices at her swearing in as secretary of the interior by another female first, Vice President Kamala Harris. Haaland chose to wear a ribbon skirt decorated with butterflies and a cornstalk created by Indigenous artist Agnes Woodward. A sense of history permeated those actions—she used the moment to echo historical visits of tribal delegations arriving in Washington to represent their nations, reject federal boarding schools policies that forced Native children to change into "civilized" clothes as symbolic means of shedding their cultures, and celebrate the ongoing creativity and strength of Native women and their communities. This anecdote sets the tone for the rest of the book, which centers Haaland's Indigenous identity in explaining how her policies have been shaped.

The third book, *My Name is LaMoosh,* by Linda Meanus (Confederated Tribes of Warm Springs) has a fascinating backstory. In 1956, Meanus was the subject of *Linda's Indian Home,* a children's book written by Martha McKeown, a non-Native educator who was friends with Linda's grandmother, elder Flora Cushinway Thompson. McKeown wrote the book "to dispel myths about Native Americans and call attention to Columbia River tribes as new hydroelectric dams destroyed centers of fishing like Celilo Falls" (9). Martha's husband, Archie McKeown took the photographs of Linda, her family, and the pre-dam falls that illustrated the book. Linda's grandmother supported this endeavor, and after publication she and Linda toured Washington state to educate non-Native children about the Indigenous nations and cultures in the state. Her grandmother instilled the importance of this work in Meanus, telling her "I wanted this book written so that people would know who we are and our way of life." As a child, Meanus admits, she didn't fully understand. In the caption for a beautiful photo of Thompson reading the book to a young Meanus, she writes, "[Grandma Flora] was trying to help me understand. I wasn't really interested. I wanted to go play. Now I'm much older and understand . . ." (11)

Now an Elder herself, Meanus carries on her grandmother's work, stating "being an Elder means it's my job to teach young people what I know." While she continues to visit schools, Meanus also sought to reach more children through a book of her own. "Grandma felt that more of these books should be written," she remembers (10).

Meanus compellingly tells her story with a gentle humor that will resonate with young readers. She writes in first-person style, addressing young people directly. She uses her own memories of childhood to connect with them. The book is just over ninety pages long, inclusive of the back matter. It is divided into nineteen short chapters covering Meanus's life from childhood to the present. The book is marvelously illustrated with black-and-white photographs. She gives readers behind-the-scenes details of some of the famous photographs of herself and adds photographs that reveal an intimate portrait of her family. With the photos and descriptions of her own childhood experiences, Meanus pulls what is often an abstract history about dispossession onto a personal level.

Her story is also the story of her grandparents, Flora and Chief Tommy Thompson, and their efforts to stop the dam and the tragic flooding of Celilo Falls in 1957. Meanus's life and the life of her nation goes on, but it was disrupted by that violent event. Told from a child's point of view, she admits she didn't always understand what was happening, but her close relationship with her grandparents grounded her in her culture and ultimately taught her lessons that she works to pass on today. She candidly shares the story of her grandfather's heartbreak and her grandmother's perseverance. She also tells her own boarding school story as well as the lessons about bead work, food, and ceremony she learned from her grandmother. Indeed, she frames her story as the continuation of her grandmother's work to maintain and transmit cultural knowledge and assert Native presence in the present. Her message is "My people have always been here. We've never left. And we'll always be here" (13).

Meanus approached Lily Hart and Colin Fogarty, members of *Confluence,* a nonprofit organization whose mission is "connecting people to the history, living cultures, and ecology of the Columbia River system through Indigenous voices," with the idea of writing a book that told her story from her point of view.[6] They were joined by Dr. Katy Barber, author of *In Defense of WeWyam: Native-White Alliances and the Struggle for Celilo Village*. Through collaborative conversations and interviews using the process of "transformative listening," based on the model of *As I Remember It* by Elsie Paul,[7] they produced *My Name is LaMoosh*. They describe their role as facilitating Meanus's vision through a careful process, first listening to an earlier interview with Meanus and then conducting new interviews. Together with Meanus, they identified themes that were important to her, which they describe as "Education. Flora Thompson's legacy. Elders and the next generation. Survival." (83) They then arranged the content into chapter-sized portions. Meanus then read and edited those drafts. All of this collaboration was made challenging by the COVID pandemic and required a shift to Zoom technology, but the result is a powerful statement of survivance.

The title Meanus chose, *My Name is LaMoosh*, is in dialog with McKeown's title, *Linda's Indian Home*. McKeown's book describes Linda's life at Celilo Falls before the dam was built and ends without mention of that event. *My Name is LaMoosh* continues the story into the present and gestures to the future. In Meanus's final chapter of the same title she states that her Elders taught her to introduce herself with "her Indian name" in her Native language. In her culture, your Indian name "comes from an ancestor who's gone." Hers evokes her Grandmother Flora and reflects their shared commitment as strong women advocating for Indian people, fighting for salmon, and defending their way of life. (80)

All three of the books are meant for classroom instruction or educational use. They are all enjoyable to read and pedagogically conceived. They include dialogue boxes within the text that offer additional context, define key concepts, and/or discuss related topics. They all also include back matter with timelines and suggestions for further reading. *Super SHEroes* and *My Name is LaMoosh* also contain glossaries of terms used in the text and maps. The latter has a map of the Columbia River watershed while *Super SHEroes* includes a map of the United States identifying where the women in the book live(d).

Native women's ongoing work to maintain their cultures and defend Native people are themes shared by all three of the books. Like LaMoosh's grandmother, the authors agree that we need more of these kinds of books. They are doing the important work of replacing stereotypes and derogatory ideas about Native women with stories from Indigenous perspectives. Just as Secretary Haaland worked to rename geological features on our landscape, these authors are contributing to the important work of reshaping our historical landscape. Moreover, their choice of children's books as their medium is key. Many of the stories about Native women available for children uphold colonial tropes, such as portrayals of Sacagawea and Pocahontas that are thoroughly fictionalized and/or emphasize their cooperation with non-Native people at the expense of Native nations. These books celebrate Native women who have fought for their communities and worked to preserve and transmit their cultures while also offering examples of contemporary women who are building for the future. These representations matter and make a difference.

CATHLEEN D. CAHILL is professor of history and women's, gender, and sexuality studies at Penn State University.

Notes

1. David Wallace Adams, *Education for Extinction,* (Lawrence: University Press of Kansas, 1995, 2020), 215–16.

2. https://www.scholastic.com/aboutscholastic, accessed February 20, 2024.

3. https://cahss.d.umn.edu/faculty-staff/jill-doerfler, accessed March 29, 2024.

4. Gerald Visenor and Jill Doerfler, *The White Earth Nation: Ratification of a Native Democratic Constitution* (Lincoln: University of Nebraska Press, 2012). Despite the Constitution being ratified and approved by an 80 percent majority in referendum, this Constitution was not implemented by elected leadership.

5. Learnerbooks.com accessed March 29, 2024.

6. https://www.confluenceproject.org/.

7. Elsie Paul, *Written As I Remember It: Teachings (ʔəms taʔaw) from the Life of a Sliammon Elder* with Paige Raibmon and Harmony Johnson (Vancouver: UBC Press, 2014).

KATRINA M. PHILLIPS

"The Kind of People That We Are": The Critical Role of Children's Literature in Native American and Indigenous Studies

Kindred Spirits: Shilombish Ittibachvffa
by Leslie Stall Widener and Johnson Yazzie
Penguin Random House, 2024

How the Birds Got Their Songs
by Travis Zimmerman and Sam Zimmerman
Minnesota Historical Society Press, 2024

IN 2016, illustrator David Huyck, in consultation with Sarah Park Dahlen and Molly Beth Griffin, released an infographic detailing the range of diversity in children's books based on 2015 publishing statistics. The results were unfortunate and likely unsurprising: a whopping 73.3 percent of the books depicted white characters, while 12.5 percent featured animals and non-human characters like trucks. The remaining results were sobering: 7.6 percent of books included African or African American characters, 3.3 percent included Asian Pacific or Asian Pacific Americans, and 2.4 percent included Latinx characters. A mere 0.9 percent of books included characters who were Native American or Indigenous.[1]

Huyck, Dahlen, and Griffin released an updated infographic in 2018. While the number of white characters dropped to 50 percent, the number of animal and nonhuman characters increased to 27 percent. The remaining changes were minimal, with Native American and Indigenous characters now depicted in 1 percent of children's books.[2] Additionally, the staff at the *School Library Journal* cautioned its readers that these shifts, however large or small, may simply reflect the quantity, not the quality, of children's literature.[3]

The push to diversify children's literature is not new—nor is the research showing the importance of allowing all children to see themselves in the books they read or listen to.[4] In 1990, Rudine Sims Bishop—known as the "mother of multicultural literature"—wrote that books may be windows, "offering views of worlds that may be real or imagined, familiar or strange," or sliding glass doors where readers can "walk through in imagination to become part of whatever world has been created or recreated by the author." More importantly, though, Bishop argued, a window can also be a mirror: "Reading, then, becomes a means of self-affirmation, and readers often seek their mirrors in books."[5] Even more critically, what may be mirrors for some students may be windows for others, which, as Heineke et al. contend, can lead to "rich discussions, deeper understandings, and enhanced empathy."[6]

The field of children's literature has seen some monumental shifts over the past few decades, but that progress is not exactly linear—especially when it comes to the representations of Native American and Indigenous people. The rumblings around Laura Ingalls Wilder's openly racist writings about Native people in her *Little House on the Prairie* series, for instance, led to the 2018 removal of her name from a book award.[7] Wilder biographer Caroline Fraser was among those who questioned the decision, noting that "no white American should be able to avoid the history it has to tell."[8] On the other hand, the continued collective affection for Scott O'Dell's 1960 *Island of the Blue Dolphins*—which won the Newbery Medal in 1961 and had a fiftieth anniversary edition published in 2010—caused Nambé Pueblo scholar and educator Debbie Reese to rightly contend that "sentiment is no excuse for ignorance."[9]

Those of us who grew up with books like Wilder's Little House series and *Island of the Blue Dolphins;* Holling Clancy Holling's *Paddle-to-the-Sea* (1941); Tomie de Paola's *The Legend of the Indian Paintbrush* (1988); and Susan Jeffers's *Brother Eagle, Sister Sky* (1991), among others, may now have young readers in our lives who have access to the kinds of books we could have only dreamed about. I've watched my own children, who are currently 11 and 8, devour Traci Sorell's *Contenders: Two Native Baseball Players, One World Series* and *Classified: The Secret Career of Mary Golda Ross, Cherokee Aerospace Engineer.* They scour the shelves of our local library for books like *Who Was Sitting Bull?, Who Was Jim Thorpe?,* and *Who Were the Navajo Code Talkers?,* whisper-yelling "Mom! Look what I found!" as if they'd stumbled on a Golden Ticket.

My sons are not alone in their ongoing quest for books that depict a wider range of subjects and characters, nor are they the only young readers who actively look for books that complement their own backgrounds and histories. The two books at the heart of this essay are part of a growing subfield within the body of literature for children and young adults that center Native American and Indigenous stories and subjects. Carole Lindstrom and

Michaela Goade's *We Are Water Protectors* won the Caldecott Medal in 2021, while Angeline Boulley's *Warrior Girl Unearthed* topped the New York Times Bestseller List in 2023. Some, like Christy Jordan-Fenton and Margaret Pokiak-Fenton's *When I Was Eight* (2013), Jenny Kay Dupuis and Kathy Kacer's *I Am Not a Number* (2016), and Melanie Florence's *Stolen Words* (2017) teach younger readers about the histories and horrors of boarding and residential schools.

Others, like Brenda Child's *Bowwow Powwow* (2018), Kevin Noble Maillard's *Fry Bread* (2019), and Denise Lajimodiere's *Josie Dances* (2021), draw inspiration from both fictional and nonfictional motifs in crafting their stories.[10] Still more are adaptations that expand a book's reach and audience. Roxanne Dunbar-Ortiz's *An Indigenous Peoples' History of the United States,* for instance, has been adapted into both a young reader's format and as a graphic novel. Anton Treuer's *Everything You Wanted to Know about Indians but Were Afraid to Ask,* first published in 2012 and revised in 2023, was adapted for young readers in 2021. Similarly, the young adult version of Robin Wall-Kimmerer's best-selling *Braiding Sweetgrass: Indigenous Wisdom, Scientific Knowledge, and the Teaching of Plants* has won nearly as many awards as the original.

Literature aimed at children and young adults, particularly in the realm of historical fiction and nonfiction, holds the key to a new world for young readers. Like the field of Native American and Indigenous studies writ large, these books often push back against the triumphalist narrative of American exceptionalism. One of the books at the core of this review, Leslie Stall Widener's *Kindred Spirits: Shilombish Ittibachvffa* (illustrated by Johnson Yazzie), tells the story of the long-lasting relationship between Irish people and the Choctaw Nation. Widener worked as an illustrator before turning to authorship, and Yazzie's career as an artist spans painting, sculpture, and illustration. The book begins in Ireland in 1845, the first year of the devastating Irish Potato Famine. Widener then moves to the forced removal of the Choctaw in the wake of the 1830 Treaty of Dancing Rabbit Creek. As news of the famine reached the United States, the Choctaw people who gathered at their agency in March of 1847, took up a collection for the people of Ireland. The collection totaled around $170, the equivalent of $5,000 today.

But Widener's story doesn't end there. In 2017, 170 years after the Choctaw people gave what they had to the people of Ireland, an Irish sculptor crafted a monument to this ongoing relationship. Nine 20-foot-tall eagle feathers came together to make an empty bowl, highlighting both the suffering of the Irish and the Choctaw and their connections across oceans and generations. While this would be a lovely book even if it ended here, Widener then takes the reader to the American Southwest in the midst of the COVID-19 pandemic. Just as news of the Irish suffering reached the Americas in the 1840s, news of how COVID affected the Hopi and Navajo nations reached well into Europe. More than twenty-six thousand Irish people—many with ties to those who were helped by the Choctaw generations earlier—raised more than $3 million for the Hopi and Navajo nations.

Yazzie's rich illustrations are a wonderful complement to Widener's simple yet unflinching narrative. Widener's ability to move across time and space allows readers to find the similarities in the stories while recognizing the unique characteristics of each event. Widener introduces readers to treaties and federal Indian policy, and Yazzie's colorful, detailed drawings bring these topics to life. This book serves as an excellent introduction to this era of Native history for young readers. The author's notes, timeline, and additional snippets of historical information, all of which are at the end of the book, help supplement the story without weighing down the main text.

In *How the Birds Got Their Songs / Gaa-pi-onji mino'amaazowaad Ingiweg Bebaamaashiwaad,* Travis Zimmerman and his cousin, Sam Zimmerman/Zhaawanoogiizhik, share a story that has been passed down through their family for generations. Travis Zimmerman provides the text while Sam Zimmerman provides the illustrations, and the book also includes an Ojibwe translation from Marcus Ammesmaki/Aanikanootaagewin. Travis Zimmerman is the longtime site manager for the Mille Lacs Indian Museum and Trading Post in Onamia, Minnesota, while Sam Zimmerman is an artist based in Duluth, Minnesota. Ammesmaki is a teacher at Waadookodaading Ojibwe Language Institute in Hayward, Wisconsin.

As the story goes, the earth was very young. It was very quiet. The Great Spirit called the birds together, telling them he'd give each of them a special song. The higher they flew, the prettier their song would be, and they'd learn their song on their return to the earth. The eagle was sure he'd have the prettiest song, and off he flew. He didn't realize that a sleepy little hermit thrush had tucked itself into his feathers, even as he flew so close to the sun that his feathers burned and turned black. As he started his descent, the little hermit thrush woke up and started flying, looking for her own song. The hermit thrush flew into another world through a hole in the sky, only to return with the most beautiful song. Afraid of the eagle, the hermit thrush hid deep in the forest and only sang when she knew the eagle was far away.

Each element could stand on its own—Travis Zimmerman's lilting prose, Sam Zimmerman's intricate paintings, and Ammesmaki's Ojibwe-language text—but together the three components weave a beautiful retelling of this story that extends beyond the bounds of language alone. Sam Zimmerman's artwork is breathtaking (to the point where I'm tempted to email the press to ask if they'd consider selling prints of the individual illustrations), while the decision to page-set the Ojibwe language text directly under the English text offers the chance to see the languages simultaneously. The book is easy to read, making it a perfect choice for read alouds, and young readers—and young listeners—will be captivated by the illustrations.

Together, these two books help highlight the depth and breadth of Native American and Indigenous children's literature. My eight-year-old is immersed in the Zimmermans' book as I write this, while the eleven-year-old has reluctantly (and only temporarily, he reminds me) relinquished *Kindred Spirits* so I can finish this review. It's evident that the rise of books that center Native and Indigenous voices, cultures, and histories are the windows, the sliding glass doors, and the mirrors for young people, and it's no different for Native American and Indigenous readers. I've told this story many times, but I published my first children's book—a book about Indigenous Peoples' Day—in 2022. Like I do every year, I'd emailed my sons' teachers at the end of September to ask if I could send in some books for Indigenous Peoples' Day and Native American Heritage Month, and both teachers enthusiastically agreed.

I tried to play it cool when I picked up my kids on Indigenous Peoples' Day, doing my usual "So how was school?" routine. But that day was different. Our older son—then a third grader—said, "It was great!" He told me how his teacher had read my book out loud to the class, and that his classmates asked him questions about what it was like to be Ojibwe. He's always been a confident kid, but it was evident that his childhood was already being shaped in ways that far exceeded my own elementary school experiences. Our younger one was in kindergarten at the time, and he was a little more succinct. "It was good," he said. "My teacher read us the book you wrote about . . . the kind of people that we are." They now ask me what books I'm going to give to their teachers every year, and they even offer their own suggestions. As my own sons' experiences remind me, children's books allow young readers to develop their language skills, their imaginations, and their understandings of the world around them. With books like *Kindred Spirits* and *How the Birds Got Their Songs* as part of this ever-growing canon, young readers have even more opportunities to learn about Native histories, Native cultures, and Native peoples.

KATRINA M. PHILLIPS (Red Cliff Ojibwe) is an associate professor of history at Macalester College.

Notes

1. David Huyck, Sarah Park Dahlen, Molly Beth Griffin, *Diversity in Children's Books 2015 infographic*, https://readingspark.wordpress.com /2016/09/14/picture-this-reflecting-diversity-in-childrens-book-publishing/. Statistics: Cooperative Children's Book Center, School of Education, University of Wisconsin—Madison: https://ccbc.education.wisc.edu/literature-resources /ccbc-diversity-statistics/books-by-about-poc-fnn/.

2. David Huyck and Sarah Park Dahlen, *Diversity in Children's Books 2018 infographic*, https://readingspark.wordpress.com/2019/06/19/picture-this -diversity-in-childrens-books-2018-infographic/. Created in consultation with Edith Campbell, Molly Beth Griffin, K. T. Horning, Debbie Reese, Ebony Elizabeth Thomas, and Madeline Tyner; statistics: Cooperative Children's Book Center, School of Education, University of Wisconsin—Madison: https://ccbc.education.wisc.edu/literature-resources/ccbc-diversity-statistics /books-by-about-poc-fnn/.

3. SLJ Staff, "An Updated Look at Diversity in Children's Books," *School Library Journal,* June 19, 2019, https://www.slj.com/story/an-updated-look -at-diversity-in-childrens-books.

4. Amy J. Heineke, Aimee Papola-Ellis, and Joseph Elliott, "Using Texts as Mirrors: The Power of Readers Seeing Themselves," *The Reading Teacher* 76, no. 3 (2022): 277.

5. Rudine Sims Bishop, "Mirrors, Windows, and Sliding Glass Doors," *Perspectives: Choosing and Using Books for the Classroom* 6, no. 3 (Summer 1990).

6. Heineke et al., "Using Texts as Mirrors," 278.

7. See Caroline Fraser, "Yes, 'Little House on the Prairie' Is Racially Insensitive—but We Should Still Read It," *Washington Post,* May 13, 2018, https://www.washingtonpost.com/entertainment/books/yes-little-house-on -the-prairie-is-racially-insensitive--but-we-should-still-read-it/2018/03 /12/8e021422-1e40-11e8-9de1-147dd2df3829_story.html.

8. Fraser, "Yes, 'Little House on the Prairie' Is Racially Insensitive."

9. Debbie Reese, "A Critical Look at O'Dell's *Island of the Blue Dolphin*," *American Indians in Children's Literature*, June 16, 2016, updated September 24, 2018, https://americanindiansinchildrensliterature.blogspot.com/2016/06 /a-critical-look-at-odells-island-of.html.

10. Gillian Newland illustrated *I Am Not a Number,* while Gabrielle Grimard illustrated *Stolen Words* and *When I Was Eight. Bowwow Powwow* was illustrated by Jonathan Thunder and translated by Gordon Jourdain; Angela Erdrich illustrated *Josie's Dance;* and Juana Martinez-Neal illustrated *Fry Bread.*

LINDA PEAVY

Native Ball: Legacy of a Trailblazer
directed by Megan Harrington and Jonathan Cipiti
Family Theater Productions, 2023

In Memoriam

Over the course of filming *The House that Rob Built* and *Native Ball*, Malia and I forged a deep friendship. She had a quiet, humble heart and loved young and old and everyone in between. I learned by her example and words what resilience looks like. I don't think she truly realized the significance of her historic accomplishments until the film was released, and it was beautiful to watch her take in all the accolades, knowing she didn't want any of the glory for herself.

Malia was a bright light, a beacon of kindness to all who crossed her path. As her earthly time drew to a close, the Lady Griz family shared stories around her hospital bed and reminisced over old photo albums. There were tears and heavy hearts in visits peppered with laughter.

Over twenty-three former Lady Griz, from five states, including Montana, traveled to Browning to attend her rosary and funeral mass on January 7 and 8, 2025, with Coach Selvig at the helm. We showed up to honor our warrior and stand beside her husband, kids, mom, dad, siblings, aunts, uncles, cousins, and Blackfeet Nation. The picture of all of us decked out in Lady Griz attire and holding Malia's photo says more than words could ever convey.

The fact that Malia's story is memorialized on film is a great example of how God is sometimes working through you to do things much bigger than you can even imagine; we had no idea we'd say goodbye on this side of Heaven so soon. We weren't just making a film: we were capturing a trailblazer's life for the ages.

A "Malia Kipp Memorial Scholarship" is being created in her honor at the University of Montana. A fitting tribute to a selfless person who was always lending a hand to pull the next woman up the ladder. Godspeed, Malia.

—MEGAN HARRINGTON

THIS SHORT DOCUMENTARY tells the story of a young woman, Barbara Malia Kipp, from the Blackfeet Indian Reservation, who became the first girl from her Tribe to be offered a full-ride basketball scholarship by a Division I NCAA team. That, in itself, would be an accomplishment, but it is the heart and soul of Malia Kipp that is the real subject of this film. Created by Family Theater Productions, this work captures the philosophy and character of its central figure, and it's possible that only her one-time teammate on the University of Montana Grizzly squad could have known the world of Montana basketball and reservation life well enough to have told this story.

There is a freshness and openness surrounding the modest hero of this documentary: a sense of wonder, joy, and delight at the good fortune of being able to spend hours and hours shooting, dribbling, and executing old-school basketball moves learned from her father. Born on a reservation so isolated that the nearest mall or movie theater was two and a half hours away in any direction, Malia Kipp, like her friends, benefited from the fact that basketball provides children and adults alike with something to hope for, something to achieve, and something to be proud of.

"Basketball?" Kipp muses, "I think it is in my genes." Her feeling is echoed by a group of young women who follow in her footsteps a few years later. "If you live on the reservation, you play basketball," Shanae Gilham attests. Yet until Malia Kipp proved that Native American girls could play basketball after high school, "rez" ball was just something you did. This is not a fairy tale in which Malaya Kipp felt immediately empowered and easily achieved success on the college court. Rather it is a story of resilience and perseverance, a story in which an encouraging but demanding coach taught her to believe in herself, to believe that she deserved to play at the university level and that with hard work she could excel.

From the first, Malia had realized that she *must* succeed, for if she failed, those coming behind her would not likely be given the same opportunity she had been offered. She was thinking not only of her younger sister, who already played almost as well as she did, but also of all the youngsters coming to the gym to see her play, thinking "Maybe I can do this, too." She knew she had to succeed not only for herself and her family but for all those kids who wanted a chance to follow in her footsteps.

She played for the Blackfeet Nation and for all Native Americans. She was a warrior in every sense of that word. Chief Earl Old Person had presented her with an eagle feather, the highest honor one person could give another, for her leadership during her high school years in Browning. During her senior year at the University of Montana, he brought the Rawhide singers and drummers to the gym, where he explained to the crowd that this band usually honored returning veterans, warriors in battle, and that they were now honoring Malia, who had given herself fully to becoming the best basketball player and the best role model she could be.

Her quest for success did not end on the court. She had gone to the university not only to play ball but to get an education. She knew she must succeed in the classroom as well as in the gym. It didn't help when one professor told her she was not smart enough to pursue a degree in sports medicine. A lesser person might have given up after that harsh assessment, yet Malia was determined to prove him wrong. It is a testament to her character that years after her graduation from college with a degree in nursing and a decade of work with the Indian Health Service—most recently as a gerontology specialist, a role that allowed her to give back to the Elders who had given so much to her—looking back at that professor's remark she says she would just like to say, "Look where I am now." Her smile makes it clear this is not a bitter observation. It's a simple statement of fact. She let nothing stand in her way of accomplishing her goals.

To those looking for a sensationalized tale centered on reservation hardships and inequalities, on broken families and heroes who faltered and failed, *Native Ball* might well be a disappointment. Filmmakers and writers, like other artists who tell stories, make choices that reflect their own values. Perhaps only Megan Harrington of Family Theater Productions could have had the insight and sense of purpose to have produced *Native Ball*. Indeed, it's quite likely that only Harrington could have persuaded modest Malia Kipp to take center stage in a documentary.

This is a film about faith. Malia herself says that at one point when she was deeply frustrated, thinking she just wasn't going to make it in the classroom, she remembered Gram, her grandmother Kipp, saying, "Babe, God doesn't put things in our way to break us. Those things you perceive as burdens, they're a reminder that he's asking you to do this because you can do it. So, you remember that. And you just keep going forward, and you take care of business."

It is this kind of faith in forces beyond family and tribe, forces beyond human understanding, that helped Malia Kipp remain true to herself and her traditions as she overcame her fears ad learned to believe she was doing what she was intended to do—not only as a stellar basketball player but also as a skilled and compassionate nurse whose contributions to the health and well-being of fellow Native Americans are the stuff of legend.

This is the legacy of a true trailblazer.

LINDA PEAVY is an independent scholar and co-author (with Ursula Smith) of *Full-Court Quest: The Girls from Fort Shaw Indian School, Basketball Champions of the World.*

LISA UPERESA

The Imperial Gridiron: Manhood, Civilization, and Football at the Carlisle Indian Industrial School
by Matthew Bentley and John Bloom
University of Nebraska Press, 2022

THE IMPERIAL GRIDIRON by Matthew Bentley and John Bloom offers a deep treatment of the use of football at the Carlisle Indian Industrial School that disentangles some of the important contradictions in the "central goal of a Carlisle education: the destruction of the Indian to enable the creation of a 'civilized man'" (2). With carefully assembled and analyzed primary source material, the book gives an excellent view into the school, the role of football in gendered and racialized projects of "civilization," and how both were shaped by and responded to contemporary politics of the time.

At Carlisle under Capt. Richard Henry Pratt, football was a compelling site for both manliness and masculinity in the "civilizing" project—the latter claimed in and through the physical toughness of the game; the former achieved through a kind of restraint and sportsmanship in the context of the raw violence and spectacular traumatic injuries of the early years of the game. Football was seen as a tool to "train young white men to maintain their vitality by bringing out their inner 'savage'" (6) so they could not only compete with but dominate African American and Indigenous populations. For Indians it was the opposite; the training of the body and comportment would domesticate the "inner savage" so they could function within "civilized" society. Yet despite the expectations to adopt white middle-class restraint, Bentley and Bloom note that the students were never prepared to enter the middle class, trained as they were for working-class occupations. Football, then, was used to earn money, gain publicity, and demonstrate the school's ability for racial transformation (stripping students of Native languages and ways of being in the world and assimilating them to whiteness) while leaving racial hierarchies intact.

Drawing on primary source material, the authors show how the students were subject to constructs of white saviorism and authority while racist media coverage focused on physicality and exoticized Indians for their perceived savagery. Interestingly, with the founder's departure, the ideological project of "civilization" through football was dropped in favor of the explicit exploitation of football for financial gain. In the rise of "athletic manhood" at the school and the program run by Glenn Scobey "Pop" Warner, the pretense to manliness gave way to a focus on winning and professionalism. "Carlisle's football team became more important than the school itself" (82). Carlisle's winning team was a source of pride for its players even as it reproduced denigrating stereotypes already in circulation. As with other examples of Indigenous achievement in sport (like Hopi runner Lewis Tewanima who also joined the school), there were two competing frameworks operating at the same time: one portraying the star athletes as exemplars of colonization and another in which success in athletics energized Indigenous communities and proved the lie of racist American ideologies. In the end, students themselves brought about an end to the boarding school. Their petitions prompted congressional hearings that exposed abuse, corruption, and the incompetence of its leadership while shining a revealing spotlight on the football program. The chapter on the 1914 congressional hearings provides key insight into the problematic workings of the school, the students' experiences, their critique of athletics on campus, and Warner as an abusive coach. While the students successfully employed a "civilization" discourse, the authors point out that it was also suffused with patriarchal whiteness.

Aside from the detailed historical material presented, one of the book's contributions is its attention to shifts over time that respond to key lines of contradictory thought about football in America still with us over a century later. The field, seen as an ideal training ground for fair play and sportsmanship, is also one in which virile physicality routinely veers into denigrating domination. The visibility of sports as a platform is also rife with potential for corruption and abuse: the joy and happiness of players and their communities can be overshadowed by the sacrifice of players to the larger goals of the institution or personal prestige projects of coaches. Further, the potential to challenge racialized discourses about Native peoples is often (though not always) limited by encompassing long-standing racial hierarchies in the U.S. The book also offers a potent reminder of the key role of leadership in shaping school and athletic cultures given the malleability of sport and the range of projects to which it can be tied. In that, it provides a challenge in the contemporary moment where the myth of amateurism is all but dead. Following decades of exploitation of athletes for financial gain, recent changes in sport governance offer more agency for athletes while opening new avenues of potential exploitation—a familiar theme addressed in the book. Of interest to historians, scholars of sport, gender, American studies, Indigenous studies, and learned fans of the game, *The Imperial Gridiron* is a valuable addition to critical histories of sport and Indigenous Peoples.

LISA UPERESA (Samoan) is associate professor of Asian American studies and Pacific Islander studies at UCLA.

GLORIA E. CHACÓN

The Serpent's Plumes: Contemporary Nahua Flowered Words in Movement
by Adam W. Coon
SUNY Press, 2024

ADAM COON'S *THE SERPENT'S PLUMES* is a key contribution to the study of contemporary Indigenous literatures of Abiayala. Coon initiates the discussion by leveraging the symbol of the serpent, so central to Mexican state promotion of nationhood, and demythologizes its non-Indigenous appropriation throughout the volume by offering an analysis of contemporary Nahua writing. The "plumed serpent" as precolonial symbol and eponymous title of multimedia artist Mardonio Carballo's work furthers the multiple linguistic play of serpent and quills (although it works better in Spanish) to sign, signify, and resignify contemporary Nahua writing. The book is divided into six chapters with an introduction and conclusion. The author focuses mainly on the works of Natalio Hernandez, Martin Tonalmeyotl, Ethel Xochitiotzin, Judith Santopietro, Mardonio Carballo, and Ateri Miyawatl. The chapters offer a balanced engagement with male and female authors, established and up-and-coming poets, as well as contributors with fluency and distance to Nahuatl. Adding to previous studies published in English that focus on theorizing contemporary Indigenous literatures, Coon works from Indigenous language and Indigenous analytical concepts to discuss contemporary literature.

Coon displays analytical dexterity by introducing ixtlamatilistli, yoltlajlamikilistli, and tlaixpan throughout the volume as philosophical concepts, helping readers understand their function in the poetic work of distinct generations from different geographically situated Nahua communities. The concepts serve as a lens to delve into multiple Nahua texts and further propose decolonizing strategies in Indigenous literatures. In other words, these philosophical and analytical concepts allow the author to engage various styles of Nahua poetry. The first concept, ixtlamatilistli, represents knowledge with the face, highlighting personal experience; the second concept, yoltlajlamikilistli, embodies knowledge with the heart, signaling effective intelligence, and the last one, tlaixpan, expresses a view of the past as not behind but in front of an individual. Together, they enable Coon to upend the narrative of the vanquished Indian or the idea of Nahua peoples as historically absorbed by national mestizaje.

The Serpent's Plumes underlines the diversity of voices in contemporary Nahua literature. These differences are not solely the outcome of generations, but also of migration, gender, sexuality, language, diasporas, and violence. A main distinction between the older and younger generation is that the latter have had less ties to the neoliberal state and have self-constituted with limited support post-2000. Chapter 1 centers on Natalio Hernández, while the second examines a younger generation of male writers represented by Martin Tonalmeyotl. Coon argues that Hernández's literary production deconstructs a national discourse that associates full citizenship with a Castilian speaking, mestizo identity distanced from native practices (38). Then, he approaches Martin Tonalmeyotl's Tlalkatsajtsilistle as projecting an anticolonial stance against government encroachment in his homeland of Guerrero.

The third and fourth chapters focus on Nahua women poets and their perceived absence in this literary corpus. The sections that address these issues in chapter 3 could have been better organized with the discussion of social predicaments faced by women poets before the poetry analysis. Coon addresses the vexed issue of feminism in relation to Indigeneity and notes that women poets have had to experience opposition and criticism in and outside their communities. The author observes that while women pass on language socially and historically, it is through men that language becomes literature.

Chapter 5 returns to the symbol, metaphor, key, and synecdoche of the feathered serpent discussed in the introduction. Coon draws on Carballos's *Las Plumas de la Serpiente* and his radio broadcast, offering an interesting take on the code switching known as Nahuañol/Spanahuatl in this multimedia text. The author argues that Carballo's *Las Plumas de la Serpiente* (2012) promotes an acoustic ecology against the backdrop of media colonialism (183).

Chapter 6 focuses on the work of Ateri Miyawatl and is representative of Coon's expert analysis. The chapter begins with a sensationalized interaction between the poet and the internationally recognized Maya K'iche' activist, Rigoberta Menchú, who was challenged by Miyawatl for being at the service of the Mexican government. It is an excellent aesthetic and political reading of Miyawatl's work.

The conclusion offers avenues for further dialogue among and between Indigenous Peoples in the north and south, as well as between queer/cuir people. Coon problematizes Indigenous literatures and asserts that contemporary Nahua writers need not be linked to the precolonial period, but the book itself proves this is more of a rhetorical than theoretical exit. Despite a nod to Nahua philosophy, there is little engagement with philosophers. Nonetheless, it will be an influential and important compendium to the study of Indigenous literatures and their theorization.

GLORIA E. CHACÓN (Maya Ch'orti' and campesino origin) is professor in the Literature Department at University of California, San Diego.

JESSICA HALLENBECK *with* SIKU ALLOOLOO

Settler Aesthetics: Visualizing the Spectacle of Originary Moments in
The New World
by Mishuana Goeman
University of Nebraska Press, 2023

IN **SETTLER AESTHETICS:** *Visualizing the Spectacle of Originary Moments in The New*
World, Mishuana Goeman takes up a detailed analysis of the 2005 film *The*
New World (TNW), a retelling of the story of Pocahontas by renowned director of the New Hollywood era, Terrence Malick. Goeman analyzes *TNW* as a
spectacle of encounter, working across cultural theory, environmental history, geography, and Indigenous feminisms to read the film's imbrication
in ongoing structures of settler colonialism. Throughout, Goeman demonstrates how the settler aesthetics of *TNW* support regimes of power that
sustain settler colonialism. Taking on terrain that is admittedly already
crowded—both in terms of the Pocahontas story and its circulation within
settler colonialism, and analyses of Malick's filmmaking—Goeman argues
that it is the duty of Indigenous feminist analysis to intervene in the ongoing
harm of the foundational narrative of America.

Goeman begins by showing how the Pocahontas story is central to American settler colonialism, pointing toward how "the circulation of the story,
imbued with the discourse of nobility produces the social life of American personhood while marking the native body for absorption and death"
(39). Perhaps most compelling is Goeman's adept work in unpacking the
way that landscape—and its destruction—propels the affective state of the
film and the audience forward while simultaneously perpetuating settler
narratives. This is a particularly useful intervention into the defining feature of Malick's work—that of how he represents land / landscape in his
films—and how this in turn establishes the visual and sonic narrative of the
birth of America.

What is striking about *TNW* is that Malick is mourning for a utopia that
was glimpsed by the colonizer and then foreclosed through environmental
destruction, enclosure, and greed. It is clear that, for Malick, Indigenous
people—in this case, the Powhatan—offer(ed) a different path. In this sense,
the film holds up a mirror to the deranged, remorseful, and romanticized
narrative of settler colonialism and its originary moment. Goeman pushes
further, arguing that while Malick's landscapes in *TNW* offer a way to think

through how humankind has become immoral, they simultaneously function to evacuate Indigenous agency, stewardship, and scientific knowledge from land and personhood (72). For Goeman, *TNW* represents a filmic apology detached from actual responsibility or repair, instead creating an affective field that is steeped in regret for Smith's actions and those of the other colonizers. Characterising *TNW* as an "Indian sympathy film," Goeman's argument then becomes a temporal one (95). The film is clearly directed from a point of view in the present, looking back at this originary moment; yet the Indigenous Peoples remain suspended in the past, so close to nature that Pocahontas herself seems entwined within it.

While the film's narrative and visuals are steeped in an aesthetic of settler mourning, Goeman goes further, seeking to determine whether a more reparative framework was used in its making. Goeman researches the directorial choices in the context of the Indigenous actors in the film, the Nations who consulted in its creation, and the Pamunkey Tribe's ongoing engagement with the Pocahontas story to read Indigenous agency into and beyond the film. Goeman notes that despite Malick formally approaching the Virginia Council of Tribes for support, that the Pamunkey and Mattaponi tribes—those most connected to Pocahontas—withheld their participation in the making of the film. In the final chapter, Goeman argues that the film missed a critical opportunity to move from simply acting as a mirror to actually becoming a representational practice of repair, bringing cultural work and authenticity into being through the making of the film itself. Goeman details that despite the main actors, Wes Studi and Q'orianka Kilcher, learning Algonquin and consulting tribes being promised that a third of the film would be in Algonquin, the majority of the Algonquin dialogue—and conversations between the Indigenous actors in the language—were removed in the editing of the film.

Goeman concludes that *TNW,* despite the promise that it would "be a better version of dominant, mainstream settler history," continues to exist within a context of "violent ongoing settler transaction" (150). Yet, she also carefully reads the attention to language and to the authentic portrayal of Powhatan Peoples in the film as a political strategy on the part of the tribes involved, many of whom (including the Pamunkey) were seeking federal recognition as well as promised money once the film achieved box office success. This context affirms Goeman's argument that visual sovereignty is "not just . . . making our own arts and films but also as reframing, reclaiming and reformulating perceived images into indigenous world views" (13). Throughout *Settler Aesthetics*, Goeman points to these moments of rupture; in refusals to participate in the making of the film, in public statements made about the film, and in political actions that point to Indigenous agency that exceeds and contests its onscreen representation. In so doing, Goeman shows how the affective structures of settler colonialism within and outside *TNW* are effectively circumvented.

JESSICA HALLENBECK is an independent scholar and filmmaker (Lantern Films).

SIKU ALLOOLOO (Inuk/Haitian/Taíno) is an independent writer, artist, and filmmaker.

CHADWICK ALLEN

Lynn Riggs: The Indigenous Plays
edited by James H. Cox and Alexander Pettit
Broadview Press, 2024

PUBLISHED SCRIPTS can be great additions to the Indigenous literary studies sylla-bus and classroom. More so than typical novels and short stories, the skeletal forms of scripts—with their emphasis on dialogue rather than exposition—ask readers to engage their imaginations to fill in specific details about char-acters, settings, and actions. Scripts also invite readers to exercise their own voices and bodies and explore their immediate surroundings to bring the outlines of a playwright's story to life. Ideally, one reads scripts in antic-ipation of performance—from a minimally rehearsed stage reading to a full production with costumes and lighting—whether in the role of actor or audi-ence (or both). Students at all levels respond well to the incompleteness and mutability of scripts, especially if they are given opportunities to make dra-matic works their own through creative staging, casting, or adaptation.

James Cox and Alexander Pettit's edited anthology of three stage plays by Lynn Riggs, an understudied queer Cherokee author, is a welcome addi-tion to the Indigenous literary canon—and should become required reading for any student (or scholar) of Indigenous drama. Riggs was born in 1899 in the Indian Territory, which the U.S. government had codified as the destina-tion for the forced relocation of the Cherokee and other Indigenous nations in the 1830s. As a child, he lived through the territory's forced reimagin-ing as the settler state of Oklahoma, which was brought into the Union by presidential proclamation in 1907. Today, Riggs is perhaps most remem-bered for *Green Grow the Lilacs,* his early stage play about the formation of the "brand new state" (first performed in 1931), which became the basis for Rodgers and Hammerstein's extraordinarily popular Broadway musical *Oklahoma!* (first performed in 1943). But Riggs was part of the broader lit-erary movement known as modernism, and his larger corpus is edgier and more interesting in its engagements with the politics of geography, Indige-neity, race, and sexuality than the musical adaptation of one of his early suc-cesses might suggest. *Lynn Riggs: The Indigenous Plays* adds to an increasing appreciation for the sophistication and subtlety of Riggs's dramatic works beyond *Green Grow the Lilacs* but also to an increasing acknowledgment of what these complex, often violent, highly nuanced, and somewhat enigmatic works can teach us about the affective histories of the Indian Territory and the aftermath of its transformation into the state of Oklahoma.

Along with a substantial preface written by the Cherokee literary scholar Daniel Heath Justice, the contextualizing apparatus provided by Cox (a non-Native scholar of American Indian literatures) and Pettit (a non-Native scholar of modern drama) help to rescue Riggs from his relative obscurity within the American and American Indian literary canons and from his undeserved reputation as something of an oddity or melancholy outsider. As Justice notes in his preface: "While it's a firm cliché to say that an artist is 'before their time,' it certainly feels at least partially applicable to Riggs, whose subject matter and frank explorations of the shadow-side of humanity frequently scandalized his more conservative audiences while being hailed as revolutionary by his admirers" (13).

Cox and Pettit have chosen scripts for three of Riggs's stage plays that "foreground" Indigenous history and Indigenous families "in ways that Riggs's other plays do not": *The Cherokee Night,* the script beyond *Green Grow the Lilacs* that has received the most attention from Indigenous studies scholars thus far, along with the lesser-known (although no less interesting) *The Year of Pilar* and *The Cream in the Well* (25). Cox and Pettit offer extensive framing for each script, including histories of each play's production and publication as well as detailed accounts of the relevant historical and geographical contexts for each play's conception, writing, and staging. The scholars also provide a brief chronology of Riggs's fascinating life, which took him away from Oklahoma to New York, Hollywood and Santa Fe, and of his broader literary history, which included writing not only stage plays but also screenplays, poetry, and essays. Importantly, Cox and Pettit situate the reception of Riggs's work within contemporary scholarly conversations and debates.

Beyond the scripts themselves and the contextualizing apparatus for each play, readers will appreciate Appendix A, "Lynn Riggs on the Performing Arts," which gathers together nine of Riggs's short writings about theater and poetry. These hard-to-locate pieces will be especially useful to those interested in teaching or writing about the plays. In addition to providing insights into Riggs's thinking about his own and others' playwrighting across the mid-twentieth century, the essays help to more clearly link Riggs to other Indigenous and U.S. minority writers of his era.

CHADWICK ALLEN is professor of English and adjunct professor of American Indian studies at the University of Washington.

SOPHIE McCALL

Empty Spaces
by Jordan Abel
Penguin Random House Canada, 2024

IN *EMPTY SPACES*, Nisga'a writer Jordan Abel engages in a process of "writing over, through, and beyond"[1] the endless descriptions of "empty" land in James Fenimore Cooper's 1826 novel *The Last of the Mohicans.* Cooper's novel, as Roxanne Dunbar-Ortiz has argued, became instrumental in genocide by perpetuating the settler fantasy of *terra nullius.* Abel demonstrates that these landscapes are not empty at all—they are full of other-than-human beings, including animals, birds, fish, insects, rocks, trees, and bodies of water. Abel's challenge then becomes how to write a novel without centering human protagonists and ways of knowing and how to write from the perspectives of other-than-humans, including the land itself.

When Abel visited my graduate class in March 2024, he shared with us three diagrams that graphically represent the novel's narrative movement, perspective, and structure. The first is a representation of the changing elevations in the novel. The land is at once setting, plot, and protagonist: "There is a gust of wind that follows the curvature of the valleys and glides up to the black clouds one hundred feet up in the air" (12). The diagram looks like a tide chart with high points of one hundred feet in chapters 1, 7, and 13 in the shape of a *W.* The novel moves vertically more than it does horizontally; it moves backward more than forward. Standard reading practices risk entrenching a notion of linear time—and by extension a colonial notion of progress. Abel's novel instead moves up and down through a dizzying vortex of elevation, rapidly ascending and plummeting in a repeated wave formation. The feeling and experience of reading this novel is that of shifting tides, in which change is continuous, yet larger patterns remain the same: "In six hours these waters will rush in. And in another six hours, these waters will rush out" (4).

The second diagram that Abel shared with us is a Venn diagram, labeled "Polyperspectivity," with the three rings identified as "human," "non-human," and "land." The middle, shared section of the three rings is marked as the perspective of "we / us," the speaker. Narrated in the first-person plural, this novel is a viscerally felt experience of inhabiting nonhuman perspectives, which slide erratically in and out of human perspectives. The reader encounters fractured fingers, severed arms, and hears voices and laughter.

While fingers, arms, and voices are often hallmarks of human presence, they may also belong to bodies of water, wind, and trees. Other body parts such as antlers, wings, scales, and claws tumble together in disconcerting piles. These piles grow ever larger as the novel's action moves from rivers to roads, from forests to towns, from cliffs to apartment buildings. The novel's plot is the unfolding of an apocalypse in multiple time frames. Though not spelled out or explained, terrible things happen in this novel. Ordinary things happen too: Seasons change. Life continues in the wake of unspeakable destruction, constant renewal, and change.

The third diagram, labeled "Structure," defamiliarizes the reading process by moving "backwards." The first of five parts of the novel, entitled "Backscattering"—defined as "a deflection (of radiation or particles) through an angle of 180°" in Wikipedia—describes Abel's process of reflecting upon, retaining, or discarding images within each sentence. *Empty Spaces* is not, strictly speaking, an Indigenous text "writing back" to the colonial fallacies in *The Last of the Mohicans*. Only the first chapter could be called a rewriting of Cooper's text; the other twelve chapters are Abel's rewritings of his own rewritings. Each chapter ends with a hinge, at which point the novel turns back upon itself and moves through its sentences and its land formations in reverse order. The novel is largely descriptions of multiple reflective surfaces created by water, air, light, and carbon. Likewise, Abel reflects upon his own sentences over and over, repeatedly returning to the same sentences and the same landscapes, yet also warping them into uncanny formations. In the first chapter, a reader might recognize rocks, chasms, rivers, and waterfalls from Cooper's novel; but Abel finds other pathways through these literary landscapes, writing unpossessed by Cooper's colonial representations.

The experience of reading Jordan Abel's *Empty Spaces* is an intensely visceral one, engaging all of the reader's senses. Fragments repeat, collide, morph. As disorienting as the space in *Empty Spaces* is at times, there is an unwavering attention to balance, design, patterns, texture, color. Ultimately the fragments come together to form a powerful, cohesive whole. There is a terror and a beauty in Abel's resonant repetitions. There is hope for "another softer place." There is fear that "some other, softer place is not softer at all" (14).

SOPHIE McCALL is professor of English at Simon Fraser University.

Note

1. From Abel's "Empty Spaces," an artist's statement, *Capilano Review* 3, no. 45 (Fall 2021).

BRADLEY DUBOS

Samson Occom: Radical Hospitality in the Native Northeast
by Ryan Carr
Columbia University Press, 2023

THIS MARVELOUS NEW STUDY of the Mohegan/Brothertown minister Samson Occom—the first monograph devoted to Occom in nearly a century—offers a fresh, illuminating account of perhaps the best-known Native North American author from the eighteenth century. Despite Occom's distinguished literary reputation, author Ryan Carr observes most of his writings have received little scholarly attention, particularly those sermons, letters, and other texts focused on religious topics rather than explicitly "Indigenous" themes. Carr's book zooms out to give a wider view of Occom's body of work, showing that Occom's deep commitments to Indigenous sovereignty, self-determination, and Northeast Native traditions of hospitality infused nearly everything he wrote. Foregrounding Occom's deliberate use of language to extend hospitality to a broad public of "strangers," in his time and ours, Carr argues that "Occom's evangelicalism was never anything other than a way of expressing his traditionalism"—of carrying forward "his people's ancestral customs of kindness to people of all nations" (9).

Two opening chapters lay methodological groundwork to make the case that Occom's traditionalist social ethic dwells on the surface of his writings. First, Carr outlines the historical and political contexts needed to situate Occom's traditionalism amid the "multiple traditionalisms" that thrived at Mohegan and Brothertown during his era (13). Understanding Occom requires approaching "tradition" not as a frozen category that Indigenous people are "stuck" to but rather something they "'stick to' through their own agency" (34)—a point evidenced in the book's foreword, where Brothertown Indian Nation researchers Megan Fulopp and Amy Besaw Medford describe ongoing practices of "stranger-love" in the context of a present-day book club (vii).

Second, Carr advocates a practice of "reading obviously," a conscious departure from esoteric interpretations of Occom that search for some "hidden Indigenous knowledge" buried beneath his evangelical persona (66). Carr instead models how to read Occom's texts according to the expectations Occom himself communicated about how "strangers," including nontribal readers, should interpret and interact with his words. Carr frames this approach (following Audra Simpson and Robert Warrior) as a question of acknowledging

Indigenous authors' "literary sovereignty," a provocative suggestion that indicates how Native American and Indigenous studies (NAIS) scholarship can put pressure on literary theory's sometimes overzealous bracketing of authorial intention in ways that literary scholars should find challenging and productive. Taking Occom at his word (which does not mean ignoring how his thinking changed over time) also enables Carr to challenge some long-running assumptions in the historical literature: for example, the mistaken view that Occom was an "Indian Moses" who sought to shepherd his community toward a new relationship with the land modeled on Anglo-style farming.

The remaining four chapters unfold largely through a series of close readings that unpack Occom's unique style of evangelicalism, examining his theological innovations, his public displays of piety, and his theorization of reading as a tool for (re)awakening one's senses to the sacredness of the world. Chapter 3, which carefully analyzes several of Occom's sermons to flesh out his anticolonial and heterodox "theology of land and peoplehood," is frankly the most convincing account of Occom's religious thought I have read. Carr's archival research shines through in chapter 5, another highlight, where he recounts a collaborative investigation into Occom's 1768 autobiographical manuscript that suggests it circulated in Native spaces beyond what scholars previously imagined.

Carr opts for a conversational tone throughout, a refreshing choice that reflects Occom's own preference for "plain, every-day talk" (24). That said, as the analyses grow increasingly creative in later chapters, they occasionally veer toward less "obvious" conclusions—particularly when chapter 6 interprets some slippery syntax in an Occom-authored petition as gesturing to a kind of precolonial Christianity—which can sometimes feel at odds with the spirit of reading "obviously." And while Carr writes thoughtfully and sensitively about his own positionality as a "non-Indigenous knower," I would have liked more clarity on the relationship between "Indigenous knowledge" and "Native cultural perspectives" vis-à-vis the disciplinary goals of NAIS (56—57). By and large, however, Carr's impressive research and perceptive readings succeed at elucidating "what Occom was usually up to when he put pen to paper" (7).

Samson Occom is one of those rare studies that transformed how I experience the primary materials. Now, seeing strangerhood and radical hospitality just about everywhere in Occom's writings, I wonder how I ever missed it to begin with. Carr's book is essential reading for anyone who studies Occom or Brothertown history, and it will be highly useful for students and scholars with general interests in the Native Northeast, early American religions, and Native literary history.

BRADLEY DUBOS is assistant professor of English at Ohio State University.

CRYSTAL GAIL FRASER

Crooked on the Stretcher Board: Collected Essays on Gwich'in History, Language, and Folk Culture
by Craig Mishler with Kenneth Drizhuu Frank
IPI Press, 2023

ONE CRITICAL TEACHING that I have learned from my Dinjii Zhuh Elders and relatives is the importance of sharing in our culture. And when I read collections like *Ch'ats'ą' Vizhit Teech'iriikii* by Craig Mishler, I am grateful that our people shared their knowledge, wisdom, experiences, and insights with newcomers. Craig Mishler is an anthropologist and has dedicated his life to living and working in the North. He calls the book a collection of "ethnographic samples of Gwich'in folk culture," which were taken from his "personal experience visiting and observing the Gwich'in over a period of fifty years" (21). I see the principles and values of generosity, respect, and sharing in this book that are so prominent in Dinjii Zhuh communities.

Over its 373 parages of narrative, the book is divided into four thematic sections: "History and Biography," "Language," "Folklore and Folklife," and "Rituals and Festivals." In Mishler's words, the papers, "taken collectively, provide a deep look and multiple points of entry into Gwich'in daily life as I saw it and knew it over five decades" (25). The sharing of this knowledge is especially important given the increasing number of Dinjii Zhuh who live outside of our traditional homelands and perhaps do not have access to Elders, community teachers, or other methods of learning our culture and language. Mishler himself notes this, that each essay "makes parts of Gwich'in folk culture 'visible' to those living outside of the homeland and outside of the culture" (24).

This collection features essays and papers that were either previously published in academic journals or delivered at conferences. Academic publications are not always easily accessible, and so it is possible that this anthology provides communities an opportunity to read these essays, perhaps for the first time. Despite this, I fear that many of the chapters will only resonate with academic and technical audiences. For example, not all are familiar with anthropology jargon, such as "emic" and "etic" (27). The section of "Language" might only appeal to either fluent Dinjii Zhuh Ginjìk speakers, linguists, or others with specialized training in languages. Nevertheless, the book's diverse chapters ensure that no reader will be disappointed.

Mishler and his collaborator Frank discuss a wide variety of topics, such as the arrival and influence of early missionaries and fur traders, biographies of prominent Dinjii Zhuh community members, the importance of storytelling and orality, traditional naming practices, linguistics, and topics in popular culture such as pastimes, humor, and seasonal celebrations. Importantly, Mishler publishes the words of the people and alerts the reader to where crucial collections are housed.

The insert of black-and-white and color photographs is a beautiful addition to the book, and I wish there were more. Dinjii Zhuh are not only oral people but also visual people. Being able to see renditions of our ancestors, Elders, and community members has the ability to bring words alive as we read them. For community members, the images themselves tell a different kind of story that cannot be captured in text.

It is clear that Mishler has knowledge about Dinjii Zhuh women, and I wish he would work with the community to publish or share more about this. Readers are only given snippets of topics focused on women, such as the life of Julia Kuttug (chapter 1, "Missionaries in Collision"), the importance of women as translators during the fur trade era (chapter 10, "That's a Rubbaboo"), the role of women in riddles (chapter 12, "Telling About a Bear"), gendered social practices at New Year's celebrations (chapter 16, "Saturnalia in the Subarctic"), or the particulars about girls' menstrual caps (chapter 19, "Tr'igwitil"). There are also no entries for girls, women, or gender in the index. This may be a reflection of Mishler's friendships and community relationships, what he thought appropriate and not appropriate to publish, or a reason unknown. Still, more knowledge about our female ancestors would have been appreciated and valued.

Readers will value this book. They may be Dinjii Zhuh, newcomers to the North, undergrad or graduate students, specialists who work in northern contexts, or a general audience who wants to better understand Dinjii Zhuh histories in both American and Canadian contexts. Craig Mishler and Kenneth Frank are among the best-known researchers in Dinjii Zhuh studies, and that a wide breadth of their work is available in a collection like this demonstrates the sophisticated history and culture of Dinjii Zhuh but also the work that remains. This is a stellar example of community and academic collaboration.

CRYSTAL GAIL FRASER (Gwichyà Gwich'in from Inuvik and Dachan Choo Gèhnjik) is associate professor in the Department of History, Classics, and Religion and the Faculty of Native Studies at the University of Alberta.

PHILIP BURGESS

The Rocks Will Echo Our Sorrow: The Forced Displacement of the
  Northern Sámi
by Elin Anna Labba
University of Minnesota Press, 2024

SOMETIMES EXTRAORDINARY HISTORIES are simply waiting in plain sight for the right person to tell them. This feels like the case with this extraordinarily moving translation from Swedish of Elin Anna Labba's history of the forced displacement of the Northern Sámi from their ancestral reindeer pastures on the coast of northern Norway.

In 1905, Norway wanted to assert its newfound independence, especially in the North where Sámi reindeer herders had been migrating across the border to Sweden for centuries. Herders were now seen as bringers of a "reindeer plague," practitioners of a way of life that was sure to die out. Official state policy became focused on moving these herders and reindeer to what they termed "vacant" areas in Sweden. While this was supposed to be according to the free will of herding families, in reality, they had no choice.

Between 1919 and the early 1930s, Norway collaborated with Sweden in forcibly relocating reindeer herding families—who, since time immemorial, had been using the lush and insect-free summer pastures on the coast—into completely different landscapes in central Sweden. This area already had other Sámi herders living there who weren't thrilled to suddenly have strangers from the North using their pastures. Entire Sámi families stumbled into an unknown space, without maps, names for places, without *joiks* for the rocks and trees, into a landscape devoid of the stories that bound their families and livelihood together. Most importantly, they were without the extended family networks that lie at the heart of Sámi life. As Labba puts it, when families are separated, protections are lost.

For Labba, this is a deeply personal history, as her family was one of those relocated. She opens the book with a tribute for those landscapes that are a part of her, but she does not know. The famous Sámi poet, artist, and musician Áillohaš wrote that home is where the heart is. Labba asks if this is still so if you were forced to leave. Can you mourn a place that you never lived in?

Labba brings a personal and often poetic touch to this painful story that enlivens the dilemmas faced by these families as they bade farewell to stones and birch trees they knew they would never see again. She switches between imagined dialogues, interviews, and archival research. Some had to leave babies with settled families on route, picking them back up years later when their child no longer knew them and no longer spoke their language. Today we might talk about resilience and adaptation. Labba takes you on a more poetic journey and engenders a profound understanding of how much these families lost and how they somehow survived.

Labba includes solid archival research, reading through the countless official letters that were filled with cruelty, and trawled through letters and photographs from the period, coupled with countless interviews up and down the length and breadth of Sápmi: all of which make this a singular history of a traumatic event that few in Fennoscandia have heard of and is not widely known even inside Sámi circles. This sad personal story is also a damning account of two states' callousness toward an Indigenous people.

The official language of "relocate or face a cull of your herd" by the so-called Lapp Authority finds its echoes in today's Norway, where talk of forced reindeer culls has resurfaced in recent years. While Sámi have achieved some political autonomy in all three Nordic countries, all states continue to police traditional livelihoods with a heavy hand, and pressures from industrial land uses such as forestry, mining, and windpower, now cloaked in the language of the green shift, have meant that reindeer herding continues to be squeezed.

More detailed maps would have been helpful as there is only one—and it is rather stylized with few details. The book is richly illustrated with archival photographs, which have a freehand-style font with the names of those pictured. I assume this was to counter the "nameless Lapp" image so prevalent in the past, but the font style and color render them hard to read. There is a wealth of information in the appendices that is well worth diving into. The translation is excellent, apart from one jarring reference to Nils Aslak Valkeäpää as a Finno-Sámi poet. It would be hard to think of a more pan-Sámi figure.

PHILIP BURGESS is a project planner at the Arctic Centre, University of Lapland, Finland.

COEN HIRD

Haunting Biology: Science and Indigeneity in Australia
by Emma Kowal
Duke University Press, 2023

IN *HAUNTING BIOLOGY,* Dr. Emma Kowal examines a central question: "*How are we to understand Indigenous biological difference in the twenty-first century?*" Kowal uses a fragmented approach, bringing together multiple histories of "Western" (or globally dominant) scientific studies on the racial difference of Indigenous Peoples. Kowal critiques these narratives using sociological theory, which also frames conceptualizations of "haunting" imbued within the book. Her work brings the limitations of leaning on Western theorists to the fore. This is important as *Haunting Biology* does not engage deeply with Indigenous analyses of racialized violence in scientific spaces. Though, Indigenous philosophers and scholars of race hold the keys to better understanding Indigenous racialization in Australia. *Haunting Biology* cogently demonstrates that Western scholars in so-called Australia have not yet transcended the division between social and biological inquiry to interrupt the "cycle of periodic crises" within racialized biology. Kowal works against this by bringing into view some of the racialized political dimensions within contemporary and historical biological sciences as an important act of truth-telling in this moment.

Haunting Biology wisely resists a straightforward orientation to Indigenous biological difference as myth or biological reality. Instead, Kowal asserts a fundamental point: that the supposed emancipatory promises of contemporary racial science are best explored by the people they may serve. Chapter 1 briefly explores this assertion in contemporary Indigenous genomics, while also giving some space for existing arguments that Western scientific ideas of biological inheritance are colonial impositions and not always compatible with kincentric worldviews. These arguments extend well into the scientific study of more-than-human kin in Western science, which is still largely seen by the scientific community as separate from social contexts. However, *Haunting Biology* focuses sharply on human research. And here, Kowal lays the sociological groundwork for concepts of "haunting" that imbue the book.

Chapter 2 brings forward Western scientific histories of bones and blood used to define race science in this place for centuries. The repatriation of bones is a well understood project today, but Kowal points out that blood is epistemologically separated from bones in Western thought, largely defining attitudes around its scientific study and storage. This is important because Indigenous epistemologies are often incongruent with this position, and Kowal brings forward the tensions this raises with reference to blood banks. Chapter 3 extends the epistemic distance between bones and blood by providing critique for the famous and problematic story of the Golden Ridge Station hair sample that contributed to the study of racial difference across multiple paradigms of Western scientific thought.

Chapter 4 interrogates the history of the "archaic Caucasian" theory—a notion of Indigenous folks in so-called Australia as basal ancestors of white settlers—to conceptualize how these histories contributed to settler belonging at a key point of the colonial Australia nation-building project. Kowal realizes how historical Western scientific understandings of race were weaponized to enable and support racist, genocidal, and assimilationist government policies. Chapter 5 provides an account of physiological research into Indigenous metabolism. Kowal positions these narratives within the wider context of the colourful history and political shifts of the AIAS (now AIATSIS) and Aboriginal studies in Australia. Chapter 6 departs from narratives of biological "samples" to explore the life of a museum prop through differing lenses of postcolonial and decolonial thinking. Kowal argues that Indigenous objects and nonlocal communities are invisibilized in museums today, largely through attempts of well-intentioned settler museologists in positions of power attempting to "decolonize" museums, perhaps missing the mark on what real decolonization would look like. Kowal's analysis provides critical reflections on what decolonial museology practice could move toward.

Haunting Biology is not only meant adjectively, but it is the central aim of the book: to haunt contemporary research into Indigenous biological difference and human biological research in general. Kowal's aim is admirable in the pursuit of a bioethical "good science," and convincingly asserts that contemporary researchers need to be cognizant of their recent and more distant predecessors. Kowal argues for living with and embracing the ghosts of racial science rather than taming them or leaving them undisturbed. While Kowal provides a convincing sociological analysis for this position, ultimately Indigenous communities need the power to address their ghosts in ways rooted within their own knowledge traditions. Emerging fields such as Indigenous health humanities and Indigenous genomics provide spaces for Indigenous Peoples to offer such decisions. Regardless, *Haunting Biology* plays an important role in bringing these ghosts into the light and illuminating the paths we might take moving forward.

COEN HIRD is a lecturer in the School of the Environment at the University of Queensland.

JULIANNE NEWMARK

Book Anatomy: Body Politics and the Materiality of Indigenous Book History
by Amy Gore
University of Massachusetts Press, 2023

AMY GORE OFFERS A CAUTIONARY DIRECTIVE in the conclusion to her 2023 monograph *Book Anatomy:* "When we read a book for its narrative content only, we miss half the story" (125). I know from my own personal experiences of moving with and across the text's analytical arc that engaging with a book is a bodily act, an act that engages my sensorium as I touch pages, hold my pen, craft marginal notes, consult the front and back matter, and study the image(s) chosen for the cover and as the book's internal figures. Because Gore calls our attention to all of these textual and paratextual elements, which create a reader's experience, she is also able to powerfully situate such phenomena as important and empowering parts of multifaceted authorial experiences in Indigenous book history.

Books and other textual outputs are material relations—tangible community members and persuasive travelers. Gore's title brings forward the theme of examining books as bodies, bodies with agency. She asserts that "the composition of the book testifies to physical and social violence inflicted upon Indigenous bodies and, in many cases, also creates the space for Indigenous assertions of . . . bodily sovereignty and bodily experiences under colonization" (9). Put plainly, *Book Anatomy* is concerned with paratextual elements, as she explains in her introduction. Her work "looks to the book itself and its paratextual elements—its graphic design, illustrations, typefaces, prefaces, appendices, copyright, frontispieces, and so forth—as an embodied expression of print culture power relations" (2).

Across a robust and theoretically well-supported introduction, four compelling internal chapters (discussing John Rollin Ridge, Sarah Winnemucca, and S. Alice Callahan, Pretty Shield, and D'Arcy McNickle), and a brief, future-oriented conclusion, Gore offers her readers insights, textual and paratextual readings and discernments, and strategies to understand books as not only "method[s] of colonization" but "simultaneously" as "material manifestation[s] of Indigenous resistance against systemic oppression" (11). To read Gore's book is to participate in a project of reading *against* the very formal conventions of books (even though her book, perhaps winkingly, reflects these traditional conventions—in its size, its university-press conventions, its organization, and more). She engages with these conventions differently, knowingly—as figurative and literal features of a *body* of work. Gore helps us as readers recognize meaning and message in the spaces and domains of texts that have historically been deemed "marginal," compared with the center-of-page body text. There is so much more to *read* beyond words; Gore shows us how.

Gore's examination of 1932's *Red Mother: The Life Story of Pretty-Shield, a Medicine Woman of the Crows* (a title later changed to *Pretty-shield: Medicine Woman of the Crows*), demonstrates Gore's keen reading of primary materials, her ability to assess social and market changes relative to book production over time, and her sensitivity to established readings of collaborative Indigenous works, against which she brings forward her own analyses. As an "ethnographic collaboration," wherein a "non-Native recorder," Frank B. Linderman, recorded in the text the words of a "Native informant," Pretty Shield, Gore draws our attention to the work's "most unique feature," which "comes from the paratextual insertion of Pretty Shield's thumbprint as part of the opening matter of the book" (73, 81). Gore understands Pretty Shield's thumbprint as an index of complexity: it is bodily (of course), it is cipher, it is authoritative, and it evidences the transactionality of book production and authorship. Her consideration of *Pretty-shield* honors the "complexity within Indigenous literary criticism" (95). Indeed, if we don't grapple with the difficult nature of such works, we fail to recognize within them indices of "Indigenous agency" and miss the contributions of these texts to our field.

Gore's grappling with the concept of "blank space" is compelling. Relative to Sarah Winnemucca and S. Alice Callahan, Gore writes in her book's second chapter about "blank space," propelling both authorship and colonization, whether this blank space was imagined on maps or perceived as the vacant space of a "virgin" page, prior to its inscription. Gore writes that "in the face of the rising onslaught of colonization," Native authors—and many of the authors she studies are women authors—inserted "marginal, handwritten marks" that "assert the continuing presence of Native peoples, bodies, and communities embedded in the book object"—and beyond it, spatially and temporally (42).

I could not help but assess my own paratext once I finished reading *Book Anatomy.* I crafted a blizzard of marginalia, curving text across inch-wide margins, adjacent to horizontal underlining, pressed upon the pages with a black ballpoint pen. Gore offers a tightly wrought theoretical frame and a useful vocabulary—and, as a reader, I was deeply engaged. While challenging the reader to consider an array of textual aporias, Gore's elegant writing unspools a careful account of reading practices that are *beyond* textual.

JULIANNE NEWMARK is director of technical and professional communication and assistant chair for core writing at the University of New Mexico.

TSIM D. SCHNEIDER

Indigenizing Archaeology: Putting Theory into Practice
edited by Emily C. Van Alst and Carlton Shield Chief Gover
University Press of Florida, 2024

EDITED BY Emily Van Alst and Carlton Gover, *Indigenizing Archaeology: Putting Theory into Practice* features new and rising voices in Indigenous archaeology (the body of scholars, theories, and techniques unified for twenty-five years around the theme of responsible and relevant archaeology "with, for and by" Indigenous communities). An introduction and eleven chapters are book-ended by Roger Echo-Hawk's foreword and an afterword by Joe Watkins—two Indigenous archaeologists whose lengthy careers add context to the growth and continuing work of decolonizing and Indigenizing efforts within Americanist archaeology. For folks unfamiliar with recent advances in archaeology beyond the discipline's well-founded Indiana Jones-esque reputation for extractive, destructive, and irresponsible work at the expense of our ancestors and cultural places, the perspectives gathered together in *Indigenizing Archaeology* gift fresh wisdom and renewed celebration of an archaeology that can truly benefit Native and Indigenous communities. Van Alst, Gover, and colleagues are not only continuing to make space for Indigenous knowledge in archaeology, they are advancing methods for remaking the field.

Van Alst and Gover's introduction traces key pulses of consultation, collaboration, and braiding in Indigenous archaeology. The volume's three parts include separate case studies that operationalize, or put into practice, Indigenous knowledges that are unique to the communities the authors partner with and/or belong to. Four chapters in Part I, "Recontextualizing Archives of Knowledge," offer chilling and powerful examples of research in archives—"haunted" spaces, Zoë Eddy shares, that reflect and perpetuate violent legacies of collecting. Essays by Kay Mattena, S. Margaret Spivey-Faulkner, and Lydia Curliss, as well as Mattena's gorgeous artwork featured throughout the book, show that museums and archives can also be emergent and empowering spaces for healing and rebuilding.

Part II centers on "Reclaiming Cultural Heritage." Patrick Cruz and Nicholas Laluk speak to the delicate line walked by Native archaeologists as they advocate for their communities in archaeological settings while simultaneously maintaining good relations with home and place. Honey Constant-Inglis discusses the power of tribal-led research, stewardship, and interpretation at a soon-to-be UNESCO World Heritage Site. In addition to advocating for more room to build and attend to relationships in NAGPRA work, Ash Boydston-Schmidt's point that "we cannot leave our work at work. It lives with us" (106) prompts further reflection on disparate experiences of "archaeology *by*" versus "archaeology *with*" Indigenous Peoples.

Rounding out the volume, Part III focuses on "Retelling Indigenous Stories." Three chapters provide instructive examples for responsible and collaborative braiding of Indigenous knowledges and Western science in rock art research (Van Alst), storywork (Ashleigh Thompson), and radiometric dating (Gover). They are also profound examples of archaeologies centered on being a good relative and not things alone. But what does it mean to "Indigenize" archaeology? Readers searching for a cut-and-paste definition might be disappointed and, while enhanced conversation across the eleven chapters might have prompted a more emphatic call to action, I walk away from this book enlightened and eager to further Indigenize my craft through heightened attention to relationality, reclaiming Native knowledge, and the healing that can flow from good relations, trust, and sharing.

While reading *Indigenizing Archaeology,* I found myself recalling moments from my early education. As a university student majoring in anthropology during the late 1990s, I grew increasingly interested in the archaeology subfield as a way to learn more about the history of my Coast Miwok ancestors and our present-day community. You can imagine my alarm after reading the pronouncement of some long-ago anthropologist that Coast Miwok culture had gone extinct. End of story. The archaeology I was being trained in—a destructive and extractive practice witnessed by my Elders back home—could not help contextualize this harmful statement. *Indigenous Archaeology* (2000) by Joe Watkins had not yet been published. I do not recall any Native authors in my course syllabi, and words like "collaborative" and "decolonization" had not yet filtered into archaeology's lexicon. But I had a supportive family, my (very much living) tribal community back home and, as one of the most crucial takeaways from this volume shared by Constant-Inglis, I had a mentor who helped build a safe space and "change the cycle" (120). Archaeology can be more, Watkins notes in the afterword, but not "without archaeologists who are amenable to doing so" (180). Readers, especially budding Indigenous archaeologists and mentors looking for direction, will draw inspiration from the experiences and expertise thoughtfully brought together in *Indigenizing Archaeology.*

TSIM D. SCHNEIDER (Citizen of the Federated Indians of Graton Rancheria) is associate professor of anthropology at the University of California, Santa Cruz.

COURTNEY LEWIS

Engraved on Our Nations: Indigenous Economic Tenacity
by Wanda Wuttunee and Fred Wien
University of Manitoba Press, 2024

THE 2024 ANTHOLOGY released by the University of Manitoba Press, *Engraved on Our Nations: Indigenous Economic Tenacity,* is a well-curated survey of the current state of First Nations economies. Edited by Wanda Wuttunee (Red Pheasant First Nation citizen) and Fred Wien (non-Indigenous), this work attempts to counter the seemingly ceaseless settler colonial positioning of Indigenous economies from a deficit perspective—a positioning that erases the historic and current resilience, tenacity, and agency that have enabled Indigenous Peoples to not just survive, but to thrive, despite continued economic suppression.

While this is not a new approach, as many Native American and Indigenous studies (NAIS) academics and professionals have written about Indigenous economic agency, Wuttunee and Wien bring a long history of their own work to this anthology, alongside other well-established researchers, such as David Newhouse (Onondaga citizen). Care was clearly taken in choosing the contributors, which include First Nations writers (four academics and four non-academic professionals) and four non-Native academics, individuals who represent a range of perspectives, experiences, and writing styles that come together to form a cohesive larger picture of First Nations economies today.

The book is organized into four parts that comprise eleven chapters. Newhouse begins the introduction by framing First Nations economic history through the lens of transformation, emphasizing this as a "history of tenacity." This sets the stage for the tone of the book, which squarely centers First Nations' peoples as agents of transformation who are currently pursuing ways to regain economic stewardship. Part 1 ("Strategic Leadership") includes works from Mary Beth Douchette (Membertou Band citizen) and Wien, Daniel Millette (non-Indigenous), and Charlotte Bezamat-Mante (non-Indigenous). These works focus on the projects of tribal leaders, some spanning decades or over multiple jurisdictions, thus highlighting the complexities of sustaining long-term visions and competing goals.

In Part 2 ("Culturally on Point"), Isobel Findlay (non-Indigenous) discusses the place of organization in animal trapping for First Nations' economies.

Judith Sayers (Hupacasath First Nation citizeny) highlights British Columbia First Nations communities' work in sustainable development vis-à-vis the complexities of governmental consultation, including United Declaration on the Rights of Indigenous Peoples. Clifford Gordon Atleo (Tsimshian and Nuu-Chah-nulth) then tackles a question that hangs over much Indigenous economic work, that is, whether or not there can be an Indigenous capitalism. Atleo's contribution also includes a review of a selection of literature on the topic.

The goal of Part 3 ("Family Connections") is to examine nontribal entrepreneurship; the title is an intriguing choice as there is an implication here that counters Western notions of the rugged individual entrepreneur. Chris Googoo (We'koqma'q First Nation citizen), Catherine Martin (Millbrook Mi'kmaq First Nations Community citizen), and Wien catalog stories from recipients of entrepreneurial lifetime achievement awards, exploring the factors that fuel their businesses' longevity. In contrast, Wuttunee focuses on one individual (Jim McDonald) to delve into overlaps between leadership and business leadership; she also pens the next chapter in which she explores the legacy of what began as a small convenience store (and Neechi Commons) that grew over thirty-three years.

In Part 3 ("Partnering for Success"), Jerry Asp (Tahltan Nation citizen) reports on how the lucrative Tahltan Nation Development Corporation took on the challenge of partnering with multiple companies and how these partnerships supported the Tahltan nation. Here, Wuttunee provides a third chapter, this time focusing on partnerships across initiatives, municipalities, and communities, some of which had a history of animosity to overcome. The conclusion takes bold stances that support wider Indigenous economic work, such as challenging the Harvard Project for Economic Development's assertion that business and politics need separation, as well as more mainstream fallacies, as in the lone entrepreneur (in practice, all entrepreneurs rely heavily on multiple systems of support).

This book will be especially useful for those in Indigenous business communities who are looking for real-world case studies and discussions of how economic change can be implemented and sustained, as well as academics (faculty, staff, and students) interested in the context of current economic First Nations movements and their trajectories over time.

COURTNEY LEWIS (Cherokee Nation) is associate professor of cultural anthropology at Duke University.

TRACI BRYNNE VOYLES

Nuclear Decolonization: Indigenous Resistance to High-Level
   Nuclear Waste Siting
by Danielle Endres
Ohio State Press, 2023

THE SUBJECT of Danielle Endres's new book is not nuclear contamination on Indigenous homelands—at least, not entirely. Without downplaying the critical urgency of understanding how, why, and where the settler state has targeted Native places for nuclear waste storage and other forms of radioactive environmental racism, Endres makes a compelling argument that the book should focus on a different topic: a highly detailed study of the Indigenous decolonization efforts that have emerged in response to nuclear colonialism. This approach addresses a discrepancy in topics that have drawn scholarly attention; as Endres rightly points out, "There has been limited scholarly engagement with the term *nuclear decolonization* and far more engagement with *nuclear colonization*" (59). Endres draws on extensive engagement with Western Shoshone, Southern Paiute, and Skull Valley Goshute lands protectors, as well as a deep well of knowledge from Indigenous studies scholarly sources, to craft a book that takes seriously the forms of decolonization activism and rhetoric that have emerged in the context of targeted exposures to radioactive harm.

Nuclear Decolonization focuses on two sites that readers of this journal might find familiar from other studies of Indigenous environmental justice movements: the Yucca Mountain high-level nuclear waste repository, located in Newe and Nuwuvi Lands in the Great Basin; and the Skull Valley Private Fuel Storage nuclear waste storage site in Skull Valley Goshute Reservation Lands. In four well-structured chapters, Endres attends to the particularities of Western Shoshone, Southern Paiute, and Skull Valley Goshute histories, environmental worldviews and practices, and contemporary politics that gave rise to nuclear decolonization movements from the 1980s to the present.

Two chapters in particular stand out as vital contributions to conversations in Indigenous environmental studies, sovereignty, and survivance: chapter 1, "From Nuclear Colonization to Nuclear Decolonization," and chapter 3, "Indigenous Lands Rhetorics." Chapter 1 makes a compelling and generative case that antinuclearism as an environmental politic should emerge directly from the work of Indigenous nations and peoples engaged in decolonization efforts that resist nuclear technologies. This chapter successfully turns our attention from the damage-centered focus on nuclear colonization (per Unangax̂ scholar Eve Tuck) to the desire-based work of building a nuclear-free, sovereign future—and, in the process, reminds us of the power of decentering settler violence and settler systems as a primary focus in Indigenous studies. Chapter 3 offers a richly detailed articulation of how antinuclear rhetoric works in these decolonization efforts. In this highly readable (and teachable) chapter, Endres resists an overarching tendency to gloss over the many diverse and nuanced ways that Indigenous environmental thinking emerges from particular place-based worldviews. Here, Endres shows the power of nuclear decolonization as a framework for sovereignty and environmental quality, in ways that are at once minutely local and movingly global.

This book will be an exciting addition to Native American and Indigenous studies courses, particularly those that seek to introduce undergraduates to the colonial politics of nuclearism (chapter 1); Western Shoshone, Southern Paiute, and Skull Valley Goshute land relations in the Great Basin (chapter 2); Indigenous rhetorical strategies surrounding land and land relations (chapter 3); and the role of nuclear decolonization movements in crafting nuanced articulations and assertions of nationhood and sovereignty (chapter 4). The book will also contribute in productive ways to vital ongoing conversations—in and beyond the classroom—about Indigenous studies research methods, particularly regarding the role of white settler researchers. Moreover, Endres's accessible writing style and use of engaging first person stories about the research experiences that shaped the book will hold readers' attention while imparting vital information and analysis.

In the preface to the book, Endres writes: "I hope that the book will contribute to anticolonial struggles within and outside the academy." She goes on, "I believe that this story needs to be told and . . . I feel a responsibility to tell it" (xvii). The book that follows these statements supports all three assertions. Endres has written a careful, nuanced, and respectful accounting of the many ways that Western Shoshone, Southern Paiute, and Skull Valley Goshute peoples have grappled with having their lands targeted for nuclear colonialism. What emerges, according to Endres's detailed accounting, has been a complex, multitudinous political framework that asserts that Indigenous sovereignty and land relations cannot be cleaved from antinuclearism. In Endres's own words, nuclear decolonization "is an insistent and powerful mode of Indigenous survivance that enacts Land protection, sovereignty, and resurgence." It would be difficult to pick up *Nuclear Decolonization* and not be swayed to agree.

TRACI BRYNNE VOYLES is professor and head of the History Department at North Carolina State University.

MANU KARUKA

*Indian Wars Everywhere: Colonial Violence and the Shadow Doctrines
  of Empire*
By Stefan Aune
University of California Press, 2023

IN HIS WRITINGS from the 1990s through the end of his life, Eric Hobsbawm
frequently returned to the insight that the human species, since the end
of World War II, has accepted a scale and regularity of violence directed
at civilians that would have been previously unimaginable. The years that
are remembered as "Pax Americana" witnessed brutality that would have
been inconceivable in earlier periods. Why is this the case? And how can we
reverse this trend? Stefan Aune's analysis in *Indian Wars Everywhere* can
help us navigate these urgent questions.

Indian Wars Everywhere covers a broad historical arc, from U.S. expansion across North America through the War on Terror. Aune contends that
Indian Wars have functioned over these years as a shadow doctrine, expressing the colonialist outlooks at the heart of U.S. culture, eventually justifying
the projection of U.S. imperial power on a planetary scale. For Aune, such
violence is inherent to the U.S. The book, he writes, "is a critique of the ways
in which the United States cannot stop refighting the Indian Wars" (15).

Indian Wars are wars to extinguish Native sovereignty. Aune describes
their driving outlook with the pungent phrase "a euthanasia politics of
colonial violence," repeatedly invoked by war planners in "efforts to wield
exterminatory violence *in the name of preventing extermination*" (25–26).
Going back to the eighteenth century, references to Indigenous fighters as
"trespassers and marauders" and above all, as "insurgents" belonged to
broader efforts to reject the military authority, and with it, the sovereignty,
of Indigenous nations. This logic, Aune demonstrates, drifted over to the
U.S. occupation of the Philippines and into the Cold War, when U.S. officials
characterized national liberation movements as insurgencies, instigated by
the U.S.S.R. The persistence of the language of insurgency in the War on Terror, and increasingly, in the domestic policing of antiracist protest, signals
the unfinished project of decolonization in our own times.

Aune reveals, moreover, that the language of insurgency reflects a particular set of approaches to warfare. U.S. officials envisioned the military
governance of Indigenous communities, blurring the line between military

and police operations on Native lands. By the beginning of the twentieth century, officials drew on these experiences in the context of U.S. overseas expansion. These histories, in turn, shaped U.S. policies during the Cold War, when political leaders committed the military to administer processes of "development" and "modernization" in the Third World (151–52). At their core, Aune explains, Indian Wars are race wars, defining Native peoples as "savages" to legitimize colonial land claims, to delegitimize the "savage" violence of Indigenous fighters, and to condone the removal of limits on violence. Participation in these race wars molded conceptions of "American" identity. Attacks on civilians and food sources were taken as evidence of "a uniquely *American* individualism" (108).

Aune discusses the depiction of Indigenous resistance as terroristic in nature. U.S. settlers demanded military protection, presenting themselves as victims of Indian aggression, while military instructors at West Point urged the army to engage in tactics like winter campaigns, targeting groups of Native families with "indiscriminate violence" (31). Aune describes how U.S. soldiers brought these tactics to the Philippines, where they looted villages and destroyed rice beds, burning everything in sight. In the context of Vietnam, he argues: "'Everything was Indian' means that everything can be shot. Everything is killable, everything is a threat, and everything poses a danger both of the immediate physical sort (they might shoot you) and the ideological sort (they opposed American power)" (165). This logic, he attests, carried forward to the War on Terror, reinforcing the claim "that it may be required to kill large numbers of the enemy to preserve one's own way of life" (196). Aune's patient and methodical tracing of this history can help us understand terrorism, the use of violence to achieve political ends, as a core strategic objective for imperialism. Counterinsurgency warfare, he insists, identifies life itself as both a justification and target of violence. "Under counterinsurgency," he concludes, "war not only makes the world safe, *it makes the world*" (217).

Aune's work offers crucial insights for the advancement of anti-imperialist critique. Students of Native studies will ask questions about resistance, for the chronicle of "Indian wars" is also a chronicle of U.S. military defeats from the eighteenth century to the present. Readers are left with crucial points of reflection: How have Indigenous nations resisted the violence of settlers and their republic? What lessons can be learned from this history of resistance? Can we develop theories of resistance without providing materials to aid the next generation of Indian war theorists?

MANU KARUKA is associate professor of American studies at Barnard College.

ANNE SPICE

Indigenous Legalities, Pipeline Viscosities: Colonial Extractivism and
  Wet'suwet'en Resistance
by Tyler McCreary
University of Alberta Press, 2024

THIS BOOK is the primer I needed before starting my own research in Wet'suwet'en territories. Drawing on over a decade of research on Indigenous-settler relationships in and around his hometown of Smithers, British Columbia (located in unceded Wet'suwet'en territory), Tyler McCreary has produced an essential text on mechanisms of colonial resource extraction and their entanglement with Indigenous laws and governance. Rigorously researched, culturally sensitive and compellingly written, *Indigenous Legalities, Pipeline Viscosities* raises the bar for responsible and engaged settler research with Indigenous communities.

Throughout the book, McCreary maintains focus on how concerns about development shape resource governance and how capitalist resource extraction in turn attempts to fuse Indigeneity and development. He starts by covering the historical context of the Wet'suwet'en encounter with colonialism, sweeping through the first century of Indigenous-settler relations and the imposition of colonial industries on Indigenous economies and seasonal rounds. Chapter two delves into the landmark *Delgamuukw, Gisdaywa* court case. Instead of extracting the legal concepts and historical precedents from the case itself to argue for its broader importance, McCreary holds the *Delgamuukw, Gisdaywa* case firmly in context in Wet'suwet'en and Gitxsan territories. In doing so, the author paints a beautifully detailed picture of how the case shaped and was shaped by land-based governance, arguing that "the effect of the *Delgamuukw, Gisdaywa* decision was not to settle the issue of competing colonial and Indigenous claims but instead to midwife the emergence of new techniques for reconciling competing claims to territory and authority" (48). These techniques for reconciliation are then traced through their deployment as part of plans for development in Wet'suwet'en territories, with a focus on the Northern Gateway Pipeline project.

McCreary's analytical sharpness cuts through industry's public relations doublespeak to the true intentions guiding their partnerships with Indigenous communities. Through integration and appropriation, industry aims to transform Indigenous relationships to the land, replacing them with the commodity form. In doing so, they neutralize Indigenous resistance to industrial development, tying Indigenous livelihoods and futures to the success or failure of the pipeline project. By laying bare this corporate strategy for Indigenous pacification, McCreary does a service to Indigenous Peoples faced with difficult decisions around the development of their territories, the risks and benefits to consider, and the enduring effects on their claims to self-determination.

The author is careful to note that Indigenous resistance and Indigenous laws and governance have had an enduring effect on industrial policies and protocols in turn. He grounds his analysis of this interplay in a discussion of the Joint Review Panel hearings for the Northern Gateway Pipeline. Borrowing from anthropologist Edward Said, McCreary applies a contrapuntal analysis to the hearings, listening for the "deep ontological antagonism in which competing regimes attempt to determine what can or cannot be" (177). The presumption of settler sovereignty underwrote the hearings themselves, and Enbridge's interpretation of clear annunciations of Wet'suwet'en law and governance neutralized their political claims by relegating statements to the realm of "opinion" or "ceremony." "Settler-state regulators," McCreary argues, "continually mistook Wet'suwet'en articulations of political ontology—statements about the relations of authority that are being enacted—for simply cultural expressions. Colonial frames of regulatory recognition thus reduced Indigeneity to a different way of knowing, not a way of enacting territorial jurisdiction" (176). Often, even sympathetic portrayals of Indigenous resistance fall into the trap of depoliticizing cultural knowledge. Not here. McCreary keeps Indigenous jurisdiction and territorial authority front and center throughout this book, and carefully unpacks all the ways it is enacted and embodied by his Wet'suwet'en interlocutors—whether through song, testimony, story, or ceremony.

Indigenous Legalities, Pipeline Viscosities left me with very little to take issue with. McCreary has clearly taken great care to understand the political weight of Wet'suwet'en ways of relating, and he tells a clear story through an archive of very convoluted and technical procedures for development. Readers may find the cover and title of the book somewhat misleading—the image of police officers suggests that the book delves into more of the direct grassroots conflicts than it actually does (the police raids accompanying the Coastal GasLink Pipeline project on the territory receive mention in the last chapter but are not the focus of the book). The concept of "pipeline viscosities" is also underexplored in the book, leaving me wondering how the concept made its way into the title. Nevertheless, this is a remarkable book, and one that I will be returning to time and again to enrich my own understanding and experience of colonial extractivism and Wet'suwet'en resistance.

ANNE SPICE is assistant professor in the Anthropology Department at the University of Toronto, Mississauga.

SABRINA LAMANNA

The Incarceration of Native American Women: Creating Pathways to Wellness and Recovery through Gentle Action Theory
by Carma Corcoran
University of Nebraska Press, 2023

INDIGENOUS WOMEN IN THE UNITED STATES AND CANADA have long been overrepresented in the criminal justice system. In *The Incarceration of Native American Women,* Carma Corcoran engages the concept of Gentle Action Theory and highlights the ways in which it can be integrated into programs for Indigenous women in prison to make space for traditional methods of healing. The idea of Gentle Action Theory was coined by David Peat, a quantum physicist and Corcoran's doctoral supervisor, based "upon his belief that solutions to societal issues, when done in a gentle way, result in forming different kinds of actions" (93). Without focusing too much on damage-centered narratives surrounding Indigenous Peoples in relation to carceral institutions, Corcoran recognizes that Indigenous Peoples, particularly women, experience the criminal justice system in distinctive ways (based on colonialism, white supremacy, and sexism). She consequently centers her research on the positive impacts of cultural and spiritual pathways to wellness and recovery to support the provision of Indigenous justice. Drawing on the work of Luana Ross (1998), Corcoran explains how Native American criminality is tied to a loss of tribal sovereignty and demonstrates that integrating Indigenous methods of healing can restore tribal agency in significantly empowering ways.

Corcoran's careful and thought-provoking engagement with settler colonial history, Indigenous research methodologies, Indigenous sociological and philosophical theories, Indigenous feminisms, and criminology make for an interdisplinary and well-nuanced text. She offers a thorough discussion of the abuse that colonial logics and carceral projects perpetrate against Indigenous Peoples. Corcoran also highlights the important ways in which traditional Indigenous methods of healing can support Indigenous wellness and recovery beyond recidivism, and toward successful reintegration, intergenerational healing, and futurity. The integration of both personal and cultural stories throughout the text (as told by the author and the incarcerated Indigenous women who participated in her research, among others) demonstrates the essence of Indigenous truth-telling and agency, which as Corcoran highlights, is supported by the use of Gentle Action Theory.

Corcoran sees a connection between Gentle Action Theory and traditional Indigenous ways of knowing as both require intentional processes, creative responses, and the restoration of balance and harmony. Retelling the Cree story of "Crow and Little Bear," Corcoran demonstrates that lessons from Cree stories offer teachings that parallel the tenets of Gentle Action Theory (99–105). Some common themes relevant to Gentle Action Theory that are offered both in the story retold by Corcoran as well as her "Healing the Sacred Hoop Workshop" include: building rapport, respectful inquisition, listening and learning, honesty, gentle advice, and mutual relational problem solving. These empowering, reciprocal, and relational values are significant to promoting Indigenous healing in general, and rehabilitation from prison specifically. Corcoran calls for more relevant programming and more accurate data collection on the demographics of Native American women in prison; something needed urgently in both the United States and Canada.

Corcoran offers much in this rich depiction of Indigenous women's experiences with and interventions in the criminal justice system. Not only does she speak to Native American and Cree women in her communities, at times Corcoran also calls in the experiences of Cree and various Indigenous women in Canada, beyond colonial borders. Her aim is to draw comparisons and contradictions between the ways in which Indigenous Peoples experience the criminal justice systems across North America. At times these points are offered more descriptively than critically, failing to consider the ways that Canadian carceral legislation and systems may look good on paper but are often not reflected in practice. Canadian systems would also benefit from following Corcoran's suggestions for transformative institutional programming by way of decolonial ideas such as Gentle Action Theory.

For Indigenous Peoples, the concepts at the foundation of Peat's Gentle Action Theory are not new or revelational; they are a clear return to Indigenous ways of providing generous space, genuine relationality, supportive accountability, and creative solutions. Using the language of Gentle Action Theory to describe transformative justice principles similar to those at the foundation of Indigenous legal orders may be one way of diffusing the perceived incommensurability between Western and Indigenous philosophies of justice. Her research also offers compelling insights in the fields of Indigenous feminisms, critical Indigenous studies, and criminology. I recommend this book to anyone seeking to gain a better understanding of the urgent need for Indigenous justice movements to be rooted within Indigenous contexts and legal orders themselves.

SABRINA LAMANNA (Ktaqmkukewa'j Mi'kmaw, Italian, Irish descent) is a Ph.D. candidate in law and society at the University of Victoria.

DAVID G. LEWIS

*Bribed with Our Own Money: Federal Abuse of American Indian Funds
    in the Termination Era*
by David R. M. Beck
University of Nebraska Press, 2024

DAVID BECK'S BOOK connects two themes in Native American history: the termination of Tribes and Indian claims made by Tribes based on the poor management of Tribal money and land mismanaged by the federal government. So many Indian claims lawsuits were filed by Tribes in the early twentieth century that the federal government had to create a special court, the Indian Claims Commission, to manage the hundreds of claims. Still, many claims made in the 1940s took decades to decide. To expedite the claims, as Beck aptly shows, Tribes were told they had to sign their termination bills and also agree to be terminated before they would be paid for their claims. Described as "blackmail" by the Tribes (41), Beck effectively targets these issues in the book, laying bare the political machinations of Congress.

Federal Indian policy relies on the premise that "Indians" are unable to manage their own affairs (53) and need to become civilized to become "Americans." Termination effects can be seen in many federal laws and policies and in formerly terminated Tribes who continue to restore their sovereign functions after twenty-five or more years of nonrecognition. Beck's scholarship parallels my own research on the termination of the Confederated Tribes of the Grand Ronde Community of Oregon, terminated in 1954 and restored in 1983 (Lewis 2009). This book fits in well with his previous work on the Coos Tribal termination in Oregon and his work on Menominee history, both of which were terminated by Congress.

As I discovered, and as Beck supports, the lengths the Indian Office and Congress went to in order to terminate Tribes were extreme, bordering on illegal, with Indian agents lying about Tribal status in Congressional hearings and presenting faulty and erroneous "evidence" of the willingness of Tribes to be terminated, even arranging for termination bill approvals without Tribal officials' testimonies before Congress (Lewis 2009). E. Morgan Pryce, as noted by Beck, manipulated the termination of the Klamath and Western Oregon Tribes, presenting termination bills that divested the Tribes of their land (82). Pryce manipulated Tribal statements of agreement by presenting documents intended for an early termination bill (1952) as Tribal approval for the 1954 termination bill, a completely different agreement, which ultimately left terminated Tribes with no land or status (Lewis 2009).

Many people in the Tribes facing termination wanted to sell their land and get out from under federal administration, but others did not, and so Tribes were split. Beck effectively addresses these political cleavages with his chapters on the Menominee Tribes (70–95) and the Klamath Tribe (96–107). Beck addresses several Tribes, Coos (54–55, 188–189), Colville (168–192), Ute (148–157), Seneca (100–142), and references other termination proceedings. Beck gets into the heart of Tribal issues, writing dramatically about the interplay between federal authorities and the Tribes.

The benefits of termination for the federal government included: relieving their budgetary pressures and freeing up resources deemed vital to the development of the nation, such as timber, natural resources, water, and access to rivers to produce hydroelectric power. Beck uncovers how termination of Tribes allowed unrestricted damming of rivers for management of water, and the production of hydroelectric power in the case of the Seneca (121–46) and the Three Affiliated Tribes of Fort Berthold (103–20). Beck's thesis easily applies to other areas of the West, where termination of the Oregon and California Tribes had the immediate benefit of allowing unchallenged building of dams on fishing rivers. Dams produced electricity and materially aided the development of the West Coast economies. Without Tribal governments to limit development in their Native lands, federal authorities had free rein to destroy pristine environments.

The book features extensive references from archives throughout the U.S., photographs, maps, tables of Tribal termination laws, and ICC cases across the nation. Beck addresses the debates between the Tribes and federal officials on the meaning of "withdrawal," with the final termination bills aimed at selling Indian lands and, in the end, the Tribes getting very little in compensation for their stake in their reservation (193). Beck's analysis of the effects of termination, however, could be more robust. He includes few direct quotes from affected Tribes. The book would have benefitted from testimonials from Tribal people on the effects of termination. As such, his concluding discussion is thin compared to the extensive research he has displayed in the book. Perhaps it is the role of the Tribes and tribal scholars to fully analyze the history of the federal policy of Tribal termination and its residual effects on Tribal sovereignty, cultures, and economies.

DAVID G. LEWIS (Santiam, Takelma, Chinook, Molalla, Confederated Tribes of Grand Ronde) is assistant professor of anthropology and Indigenous studies at Oregon State University.

References

Beck, David R.M. *Seeking Recognition: The Termination and Restoration of the Coos, Lower Umpqua, and Siuslaw Indians, 1855–1984,* Lincoln: University of Nebraska Press, 2009.

Lewis, David. *Termination of the Confederated Tribes of Grand Ronde Community of Oregon, Community, Politics, Identity.* Ph.D., Anthropology, University of Oregon, 2009.

DAVID MYER TEMIN

*Of Living Stone: Perspectives on Continuous Knowledge and the Work
   of Vine Deloria Jr.*
edited by David E. Wilkins and Shelly Hulse Wilkins
Fulcrum, 2024

IN *OF LIVING STONE*, editors David E. Wilkins and Shelly Hulse Wilkins bring
together a remarkable roster of scholars, activist-leaders, and lawyers to
reflect on the many contributions of Vine Deloria Jr., the renowned Standing Rock Sioux scholar-activist. The editors set the stage for these contributions by invoking the summer 2020 multiracial mass movements in
protest of the police murder of George Floyd in Minneapolis, Minnesota.
These movements tore down the statues of genocidaires and enslavers honoring settler colonialism, white supremacy, and racial capitalism. Wilkins
and Wilkins argue that the anthropocentric arrogance and idolatrous wor-
ship of these statues—required to "capture and silence living stone"—props
up these "intimidating reminders of who holds the reigns of power" (xiv).
In *The World We Used to Live In,* Deloria insists on the educative role that
other-than-human entities, including stones, play in many Indigenous cos-
mologies. The editors suggest that, for Deloria, stones are not there for
idolmaking but to remind humans of timescales that unsettle and even pro-
vincialize our place on the earth.

Likewise, the authors point to the many Native philosophical traditions
that show how the aspirations to absolute permanence, human supremacy,
and political domination such statues represent are illusions and that "survival, health, and fulfillment are only attainable through ongoing shared
effort and balance" (xiv). This conception of Indigenous knowledge as continuous and intergenerational yet always in flux also provides the lens through
which they invite contributors to engage with Deloria's work—to put his writings "to real use; not just [to be] parroted or lauded, but strenuously critiqued,
and then either modified for current use, or kept as memories of other times"
(xvii). The volume's aspiration to draw on Deloria's work while mounting critique where necessary makes it a novel and important addition to "Deloria
studies" and to Native American and Indigenous studies more broadly.

Across thirty-three chapters, contributors to this volume engage with
Deloria's thought, reflect on his direct and indirect influence on them as
scholars, lawyers, and/or tribal leaders-activists, and otherwise rework his

core insights for pressing contemporary questions. While it is impossible to canvass all the contributions here, several themes stand out across this volume. The first is how to build upon and further extend the institutions and philosophical framework underlying Indigenous sovereignty (Deron Marquez), such as the rights of cross-boundary Indigenous communities (Rebecca Tsosie), treaties and nationhood (Martin Case, Samuel R. Cook), defending the Indian Child Welfare Act (Céline Planchou), and the continued exclusions built into tribal sovereignty politics when it comes to anti-Black racism, gender subordination, and unrecognized tribes (Kyle T. Mays, Sarah Deer, Ryan E. Emanuel, Kiros A.B. Auld).

Another of the core concerns throughout the chapters is the importance of ("traditional") Indigenous knowledge and practices such as intergenerational kinship relations (Noenoe K. Silva, Nathalie Avalos, Margaret Hiza Redsteer, Kyle Whyte, Thomas Biolsi), and to ask how those values should (re)shape tribal governance (Gabriel S. Galanda, Jordan P. Lewis, Faith Spotted Eagle). Several essays also usefully focus on updating Deloria's philosophy of "Indian education" and academia (Gregory A. Cajete, Wendy S. Greyeyes and Tiffany S. Lee, Cheryl Crazy Bull, Paulette Steves) and his treatment of media and communication for Native mobilizations (Melanie Yazzie, Mark Trahant). Though often overlooked, both of these threads are woven throughout Deloria's writings as part of efforts to build institutions serving as bulwarks of Indigenous Peoples' freedom and sovereignty. Finally, readers interested in Deloria himself will appreciate essays that touch on less widely known topics, such as Deloria's support for the Little Traverse Bay Band of Odawa Indians (Frank Ettawageshiik) and his international reception and influence on anti-imperial solidarity work with Indigenous Peoples in France (Edith Patrouilleau with Aurélie Journée-Duez).

The strength of this volume is its tremendous range and variety and welcome invitation to learn from Deloria without engaging in idolatry of him. Unfortunately, this strength is also, at times, its weakness. The sheer length, multiple notable contributors juggling so many topics, and relatively loose organization means in practice that readers may have to work their way through a lot of material to find essays that spark their particular interest. What is more, the quality of the chapters varies significantly, amplifying the unevenness of the volume. Still, there are multiple valuable interventions here that testify to the force of Deloria's thought—even via necessary critiques—for core questions of sovereignty, self-determination, and continuous Indigenous knowledge.

DAVID MYER TEMIN is associate professor of political science at the University of Michigan.

LUIS URRIETA

Plantation Pedagogy: The Violence of Schooling Across Black and
   Indigenous Space
by Bayley J. Marquez
University of California Press, 2024

IN *PLANTATION PEDAGOGY: The Violence of Schooling Across Black and Indigenous Space,* Bayley J. Marquez (Santa Ynez Chumash) traces how the logics of slavery and settlement are historically interwoven with hegemonic notions of education in America (8). She argues that Black and Indigenous people were/ are instructed through *plantation pedagogy,* a violent form of teaching that draws on human-space relations in an attempt to transform them as well as their relations with land (4). Marquez unsettles historical accounts that distance Black and Indigenous Peoples' educational trajectories from one another by pointing to the complex interrelatedness of these communities' relationships to U.S. schooling. Specifically, she examines how "the framing and institutionalization of education for Black and Indigenous peoples has been tied to the assertions that contact with the white race, enslavement, and the settlement of Native Lands are, in and of themselves, educational activities" (8). Using water currents to theorize and historicize plantation pedagogy, Marquez organizes the book in three parts that collectively critique chronological settler time and temporal sovereignty.

Part 1 traces how through plantation pedagogy the establishment of post-Emancipation schools like Hampton and Tuskegee reinvented the plantation as educational. These schools became models for colonial schools worldwide by interweaving logics of slavery and settlement in symbolic, ideological, and material ways. Marquez details how plantation pedagogy transited along currents of colonialism and operationalizes how contact with whiteness in contexts of primitive accumulation, settlement, and chattel slavery are interconnected and then "trafficked" across geographies of settlement through schooling technologies (26).

Part 2 maps how colonial power functions in transit across the geographical reaches of U.S. settler and imperial projects. Marquez examines how industrial education and plantation pedagogy was extended to Carlisle Indian School and then spread to other Native American boarding schools and throughout Indian Country, framing reservations in relation to slavery and settlement. Proximity to whiteness and discipline through manual labor justified the land allotment process and acted as a forced project of education in "citizenship" for Native peoples (72). Marquez then examines the use of plantation pedagogy in Hawaiʻi and the Philippines, arguing that in the Pacific, plantation pedagogy justified slavery without the existence of chattel slavery; the author demonstrates that this pedagogy can only be fulfilled through genocide (104). Last, she examines Booker Washington Institute of Liberia archives to show how white philanthropists and Tuskegee administrators and graduates brought plantation pedagogy and industrial schooling to Africa to teach work and industry as "redemption" as well as to squelch decolonial movements.

Part 3 examines the components, material strategies, and artifacts of plantation pedagogy as a technology of settler schooling across geographic currents, locations, and temporalities. Marquez examines the cabin and cottage as instructional and spatial architectural method and Black, Indigenous, and land assimilation through domestic cisgender heteronormative space-making. She looks at white philanthropists' influence in Black and Indigenous teacher training and supervision. Hampton and Tuskegee teachers were viewed as technological units and their teaching through plantation pedagogy as a mode of exponential settlement expansion (203). Marquez also analyzes the linked intimacies of scientific farming, agricultural experimentation stations, and demonstration farms with schools that depended on experimentation methods across colonial transits. For example, by analyzing George Washington Carver's circulars on improved farming techniques, she shows how land itself was targeted for change through experimentation at Tuskegee.

Marquez concludes by arguing that plantation pedagogy circulates in contemporary currents of colonialism in schools. She interrogates "learning by doing" pedagogy as a continuity of plantation pedagogy and engages in a politics of "not doing" as a location of thought and a refusal to learn through "doing." Marquez admonishes that pedagogy, no matter how transformative, cannot change the material ways settlement and slavery are woven into education systems and advocates for a politic of abolition/decolonization that indexes both the end of slavery and the destruction of schools that have been built upon slavery (205).

Overall, *Plantation Pedagogy* is a powerful historical account of the interconnectedness of slavery and settlement in whitestream schooling. Marquez contributes a unique and important history of schooling focused on Black and Indigenous relationality that goes beyond the seeming difference between these communities. The theoretical and historical nuances in *Plantation Pedagogy* make wonderful and necessary contributions to education studies, Native American and Indigenous studies and African

American and African diaspora studies. Marquez's work demonstrates that refusing to "do" and refusing to "solve" is a powerful personal and collective form of abolition and decolonial politics in the ongoing currents and transits of plantation pedagogy in colonial schooling.

LUIS URRIETA (P'urhépecha/Latinx) holds the Charles H. Spence, Sr. Centennial Professorship in Education at the University of Texas at Austin.

MARY AMANDA MCNEIL

*Reading Territory: Indigenous and Black Freedom, Removal, and the
Nineteenth Century State*
by Kathryn Walkiewicz
The University of North Carolina Press, 2023

KATHRYN WALKIEWICZ'S *Reading Territory* critically contributes to ongoing discussions about the co-constitutive nature of Black and Indigenous unfreedoms, vexed histories of Black and Indigenous relations, and the potentialities of Black-Indigenous coalition.

Situated in the long nineteenth-century Southeast and Indian Territory, *Reading Territory* makes three arguments. First, Walkiewicz builds upon the work of Black studies and Native American and Indigenous studies scholars in theorizing how the nascent U.S. settler state sought to eviscerate Black and Indigenous geographies. Walkiewicz offers "Removal" as a framework that "signals how the modern world order, forged through the global projects of enslavement and colonization, made bodies marked as Black or Native movable in order to secure capitalist-colonialist accumulation" (2). Notably, Walkiewicz extends conceptualizations of Removal *beyond* U.S. federal Indian policy, instead naming a *shared* condition of Indigenous and Black dispossession/displacement.

Second, Walkiewicz centers the machinations of white settler power at the state level—not the national level. "States' rights logics," Walkiewicz argues, "are the glue that holds the U.S. colonial project together because states affirm white male possession of rights and land" (1). Third, Walkiewicz uses Black, Indigenous, and Southern settler print cultures to explore statehood and Removal. This problematizes assumptions that early Southern print cultures were nonexistent, while also emphasizing Indigenous and Black "sovereign printscapes" (2). If settler print cultures sought to concretize a temporal-spatial order where "Indigeneity [was] imagined as a precursor to statehood and Blackness signal[ed] the racialized limits of inclusion that [would] follow" (15), then, to Walkiewicz, Indigenous and Black Peoples "used print to assert notions of community and belonging that were often distinct from Dominant U.S. ones" (2–3).

Reading Territory employs a "territorial hermeneutics" and a chronological case-study approach (4). Attending to present-day reverberations of nineteenth-century statehood and treaty law, Walkiewicz begins and ends with *McGirt vs. Oklahoma,* reading the 2021 SCOTUS ruling alongside contemporary cultural representations of Oklahoma. Chapter 1 examines the emergence of states' rights rhetoric in Georgia pre-Cherokee removal, arguing that Georgia statehood "established a template for *all* future states' rights claims that followed, one dependent on an interconnectedness of anti-Black violence and Indigenous genocide" (33). Walkiewicz further argues that Georgia settlers "weaponized the *colonizing printscapes* of newspapers" by claiming Indigenous lands and by refusing to cite *The Cherokee Phoenix* and David Walker's *Appeal*—printed assertions of Cherokee sovereignty and Black freedom (33).

Chapter 2 grapples with the paucity of Black and Indigenous print culture in Florida, a place that "represented both actual and imagined collusions of Indigeneity and Blackness for a mid-nineteenth century U.S. public" (81). Walkiewicz anchors the chapter with numerous settler sources preoccupied with Indigenous and Black insurgence, asserting that the "gaps in print knowledge of Seminole, Black Seminole, and Maroon life indicate archives elsewhere and otherwise" (74). In texts such as Albery Allson Whitman's *Twasinta's Seminoles,* Walkiewicz reads the "depict[ion of] an Afro-Native territorial alternative" to settler statehood (106). Walkiewicz closes with the late Betty Mae Tiger Jumper's (Seminole Tribe of Florida) oral history, arguing that it attests to a "continued Seminole survivance" that is "grounded in the strength of women and children and the stories they carry" (110).

Chapter 3 centers 1850s debates over Kansas statehood, arguing that they were "in direct tension with schemes to annex Cuba" (114). Placing settler print culture, Black nationalist Martin Delany's serialized novel *Blake,* and white abolitionist John Brown's statehood proposal into conversation with each other, Walkiewicz problematizes the "staging [of] Bleeding Kansas as an origin story [which] eclipses the forced Removal of Indigenous peoples from the region and the discursive and geopolitical shift from 'Indian Territory' to 'Kansas Territory'" (112). Examining settler print depictions of Cuba alongside John Brougham's play *Columbus el Filibustero!,* Walkiewicz ultimately asserts that "statehood campaigns, be it in Kansas, Cuba, or elsewhere, furthered the project of U.S. empire," and "often did so under the banner of abolition or decolonization" (114).

Chapter 4 centers Black and Indigenous sovereign printscapes in early twentieth-century Indian Territory and Oklahoma Territory. Attending to Black and Indigenous newspapers' considerations of all-Black towns and the Sequoyah Movement, Walkiewicz argues that Indian Territory and Oklahoma Territory's eventual incorporation as a single U.S. state under white settler rule was not foregone. Despite the failure of Sequoyah and white supremacist settler violence's eruptions across the territories, Walkiewicz argues that Black and Indigenous sovereign printscapes constituted "other articulations of territoriality and belonging" (151), even as they "are lessons in the inability of statehood to contain Indigenous and Black freedom" (199).

Reading Territory is impressive in its nuanced argumentation and rich source base. Even as Walkiewicz offers "Removal" as a unifying framework, she does not gloss over painful histories of lateral violence that have foreclosed some possibilities of Black/Indigenous relations. I do wish that Walkiewicz ceded slightly more space to examining Afro-Native Peoples' print cultures (or theorizing the lack thereof). I am also not fully convinced that territoriality—a term so thoroughly imbued with notions of property and dominion—is entirely recuperable. Nonetheless, *Reading Territory* is revelatory, urging us to interrogate the rights discourses of settler states and to imagine possibilities beyond the state.

MARY AMANDA McNEIL (Mashpee Wampanoag) is a Mellon assistant professor in the Department of Studies in Race, Colonialism, and Diaspora at Tufts University.

KEAVY McABEE

Rehearsals for Living
by Robyn Maynard and Leanne Betasamosake Simpson
Knopf Canada, 2022

REHEARSALS FOR LIVING by Robyn Maynard and Leanne Betasamosake Simpson (2022) is an insightful text that inspired me to embrace the vulnerability inherent in engaging with nuanced and disparate ideas, while illuminating the generative possibilities of finding synergy in resistance work. Maynard and Simpson approach solidarity work with care, exemplifying relationality in practice for the reader.

Rehearsals for Living emerges from the time of the COVID-19 pandemic to envision a future built upon Black and Indigenous knowledges. In this book, Robyn Maynard and Leanne Betasamosake Simpson employ the long-standing resistance practice of letter writing, sharing their own perspectives as Black and Indigenous (Nishnaabeg) feminists and resistance thinkers. The authors' bond is sincere, modeling friendship and solidarity without shying away from tough conversations. Never asking one another to compromise their own positions and values, the authors demonstrate authentic and important forms of coalition building.

Three themes emerged from Maynard and Simpson's discussion of their connected histories, resistance practices, and visions for the future. Just as land is centered throughout their letters as a point of connection, Maynard and Simpson identify a common oppressor—the colonial state. While centering shared knowledges, the thesis of this book demands the destruction of oppressive structures to craft worlds that are new and built to hold Black and Indigenous futures.

With Black and Indigenous feminisms woven throughout their work, Maynard and Simpson deploy intersectional approaches and analyses of oppression. Connected histories ground this work, appearing as Maynard describes the ways in which the genocide of Indigenous Peoples, the theft of land, and the commodification and exploitation of Black labor are essential goals of colonialism. Simpson and Maynard detail their communities' histories of resistance, recognizing differences in their experiences but always offering connections when they can be made.

Maynard's and Simpson's letters illuminate their connectedness across resistance and activist movements. Simpson talks of Indigenous resistance as a form of inheritance, making it possible for generations of families to know their cultures and communities. Maynard's own history of resistance draws upon Black theorists and activists, which forms a shared connection between the authors and creates a foundation for intellectual discourse. The authors' participation in current resistance movements conveys both parallel and converging efforts to confront the impacts of policing, surveillance, dispossession, and subjugation—all tied to the colonial manifestations of racism, violence, and exploitation.

For Maynard and Simpson, shared futures represent a radical reimagining of our worlds, while also representing a place of careful engagement when these visions are seemingly disparate. On the surface, shared Black and Indigenous futures are complicated by visions of nationhood; however, throughout their engagement, Maynard and Simpson put forward a relational, expansive view of nationhood, revealing their desire for a future that will see people thriving.

I was left with questions regarding the role of land and language, particularly as potential sites of tension between Black and Indigenous activists. In their letters, Maynard links dispossession of Indigenous lands with the transatlantic slave trade, while Simpson illustrates the importance of land to Indigenous Peoples and brings into conversation the topic of African Indigeneity. According to Simpson, land cannot be uncoupled from Indigeneity, including Black Indigeneity. Maynard does not directly engage with either the topic of language or the topic of land within the context of Black Indigeneity, leaving me curious about her thoughts on these topics. Despite not engaging directly with all points raised in one another's letters, the authors model a deeply relational approach in this work.

Rehearsals for Living is effective in its intention to critically engage and enact coalition-building. Maynard and Simpson utilize letter writing to place Black and Indigenous feminisms *in conversation,* quite literally. For the authors, relationality becomes an act of resistance to the colonial state. The authors exemplify profound and nuanced discussions, addressing difficult topics and points of contention. It is in these places of tension that I found myself moved to embrace the vulnerability needed to achieve a deeper and more nuanced resistance practice.

Visions of futures free from ongoing colonialism, genocide, and racist capitalism ground this essential work. Building upon Maynard and Simpson's example, I am hopeful there will be more relationships built across feminisms—relationships that do not demand compromise but that embrace multiple positions, knowledges, and values.

KEAVY MCABEE is a graduate student in social dimensions of health at the University of Victoria.

MARJO LINDROTH

Indigenous Peoples and Borders
edited by Sheryl Lightfoot and Elsa Stamatopoulou
Duke University Press, 2024

INDIGENOUS PEOPLES AND BORDERS, edited by Sheryl Lightfoot and Elsa Stamatopoulou, explores the ways in which borders and border-making practices, instrumental to the creation and existence of nation-states, have overlooked and constrained the lives of Indigenous Peoples. The work also examines how Indigenous Peoples have persevered as communities and nations despite the imposition of borders and how they have forged regional and global alliances of solidarity and agency. The fourteen chapters offer a range of insightful inquiries into how borders, bordering practices and the upholding of borders, as well as different actors in border areas, have impacted Indigenous communities and how these communities have persisted under and challenged those conditions.

In a major contribution to scholarship, the book brings together the fields of Indigenous and border studies—a linkage largely undeveloped to date. The valuable insights offered will spark debates in international relations and law as they pertain to Indigenous Peoples. The salient argument underpinning the book is captured in the introduction by Tone Bleie, Sheryl Lightfoot, and Elsa Stamatopoulou when they write, "Indigenous Peoples' sovereignty, cultural integrity, connection to the land, and overall well-being continue to be threatened, defined, and constrained by borders" (2).

Laudably, the book illustrates varied perceptions of borders. For example, some studies invoke conceptualizations that go beyond state borders, such as Indigenous cosmopolitanism, introduced by Tone Bleie. Others highlight the centrality of borders as a continuous source of marginalization encumbering many Indigenous communities. In the light of the progressive global ethos surrounding the rights of Indigenous Peoples, these contributions show the role of state-sanctioned borders in the continuous disregard of Indigenous Peoples' human rights. The analyses bring to light instances where governments and other actors seeking to govern Indigenous Peoples and exploit their territories will not shrink from intimidation. Hana Shams Ahmed delves into this problematic in the case of the Jumma people of the Chittagong Hill Tracts in Bangladesh. She reveals how, despite an official end to armed conflict, the Jumma live under surveillance as national "others," facing a continuous threat of violence by the state. In going beyond borders as physical phenomena, Jacqueline Gillis discusses epistemic borders and the future of geoengineering governance, where the exclusion of Indigenous knowledge would exacerbate colonial ecological violence and add to a history of injustice.

Another valuable contribution of the book is that it sheds light on how crossing borders—negating them—serves to enable the agency of and cooperation between Indigenous Peoples and, in effect, constitutes an exercise of their self-determination. In illuminating this issue, Yifat Susskind discusses the beneficial impact of grassroots and global cross-border solidarity and exchange between Indigenous women in their pursuit of justice. For her part, Sheryl Lightfoot delves into the role of the Haudenosaunee Confederacy's passports in facilitating the everyday assertions of self-determination that gradually and quietly decolonize border crossings.

In an additional insight, the book identifies the impact of economy and globalization on the human rights of Indigenous Peoples living in cross-border regions. Speaking powerfully to this theme, Andrea Carmen discusses the cross-border transport of pesticides from the United States, where they are banned, to Mexico, a practice enabled by the North American Free Trade Agreement. Indigenous communities in Rio Yaqui, especially women and children, have been severely impacted by the use of these chemicals.

One of the strengths of the book is that it includes a wide variety of contexts and lived realities of Indigenous Peoples in different parts of the world. The editors have included as authors not only researchers but Indigenous rights practitioners which further adds to the rich empirical discussions. The book's overall contribution could have been enhanced by a concluding chapter drawing together the main findings and discussing these against the aims and conceptual background laid out in the introduction. The volume is of interest to researchers and students engaging in interdisciplinary work in fields such as Indigenous studies, international relations, international law, border studies, history, settler colonial studies, postcolonial and decolonial studies, as well as political geography.

States' close guarding of their sovereignty is still evident in political and legal arenas that claim to include Indigenous Peoples yet continue to exclude their agendas and situations. This being the case, the book's focus on borders affords a much-needed tool in probing how colonial practices persist and change form. This insightful perspective also reveals a different dynamic: how Indigenous Peoples live and enact their own sovereignty by going across and beyond state borders in their everyday lives and by forming cross-border alliances.

MARJO LINDROTH is a researcher at the Arctic Centre at the University of Lapland.

ROBERTA RICE

Global Networks of Indigeneity: Peoples, Sovereignty and Futures
edited by Bronwyn Carlson, Tristan Kennedy, and Madi Day
Manchester University Press, 2023

"THE FUTURE IS INDIGENOUS." I found this statement written across a chalkboard in the meeting room of an Indigenous Peoples' organization in Bolivia while on a research trip. It stayed with me. *Global Networks of Indigeneity* helps to paint a picture of what Indigenous futures look like to Indigenous Peoples. Edited by a collective of Indigenous scholars affiliated with the Centre for Global Indigenous Futures at Macquarie University in Australia, this volume focuses on what it means to be Indigenous in a globalized world. Following a foreword by renowned scholar Maggie Walter, the editors use their introductory chapter to map out what they see as a new research agenda on global Indigenous futures based on the findings of the volume.

A number of recurrent themes emerge out this anthology. The most prominent theme is the important role that social media plays in reimagining Indigenous futures. The volume's contributors suggest that social media allows Indigenous Peoples to transcend state borders and resist settler colonialism. For instance, in their chapter on Māori relationality, Innez Haua and Dion Enari propose that "there is a new understanding of decolonisation and sovereignty: the future is network-and social media-led by new generations" (110). The second theme that arises in the volume is that of diasporic Indigeneity. Growing global migration and digital connectivity enables Indigenous Peoples to develop political communities wherever they are in the world. Ellen Marie Jensen's and Tim Frandy's chapter on Sámi migration to the United States provides excellent insight into this trend. The volume's third theme is that of the arduous journey of Indigenous scholars within academia. Full of moments of pain and joy, these stories leave a lasting impression on the reader. While the focus of the volume is the Asia-Pacific region, including the countries of Australia, Aotearoa (New Zealand) and India, a few chapters address Indigenous identity and belonging in Canada and the United States. What links these seemingly disparate case study chapters is the overarching notion of reconnection through global networks of Indigeneity.

The book's twelve empirical chapters provide an interesting mix of cases and subject matter. In chapter 2, Bronwyn Carlson examines data collected from an online survey of Indigenous respondents on how they engage with a variety of terms used to describe their identities. Chapter 3, by Tristan Kennedy, proposes that the term "translocal," as opposed to transnational, best describes contemporary Indigenous political activism. Chapter 4, by Andrew Farrell, focuses on global networks of LGBTIQ+ communities. In chapter 5, Lou Netana-Glover looks at "oceanic intimacies" or relationality between Aboriginal, Māori, and Torres Strait Islander people. Chapter 6, by Innez Haua and Dion Enari, examines relations between peoples from the Pacific Islands and Māori living in Australia. In chapter 7, Ellen Marie Jensen and Tim Frandy look at the resilience of Sámi culture in the United States. In chapter 8, Jo Anne Rey makes the case for ethical and ecological sovereignties in the face of human-induced socio-environmental changes in Australia. Chapter 9, by Bronwyn Carlson revisits the topic of social media and its possibilities for political dissent and action, both locally and globally. The focus of chapter 10, by Percy Lezard, Madi Day, and Sandy O'Sullivan, is on imagining Indigiqueer futures based on a conversation between academics. In chapter 11, Binalakshmi Nepram turns to the case of India and Indigenous women's resistance to the violence imposed by the government through its martial law act. Chapter 12 by Souksavanh T. Keovorabouth imagines a queer Indigenous multiracial future. Finally, in chapter 13, Yi-Chun Tricia Lin, Bronwyn Carlson, Coro J.-A. Juanena, waaseyaa'sin Christine Sy, and Alex Wilson provide us with four narratives on transnational Indigenous feminisms based on a digital roundtable presentation.

Global Networks of Indigeneity raises insightful possibilities for Indigenous futures that are sure to appeal to a wide audience of readers. The volume's strengths include its innovative approach to research, the timeliness and relevance of the subject matter, and its positive message for and vision of our collective future. Returning to question posed in its introduction: What does it mean to be Indigenous in a globalized world? The volume does not give us a simple answer to this complex question. Instead, it leaves us to reflect on the diverse identities, experiences, and forms of organizing contained within its pages.

ROBERTA RICE is professor and head of political science at the University of Calgary.

GERARDO ALDANA

Rethinking Zapotec Time: Cosmology, Ritual, and Resistance in
    Colonial Mexico
by David Tavárez
University of Texas Press, 2022

MODERN STUDIES of Indigenous calendars or astronomy often claim evidence of "advanced" scientific knowledge or methods within records of various kinds. Ernst Förstemann set the trajectory unintentionally with his landmark study of the Venus and Eclipse Tables in the Dresden Codex as early as 1894. Countless far less-convincing studies followed over the decades proposing patterns of dates that matched astronomical cycles—even when no text or imagery could corroborate them. The agenda was furthered by studies of architectural orientations toward celestial bodies, and then imagery with iconography that appeared to have celestial referents. I do not mean that Indigenous astronomy didn't exist or that it wasn't "advanced"—rather, I raise the concern that modern scholars often avoid more nuanced approaches to "difference" by taking a very "Western" approach of thinking in binary terms and reducing difference to "better" or "worse." In doing so, they often overlook culture, individual agency, and intellectual change over time, reducing Indigenous astronomies to clever algorithms.

David Tavárez's *Rethinking Zapotec Time: Cosmology, Ritual, and Resistance in Colonial Mexico* risks giving a similar impression of scholarly overinterpretation. Tavárez examines a collection of Zapotec language manuscripts from the early 1700s, which contain calendric information along with very simple diagrams of circles sometimes arranged in geometric shapes. These simple sketches, he claims, are versions of what we see in the Precontact Mixteca-Puebla manuscripts—those richly complex iconographic documents that include the Borgia and Cospi Codices. What separates Tavárez's work from most of the scholarship on Mesoamerican astronomies, though, is his attention to language. Tavárez is an erudite student of Zapotec languages, complemented with a strong facility in their contemporary Nahuatl. He draws on this expertise to convincingly demonstrate a strong Indigenous cultural continuity between the ceremonial work of Zapotec ritual specialists under colonial rule and their centuries-earlier intellectual ancestors.

Rethinking Zapotec Time is testament to the challenges it takes on, comprising 268 pages in eight chapters, richly illustrated, and appended with

112 pages of meticulous translations. The book is intended for the specialist, though it is complicated by the fact that Zapotec calendrics here do not make use of the "user-friendly" bar and dot notation of Mayan calendrics, or the familiar calendric iconography of Aztec and Mixtec traditions. Neither does Tavárez gently guide the reader into the challenges of interpreting the content of his specific collection of manuscripts. Instead, after the introductory chapter, he engages a debate that has raged for over a century; in chapter 1, Tavárez introduces the Zapotec 260- and 365-day counts and how they related to their parallels in neighboring cultures. Tavárez adds to the evidence that regionally synchronized counts were anomalous in Mesoamerica—much more common was variation in accordance with local needs. While compelling, the prominence of analysis seems misplaced given that Tavárez's most powerful arguments in the rest of the book do not rely on any specific calendar correlation.

Chapter 3 is equally challenging; here Tavárez takes on the linguistics of the Zapotec texts he studies, while placing them in greater contexts of Mesoamerican literacy. It may be that the challenge is heightened given that much of this material comes from wills, which emphasize legalistic issues and genealogies. Perseverance through these chapters, though, is richly rewarded with the following four. Chapter 4 initiates the book's main thrust by tracking increasingly complex relationships between content in the Zapotec manuscripts and that of the Precontact Vaticanus and Borgia Codices. Tavárez demonstrates that annotations of simple diagrams reveal the same cosmological structures as represented in the complex iconography of the centuries-earlier codices. The chapter starts with an intriguing connection between a set of "quincunx" patterns written by Juan Bautista in "Manual 11," and the cosmological house structures filled with Day Signs on two pages of the Vaticanus B Codex. This approach sets up far more powerful parallels between a diagram of circles and lines in Manual 66–1 and the "Four Fields of Creation" on four pages of the Borgia Codex. The "Field of the Burial," "Blood Field," "Field of Sharpness," and "Field of Sucklings" are briefly annotated in Manual 66–1, while fully illustrated in Borgia 29–32, which Tavárez includes in full-color plates. Here, Tavárez is at the peak of his skills, teasing out nuanced and compelling narrative, iconographic and calendric patterns between records created centuries apart.

Chapters 5 and 6 turn to descriptions of ceremonies as they were calendrically timed, and then, of communication with ancestors through songs, corresponding to translations in the book's appendix. Chapter 7 brings consideration back to the times of the scribes themselves, revealing the agency of colonial-period Zapotec intellectuals in negotiating the influence of Christianity and European culture on their religion and everyday lives. Throughout, Tavárez's analysis is dense and rigorous.

Overall, with *Rethinking Zapotec Time* David Tavárez has contributed a unique, detailed study, which endeavors to reveal and remain faithful to the intents of seventeenth- and eighteenth-century Zapotec scribes themselves. He takes no quantitative "shortcuts" to feed modern representations of esoteric Mesoamerican ritual specialists, but places their records in rich historical contexts—an achievement made possible by his investment in studying Indigenous languages and allowing their words to guide his work.

GERARDO ALDANA is professor of Chicana/o studies at the University of California, Santa Barbara.

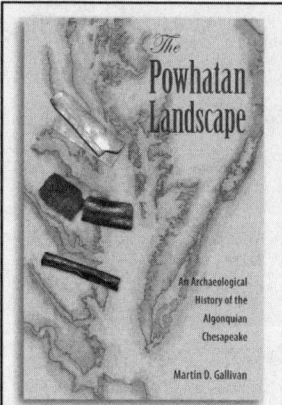

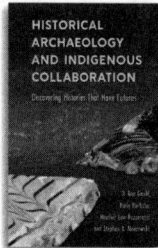

Yale UNIVERSITY PRESS

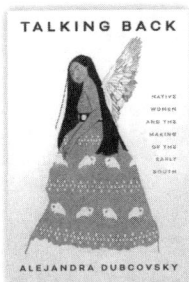

Empty Spaces
Jordan Abel

Talking Back
*Native Women
and the Making
of the Early South*
Alejandra
Dubcovsky

**Ecology
of Dakota
Landscapes**
*Past, Present,
and Future*
W. Carter Johnson
and Dennis H.
Knight

Squanto
A Native Odyssey
Andrew Lipman

AVAILABLE IN
PAPERBACK

California
*An American
History*
John Mack
Faragher

Diabetes
*A History of Race
and Disease*
Arleen Marcia
Tuchman

THE HENRY ROE
CLOUD SERIES ON
AMERICAN INDIANS
AND MODERNITY

**The Rediscovery
of America**
*Native Peoples
and the
Unmaking of
U.S. History*
Ned Blackhawk

Chitto Harjo
*Native Patriotism
and the
Medicine Way*
Donald L. Fixico

**The Makings
and Unmakings
of Americans**
*Indians and
Immigrants
in American
Literature and
Culture,
1879-1924*
Cristina Stanciu

**Indigenous
London**
*Native Travelers
at the Heart
of Empire*
Coll Thrush

THE LAMAR SERIES IN
WESTERN HISTORY

**The War on
Illahee**
*Genocide,
Complicity, and
Cover-Ups in the
Pioneer
Northwest*
Marc James
Carpenter

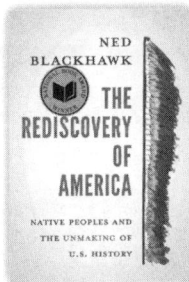

Lakota America
*A New History of
Indigenous Power*
Pekka Hämäläinen

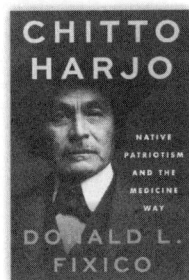

**The Business of
Killing Indians**
*Scalp Warfare
and the Violent
Conquest of
North America*
William S. Kiser

**California, a
Slave State**
Jean Pfaelzer

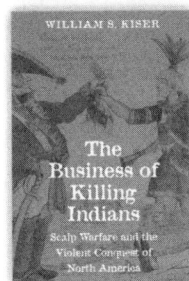

**Growing Up
with the Country**
*Family, Race, and
Nation after the
Civil War*
Kendra Taira Field

yalebooks.com

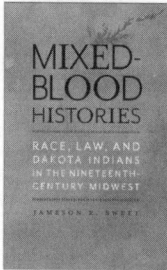

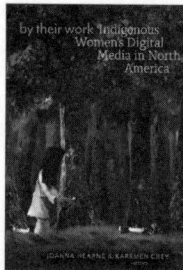

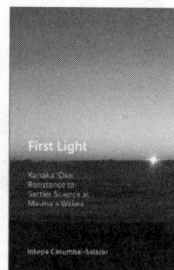